Nyasa Yoga

Kundalini, Prana, Chakra and Nadi Cultivation Techniques

William Bodri

Top Shape Publishing LLC
1135 Terminal Way Suite 209
Reno, NV 89502

ISBN-10: 0998076414
ISBN-13: 978-0-9980764-1-6
Library of Congress Control Number: 2016917346

DEDICATION

For my parents, in hopes that the merit from this book can help them reach enlightenment. For my sponsors and helpers, in hope that they can also reach enlightenment, and for my teachers in hopes that they can help many more people attain the Tao.

CONTENTS

ACKNOWLEDGMENTS

To Master Nan Huai-chin, who first told me about the *dharmakaya* and *sambhogakaya*. This book helps you to attain it starting with the development of the deva, deity or subtle body. To Sri Siddharameshwar and Meher Baba, whose combined teachings also help you to understand the bodies to be attained on the spiritual path on the way to complete enlightenment and the perfect *sambhogakaya*. To Lee Shu-mei, who supported me during my research efforts, and to my parents who never opposed my interests in spiritual cultivation. May the merit from this work go to all of them, may they all thereby attain a higher stage of the Tao, and may they supervise paths of painless assistance.

I have written this book to appeal to students of Indian yoga, who know terms like prana and *nadis*, and students of Chinese nei-gong inner energy work, who know the equivalent terms as Qi and Qi channels. These two vocabularies are used interchangeably. Because I have covered many difficult topics within this book that may contain errors because of the sophisticated correspondences, I hope that subsequent authors will use these materials as a basis to make corrections in newer and more advanced materials for the public. I thank them ahead of time for their devotion to the spiritual path and helping people attain enlightenment.

CHAPTER 1
SHAKYAMUNI BUDDHA'S
BEAUTIFIED BODY

The enlightened sage Shakyamuni Buddha lived nearly 2,500 years ago. Many people admired his body for it is said that it exhibited special marks and signs of perfection, namely thirty-two excellent marks, due to his many lives of spiritual cultivation:

1. Smooth and level feet
2. Thousand-spoked wheel sign on feet
3. Long, slender fingers
4. Pliant hands and feet
5. Toes and fingers finely webbed
6. Full-sized heels
7. Arched insteps
8. Thighs like a royal stag
9. Hands reaching below the knees
10. Well-retracted male organ
11. Height and stretch of arms equal
12. Every hair-root dark colored
13. Body hair graceful and curly
14. Golden-hued body
15. Ten-foot aura around him
16. Soft, smooth skin
17. Soles, palms, shoulders, and crown of head well-rounded
18. Area below armpits well-filled

19. Lion-shaped body
20. Body erect and upright
21. Full, round shoulders
22. Forty teeth
23. Teeth white, even, and close
24. Four canine teeth pure white
25. Jaw like a lion
26. Saliva that improves the taste of all food
27. Tongue long and broad
28. Voice deep and resonant
29. Eyes deep blue
30. Eyelashes like a royal bull
31. White ūrṇā curl that emits light between eyebrows
32. Fleshy protuberance on the crown of the head

It is also said that there are eighty minor characteristics of the body of a fully enlightened Buddha:

1. He has beautiful fingers and toes.
2. He has well-proportioned fingers and toes.
3. He has tube-shaped fingers and toes.
4. His fingernails and toenails have a rosy tint.
5. His fingernails and toenails are slightly upturned at the tip.
6. His fingernails and toenails are smooth and rounded without ridges.
7. His ankles and wrists are rounded and undented.
8. His feet are of equal length.
9. He has a beautiful gait, like that of a king-elephant.
10. He has a stately gait, like that of a king-lion.
11. He has a beautiful gait, like that of a swan.
12. He has a majestic gait, like that of a royal ox.
13. His right foot leads when walking.
14. His knees have no protruding kneecaps.
15. He has the demeanor of a great man.
16. His navel is without blemish.
17. He has a deep-shaped abdomen.
18. He has clockwise marks on the abdomen.
19. His thighs are rounded like banana sheaves.
20. His two arms are shaped like an elephant's trunk.

21. The lines on the palms of his hands have a rosy tint.
22. His skin is thick or thin as it should be.
23. His skin is unwrinkled.
24. His body is spotless and without lumps.
25. His body is unblemished above and below.
26. His body is absolutely free of impurities.
27. He has the strength of 1,000 crore elephants or 100,000 crore men.
28. He has a protruding nose.
29. His nose is well proportioned.
30. His upper and lower lips are equal in size and have a rosy tint.
31. His teeth are unblemished and with no plaque.
32. His teeth are long like polished conches.
33. His teeth are smooth and without ridges.
34. His five sense-organs are unblemished.
35. His four canine teeth are crystal and rounded.
36. His face is long and beautiful.
37. His cheeks are radiant.
38. The lines on his palms are deep.
39. The lines on his palms are long.
40. The lines on his palms are straight.
41. The lines on his palms have a rosy tint.
42. His body emanates a halo of light extending around him for two meters.
43. His cheek cavities are fully rounded and smooth.
44. His eyelids are well proportioned.
45. The five nerves of his eyes are unblemished.
46. The tips of his bodily hair are neither curved nor bent.
47. He has a rounded tongue.
48. His tongue is soft and has a rosy-tint.
49. His ears are long like lotus petals.
50. His earholes are beautifully rounded.
51. His sinews and tendons don't stick out.
52. His sinews and tendons are deeply embedded in the flesh.
53. His topknot is like a crown.
54. His forehead is well-proportioned in length and breadth.
55. His forehead is rounded and beautiful.
56. His eyebrows are arched like a bow.

57. The hair of his eyebrows is fine.
58. The hair of his eyebrows lies flat.
59. He has large brows.
60. His brows reach the outward corner of his eyes.
61. His skin is fine throughout his body.
62. His whole body has abundant signs of good fortune.
63. His body is always radiant.
64. His body is always refreshed like a lotus flower.
65. His body is exquisitely sensitive to touch.
66. His body has the scent of sandalwood.
67. His body hair is consistent in length.
68. He has fine bodily hair.
69. His breath is always fine.
70. His mouth always has a beautiful smile.
71. His mouth has the scent of a lotus flower.
72. His hair has the colour of a dark shadow.
73. His hair is strongly scented.
74. His hair has the scent of a white lotus.
75. He has curled hair.
76. His hair does not turn grey.
77. He has fine hair.
78. His hair is untangled.
79. His hair has long curls. (Buddha may be interpreted as being bald)
80. He has a topknot as if crowned with a royal flower garland.

Due to what great good karma and merit was it that Shakyamuni Buddha exhibited such beautific excellence?

First there was the cultivation practice of his present life which would produce wondrous results, but there was also the karmic merit from prior lives as well.

Other Buddhas, which means enlightened individuals, are also portrayed as possessing "beautified" bodies due to their success in reaching the highest levels of spiritual cultivation. This includes Shiva (Hinduism), Krishna (Hinduism), Mahavira (Jainism), Murugan (Hinduism), Amitofo (Buddhism), Kuan Yin (Mahayana Buddhism), Jesus (Christianity), Padmasambhava (Vajrayana Buddhism) and many other spiritual greats.

Is there a secret meaning of this list that goes beyond the surface?

The meaning is that you must cultivate each and every individual part of your body, opening up all the *nadis* within it, in order to purify the prana within it. Activating the prana within all cells of your body is how you gradually obtain a beautified body, which takes effort. By flooding your body with active prana and thereby cleansing all of your *nadis* of obstructions you will eventually generate an entirely new body within the old one and win a new spiritual life. Your entire physical body must be transformed for this to happen.

You need to cultivate every individual part of your body – through mantra practices, breath retention pranayama exercises, stretching and visualization practices that bring prana/Qi to that area, sexual cultivation and other techniques – in order to open up the *nadis* or Qi channels within that section of your body. Note: in order to transmit this information to a wider eastern audience, in this book the terms "prana" and "Qi" will be used interchangeably as will the terms "*nadis*" and "Qi channels." These terms should always be considered synonyms.

After you transform all sections of your body, all parts down to individual muscle fibers and cells (by flooding all body atoms with Qi over and over again for years) you will thereby in aggregate open up all your Qi channels, which means that you "perfect" or "purify" your entire body. At that point a deva body, which is a body double composed of prana/Qi spiritual energy, can then emerge from your physical flesh. It will emerge as if freeing itself from a casing just as normally happens when someone dies, only this body will be able to come and go as you please and will form the initial basis for a new and higher spiritual life. In a nutshell, this is the path for how you reach the highest stages of spiritual attainment.

CHAPTER 2
THE SHAKTI PEETHAS AND OTHER HOLY SPOTS

According to Hinduism, the enlightened Lord Shiva was married to the Goddess Sati. Sati is considered the principal female of Hinduism representing the feminine energies of the cosmos, called Shakti, and of the human body.

According to legend, at some time in the past Sati's father, Daksha, decided to perform a puja ceremony to take revenge on Lord Shiva, whom Sati had married against her father's wishes. Daksha invited all the deities to attend except his daughter. Shiva tried to dissuade Sati from going to her father's puja since she was not invited, but Sati decided to go anyway.

Being an uninvited guest, Daksha was not shown any respect by her father, who even insulted her husband Shiva. Sati could not bear her father's insults so she immolated herself by jumping into the ceremonial fire, thus destroying the puja ceremony, and died.

The legend goes that Lord Shiva retrieved the corpse of his wife and while carrying it upon his shoulders started dancing furiously all over the country. To bring down his anger, Lord Vishnu severed Sati's body and various pieces of the corpse fell at several spots all throughout the Indian subcontinent forming the sites that are now known as Shakti Peethas.

In other words, according to religious legend the Shakti Peethas are places where the body parts of Sati's corpse fell as Shiva carried it during his sorrowful wanderings after her death. Those locations, which have become sacred spots, are now believed to contain divine energies.

Some religious texts say that there are 51 Peethas, while others say there are more. The *Pithanimaya Tantra* mentions 51 Peethas scattered all over India, Sri Lanka, Bangladesh, Pakistan, Nepal, Bhutan, and Tibet. The *Shivacharita* lists an additional 26 more Upa-Peethas. The *Brahmanda Purana* mentions 64 Peethas while Devi Bhagavatham provides a list of 108 Shakti Peethas. The *Shakti Peetha Stotram*, written by Adi Shankara, provides a list of Peethas as well. The point is that there are innumerable places within India where special spiritual energies are available to help your cultivation; many are listed and many are not.

At each Peetha location you will usually find a temple or shrine to mark the spot. Tradition says the Peethas are overseen by enlightened spiritual protectors and devas who will help visiting spiritual practitioners to make progress on the cultivation path.

Whenever a location is identified as "sacred" in some spiritual tradition you should surmise that many enlightened spiritual beings live and work there helping locals (and travelers on pilgrimage or who simply stop by) receive assistance in their daily lives in their spiritual cultivation.

One of their goals is to help practitioners transform the prana and *nadis* (Qi channels) of their body on the way to realizing enlightenment. You have to do most of the spiritual cultivation work yourself because Heaven can only help in a limited way (never expect "miracles"), but this is why it is often of benefit to visit these locations as a spiritual aspirant. The local deva denizens and spiritual masters charged with caring for the locale, will often lend their energies to yours to help you open up your Qi channels.

The Shakti Peethas are each designated by one of Sati's body parts as follows:

Hingula, Pakistan - The Suture on the top of the head
Sharkrar, Kolhapur - Eyes
Sugandha - Nose
Amarnath Cave, Kashmir - Throat
Jwalamukhi, Kangra, Himachal Pradesh - Tongue
Jalandhar - Left Breast
Baidyanath - Heart

Nepal - Both Knees
Manas - Right Palm
Utkal Virja, Jagannath Puri - Navel
Muktinath, Nepal - Right Cheek
Bahula - Left Arm
Ujjaini, Madhya Pradesh - Elbows
Tripura - Right Leg
Chatgaon, Bangladesh - Right Arm
Shalbadi Gram, Jalpaigudi - Left Leg
Kamgiri, Assam - Genitals
Prayag, Allahabad, Uttar Pradesh - Fingers
Jayanti Hills, Assam - Left Thigh
Ksheer Gram, Bardhwan - Right Hand Thumb
Kalighat, Kolkata, West Bengal - Right Toes
Lalbagh Court, Howrah – Crown or Diadem
Varanasi, Uttar Pradesh - Earring
Kanyashram - Back
Kurukshetra, Haryana – Right Ankle
Pushkar, Rajasthan – Both Wrists
Mallikarjun Hills, Shail - Neck
Kanchi - Skeleton
Kalmadhav – Left Hip and Buttock
Amarkantak, Madhya Pradesh – Right Hip and Buttock
Ramagiri, Chitrakoot – Right Breast
Vrindavan, Uttar Pradesh - Hair
Shuchi, Kanniyakumari, Tamil Nadu – Upper Teeth
Panch Sagar – Lower Teeth
Kartoyatat, Bangladesh – Sole of Left Foot
Shri Parvat, Ladakh – Sole of Right Foot
Vibhash, Tamluk, West Bengal - Left Ankle
Prabhas, Girnar Hills - Stomach
Bhairav Parvat, Ujjain - Upper Lip
Panchavati, Nasik, Maharastha - Chin
Patna, Bihar - Right Thigh
Godavaritir - Left Cheek
Ratnavali, Chennai - Right Shoulder
Mithila, Bihar - Left Shoulder
Vairat, Rajasthan – Toes and Foot Bones
Karnat – Ears

Vakreshwar - Brain
Yashohar, Bangladesh – Left Palm
Attahas, Labhpur, West Bengal – Lower Lip
Nandipur, West Bengal - Necklace
Lanka - Anklets
Danteshwari – Teeth.

In order to cultivate and reach a high stage of spiritual attainment you need to transform your physical body by opening up its Qi channels. Without transforming your Qi channels it is impossible to attain a higher spiritual body, samadhi or enlightenment.

The first great milestone target on the spiritual path is attaining a Qi or prana body that can leave your physical body at will, from which you can cultivate the higher stages of attainment. This astral attainment, called a "will-born body" in the Buddhist *Surangama Sutra*, is only possible if you transform the Qi and Qi channels of your physical body, namely all your *nadis* and chakras.

Most people think that the "purification" or "transformation" of Qi channels commonly mentioned in spiritual texts only refers to the major Qi channels (acupuncture meridians) of the body. In actual fact, since the very first step of spiritual cultivation is to create an internal subtle body made of Qi by clearing out all of the millions of Qi energy routes within your present body – an "etheric double" so-to-speak. In other words, all your Qi channels must be transformed. Cultivation work will purify your inner Qi body that already exists in latent form within your physical body. After sufficient cultivation work, this inner Qi body can then leave its physical body casing like a bird escaping from a cage.

The physical body therefore serves as a shell, casing or incubatory vessel for the inner Qi body. This Qi body leaves the physical body upon death, but we can cultivate the ability for this subtle body to become stronger and more purified so that it can leave and re-enter the physical nature at will. This is the lowest stage of being a guru or master. All masters have this ability but will never tell you.

You already have this latent subtle body within you, for in rudimentary form this is the body that leaves upon death or is ejected during accidents and out-of-the-body experiences. It is an exact duplicate of your physical body, but it is not pure enough to achieve success at spiritual cultivation, which has the target of enlightenment or self-realization. To achieve success you need a more purified type of vessel that you cultivate by first attaining the subtle Qi body, next repeating your practices with that Qi body to attain a more purified form, and then repeat the process to attain higher and higher bodies in sequence. Some of this information can be gleaned from Meher Baba's *God Speaks* and *Discourses*.

Devas and spirits (Buddhism refers to them as Desire Realm inhabitants) all possess this body composed of impure Qi (prana), which is why they are also cultivating in various ways (under the instructions and guidance of a master) to attain enlightenment. The spiritual pathways they use are devoid of the religious sectarianism and disunity championed found in the world since devas can see everything going on in the world, including the knowing of people's thoughts, and have teachers who clearly recognize the myths and mistakes in each religion. Therefore they eschew the sectarianism for the simple direct path of spiritual cultivation.

You can only attain self-realization – which means to realize the substance of the mind that is at an energy level even more subtle than coarse Qi – by cultivating your Qi (prana) and channels. From progress at this task you will advance on the road of spiritual practice.

Regardless of your religion, "spiritual progress" requires that all the Qi channels (*nadis*) within your physical body become free of obstructions, which we term becoming purified or opened. It is possible to go about accomplishing this by concentrating on the whole body as a single unit (as if it is something inside a rubber suit that must be transformed), or by focusing on individual body parts in sections. Don't think of your Qi channels as lines, but think of them as the energy bonds between all your atoms in a pathway. Your entire body must be flooded/saturated with Qi that circulates everywhere again and again and again through many years of refinement (until a deva body can emerge from within it) so thick body sections are a preferable way of thinking about Qi channels.

In other words, if you do enough spiritual cultivation work there will come a time when your Qi begins to stir and then pass through the different sections of your body, and then through your body as a whole. When you get to any stage where your Qi begins to roll, rotate, move, orbit or circulate (however you wish to describe it) throughout your body then you are advised to stay in meditation for as long as possible to continue that process of purification. This will slowly cause a deep purging of poisons from the body. Herbal (and other) detoxification efforts are helpful in this process, and can hasten the process of transformation. *Meditation Case Studies* explains what is happeneing when you start to feel energy sensations within your body.

It is not that there are 72,000 or any other figurative number of Qi channels in your coarse physical body, such as the "350,000 *nadis*" mentioned in the *Shiva Samhita*. In "opening up," "transforming" or "purifying" your Qi channels you basically have to flood all your cells and atoms in your body with Qi to transform everything, which is what creates the independent deva body. The teachings of Vajrayana Buddhism, Taoism, Hinduism and Yoga can serve as guides for accomplishment. Very few people know how to do it correctly, which is why this book was written.

The Shakti Peethas are not by any sense all-inclusive in terms of representing the parts of your body that must be cultivated. They are just indicative of the fact that every section of your body has to be cultivated in such a way that your Qi can eventually pass freely through each section because all the energy pathways in every tissue are clear of blockages. "Cultivation" means you have to work hard at practice exercises that will bring Qi to those regions, open up their Qi channels, and purge those areas of impurities and obstructions.

At the lowest, beginning stages of the cultivation path spiritual assistance is all about affecting your body's Qi and Qi channels. This is why people mantra for spiritual help or look for a spiritual master.

THE 24 VAJRAYOGINI HOLY PLACES

There are twenty-four tantric places (energy centers) of interest to Buddhist Vajrayana practitioners - related to Mahadeva, Heruka and Vajrayogini - that are also associated with parts of the human body.

These locations, which are of importance to those who follow the Vajrayogini tradition, symbolize the body of Vajrayogini and can be used to identify internal Qi energy practice sections just as can the Shakti Peethas and list of Shakyamuni's beautified features. They include:

Puliramalaya (between the eyebrows)
Jalandhara (crown of head)
Oddiyana (right ear)
Arbuta (nape of neck)
Godavari (left ear)
Rameshvari (the hair at the center of the forehead)
Devikota (eyes)
Malava (shoulders)
Kamarupa (underarms and kidneys)
Otri (breasts)
Trishakune (navel)
Kosala (nose-tip)
Kalingkara (palate)
Lampaka (throat)
Kanchi (heart)
Himalaya (brain)
Pretapuri (genitals)
Grihadeva (anus)
Shaurashtra (thighs)
Suvarnadvipa (calves)
Nagara (fingers and toes)
Sindhu (ankles)
Maruta (big toes)
Kuluta (knees).

When spiritual practitioners have not yet attained the deva body (the inner subtle body of Qi that can leave your physical body at will), they can concentrate on these body regions in special ways to help open up their Qi channels in the vicinity and purify their Qi of impurities. That is the purpose of ancient texts plotting out such earthly locations.

THE 12 JYOTIRLINGA

India also has the twelve Jyotirlinga, which are special sacred sites where Shiva is worshipped. According to legend, at these twelve locations the energies or light of Shiva became manifest, and so there are twelve Shiva temples at these locations which are spread all throughout India.

This popular explanation of light or energy in a region is obviously a reference to either the Feng Shui energies or the energies of helpful devas and enlightened Buddhas in the vicinity, who will help aspirants with their spiritual practices once again (they will help them open up their Qi channels). Whether or not Shiva was a person/being who actually lived, you can rest assured that there are enlightened helpers at these various locations who can and will help you open up your *nadis*.

The twelve Indian **Jyotirlinga** are located at Somnath in Gujarat, Mallikarjuna at Shrishailam in Andhra Pradesh, Mahakaleswar at Ujjain in Madhya Pradesh, Omkareshwar in Madhya Pradesh, Kedarnath in Uttrakhand, Bhimashankar at Pune in Maharashtra, Viswanath at Varanasi in Uttar Pradesh, Tryambakeshwar at Nashik in Maharashtra, Vaidyanath Temple at Deoghar in Jharkhand, Aundha Nagnath at Aundha in Hingoli District in Maharashtra, Rameshwar at Rameshwaram in Tamil Nadu and Grushneshwar at Ellora near Aurangabad, in Maharashtra.

India has many other sacred places where practitioners of every religion can gain assistance for their spiritual cultivation, such as the 108 Vishnu temples (**Divya Desam**) mentioned in the works of the Tamil Azhars (saints). The eight most sacred shrines for Hindu Vaishnavas, known as **Svayam Vyakta Ksetra**, include shrines at Muktinath, Srirangam, Srimushnam, Tirupati, Naimisharanya, Thotadri, Pushkar and Badrinath. There are also the **Chaar Dhaam** which include Badrinath in the north, Jagannath Puri in the east, Dwarka in the west and Rameshwaram in the south. There are also the **Sapt Puri** or seven holy cities of Ayodhya, Mathura, Haridwar, Varanasi, Kanchipuram, Ujjain and Dwarka.

WORLD SACRED SPOTS

There are also many other locations across the world where high stage Buddhas and devas often help practitioners cultivate their Qi. Just a few indicative locations include the sacred mountain Arunachala in Tiruvannamali where Ramana Maharshi lived; Meher Baba's tomb in Meherabad; Rumi's Mausoleum in Konya, Turkey; Ramalinga Swamigal's Sathya Gnana Sabha at Vadalur, India; Sathya Sai Baba's tomb in India; Bodhgaya in India where Shakyamuni

Buddha became enlightened; the Buddhist Temple of the Tooth in Sri Lanka; the Mhajuraho Group of Hindu and Jain temples in Madhya Oradesh, India; Mount Parnassus in Greece; Boudhanath, Nepal; Angkor Wat, Cambodia; Borobudur, Indonesia; the Shrine of the Bab, founder of Babism, in Haifa, Israel; the shrine of Baha'u'llah, founder of the Baha'i Faith, near Acre, Israel; Ali Hajwari's tomb in Lahore, Pakistan; Bawaldin Zikrya's tomb in Multan, Pakistan; Shah Jalal's tomb in Sylhet, Bangladesh; the Grand Mosque in Mecca, Prophet's Mosque in Medina, and al-Aqsa Mosque in Jerusalem; the Golden Temple of Sikhism at Sri Harmandir Sahib; various Christian holy sites in Israel; the Church of St. George in Istanbul; the Tomb of Jethro in Israel, sacred to the Druze; the Cave of the Patriarchs in Hebron, Israel; Mount Haguro, Mount Gassan, and Mount Yudono, sacred to the Shugendo; the Temple of Confucius in Qufu; and Ise Shrine in Japan, sacred to Shintoism.

It is too difficult to list a mantra for the presiding enlightened Buddhas at each location, so the following is a rare list of mantras that you can use for various spiritual traditions. They are especially useful when you visit attendant spiritual locations for spiritual assistance in cultivating your Qi and channels. Anyone can use these mantras without belonging to that tradition. You are encouraged to try them and see which ones produce a result, and you should then note the ones with which you have the most energetic affinity:

Buddhism – Om Ah Lah Tah Sah Mah Rah Pah Hah Soha
Buddhism (alternative) - Om Ah Hah Sah Mah Tah Rah Mah Tha
  Sah Hung Ha
Kundalini Yoga – Om Ah Hung Ha Hung Hah Tsa Lah Rah Mah
  Tah Hung Ha Soha
Taoism – Om Ah Vah Lah Hah Mah Tah Rah Zah Mah Tah Hah
Taoism (alternative) - Om Ah Rah Pah Tah Rah Sah Hah Fah Lah
  Rah Hung
Shinto – Om Ah Rah Pah Sah Mah Tah Hah Lah Rah Mah Tah Hah
  Sah Tah Lah Rah Mah Tah Hah Sah Lah Rah Hum
Shinto (alternative) - Om Ah Rah Pah Tsa Mah Tah Lah Rah Hah
  Sah Soha
Koshinto – Om Ah Rah Pah Tsa Rah Mah Tah Hah Lah Pah Rah
  Tah Soha
Shugendo – Om Ah Rah Tah Sah Lah Mah Tah Hah Rah Sah Tah

Mah Tah Hah Lah Rah Sah Tah Soha
Yoshida Shinto – Om Ah Hung Soha
Tenrikyo - Om Ah Hung Hah Hung Om Hah Soha
Sikhism – Om Ah Rah Tah Mah Hah Sah Lah Mah Tah Sah Lah Rah
    Mah Tah Sah Hah Soha
Caodaism – Om Ah Rah Pah Tsa Nah Dee Dee Dee
Jainism – Om Ah Re-Pee Om Ah Hum Ah Tah Zah Hah Rah Lah
    Rah Mah Tah Hah Soha
Meivazhi – Om Ah Rah Tah Mah Hah Lah Rah Tah Sah Mah Hah
    Rah Mah Tah Soha
Zorastrianism – Om Ah Tah Rah Lah Mah Tah Hah Sah Rah Lah
    Mah Tah Hah Lah Soha
Yazdanism (and Yazidism) – Om Ah Tah Lah Rah Mah Tah Hah
    Sah Soha
Judaism – Om Ah Lah Rah Hah Sah Mah Tah Lah Rah Hah Soha
Orthodox Judaism – Om Ah Vah Lah Hum Ah
Wicca – Rah Mah Tah Sah Lah Hah Hum
Dahomey – Om Ah Hum Ah Rah Tah Sah Mah Lah Hah Sah Soha
Yoruba – Hah Mah Tah Sah Lah Rah Hah Tah Mah Tah Sah Lah
    Rah Hah Sah Lah Mah Tah Hah Sah Lah Tah Hah Sah Lah Tah
    Mah Sah Lah Hum
South African – Hah Lah Sah Hum

THE CHINESE SACRED MOUNTAINS

China has the four holy mountains of Buddhism – Wutai Shan, Emei Shan, Jiuhua Shan and Putuo Shan – that are "auspicious" for making progress at self-cultivation. A special energetic sensation can be felt at these mountains, which is their inherent Feng Shui energy from the earth, and this natural energy penetrates practitioners' bodies to help open up their Qi channels. The presence of natural helpful energies from the environment (or the presence of helpful devas) is often why masters set up temples in certain locations.

Whenever you visit a location with "good Qi" you are soaking in those natural energies. If they are strong energies, that extra boost of natural environmental forces will assist your own cultivation efforts by helping to open your Qi channels. If you perform pranayama *kumbhaka* (breath retention) exercises at those locations this would be especially beneficial for your progress.

These natural beneficial energies explain why practitioners like to spend time cultivating at certain sacred mountain locations. Not all of them are beneficial in this way, but you get the general idea as to why they can be important.

Basically, the energies of the mountain can be used/borrowed to augment your own efforts to open your Qi channels, and if they are "sacred" locations they are also often populated by helpful spiritual beings who might assist you with your cultivation efforts.

China also has the four sacred mountains of Taoism – Wudang Shan, Longhu Shan, Qiyun Shan and Qingcheng Shan – that function in this manner. Other Chinese mountains with spiritual significance include Mount Lao, Mount Sanqing, Mount Lu and Mount Changbai. There are even particular mantras that request Qi cultivation assistance which you can recite for some of these locations, such as:

Wutai Shan (China) – Ah Bey Rah Hum
Emei Shan (China) – Om Ah Hum
Jiuhua Shan (China) – Om Ah Hung Hah
Putuo Shan (China) – Om Mani Bey Mee Hum
Wudang Shan (China) – Om Ah Lah Rah Pah Tsah Hum
Longhu Shan (China) – Joe Lah Rah Mah Tah Hah Sah Hum
Qiyun Shan (China) – Eee Hah Lah Rah Mah Tah Sah Lah Hum
Qingcheng Shan (China) – Mah Lah Tah Rah Sah Mah Hah Hum
Mount Lao (China) – Yo Hah Mah Tah Lah Rah Hum
Mount Sanqing (China) - Yo Lah Hah Mah Tah Lah Fah Rah Mah
        Tah Hum
Mount Lu (China) – Mah Lah Rah Tah Hum
Mount Changbai (China) – Mah Lah Tah Rah Hah Sah Lah Hum

OTHER LOCATIONS

Are there other holy places throughout the world that are helpful like this?

Of course. Sacred locations may be found in mountains, islands, healing springs, lakes, special shrines, temples, monasteries and especially *the tombs of enlightened masters.*

Like the human body, the earth itself is a physical body that in special spots throws off energies particularly helpful to cultivation. Sometimes masters recognize this, which is why temples, ashrams, shrines and monasteries or nunneries were often built in certain locales. Most locations are not energetically beneficial in any unusual way, so don't expect benefits everywhere you go including when a location is considered "sacred." Most often the location was simply convenient or the residence of lots of helpful heavenly beings (devas). However, sometimes at certain locations you can tap into special environmental energies to help you in opening up your Qi channels, which is another reason sages undertake retreats in particular locales. However, no environmental Qi can open Qi channels for you. You can only borrow these energies, and must additionally do a lot of pranayama, nei-gong and other cultivation work yourself. Pranayama, where you hold your breath (*kumbhaka*) in order to force Qi channels to open internally, is particularly important in this regard.

Wherever you are right now you can also request higher spiritual beings who are enlightened (Buddhas, Bodhisattvas, Arhats, masters, gurus, tradition founders, sages, saints, etc.) for assistance in opening up your channels, which is why you normally recite prayers and mantras. This attracts the attention of higher beings to your efforts. Make no mistake in thinking you must travel elsewhere because assistance is always available if you just ask for it by working hard at cultivation, reading the right spiritual texts, and *reciting mantras asking for assistance*. Mantra recitiation is like shooting off a flare asking for spiritual assistance in transforming your prana and *nadis*.

In Vajrayana Buddhism one of the main points of emphasis is on transforming your physical body, which is necessary so that you can attain enlightenment. Therefore Vajrayana practitioners recite prayers asking for assistance on four important, fundamental matters that are relevant for all spiritual students:

(1) opening up their Qi channels so that their body becomes warmer, softer and more flexible,

(2) attaining a body that is as soft and healthy as a baby's body so that it becomes an aid rather than obstacle on the spiritual path,

(3) learning how to make their Qi begin to circulate without obstruction, which will help reduce any angry or violent tendencies, and

(4) activating and mastering the true Yang Qi, kundalini fire,

or *dantian* fire of the body in order to reach a stage of calmness, bliss and warmth and ultimately succeed in creating an independent deva body.

Another set of prayers is that (1) your energies are joyous, (2) your Qi channels open, and (3) you achieve great bliss and the emptiness-wisdom of enlightenment.

Normally when you visit the shrine of a Moslem saint, called a Dargah or Mazar (which literally means a place for visit or place of paying homage), you call on the saint's name when you need help or assistance for life, but you can ask them for cultivation assistance as well. This is the standard practice done throughout the Moslem world, such as at the Mazar of Kwaja Moinuddin Chishti at Ajmer (India); Mazar of Hazrat Nizamuddin in Delhi; the Mausoleum of Shah Gradez in Pakistan; the Mausoleum of Bayazid Bastami in Bastam (Iran); Al-Ghazali Mausoleum in Tus (Iran); or Mausoleum of Nadir Shah in Mashhad (Iran).

This is certainly an incomplete list of sacred location and by no means attempts to show favoritism to any of these saints or disparage those who Mazars are unlisted.

Whenever you find a Christian cathedral or church containing the incorruptible relics of a saint's body (which indicates that they achieved definite spiritual attainments since the delayed decomposition indicates they fully purified their Qi channels and attained a subtle deva body at minimum), then one can also call upon the saint's name for assistance as is normal in the Christian tradition.

There are many Christian saints qualified to render assistance, just as there are many qualified saints and sages from every other genuine tradition as well. If you have any doubts about the qualifications of a Christian saint, you must research their history for miracles or verify that their body showed the signs of incorruptibility after death. A short but illustrative list of such Christian saints can be found in The *Incorruptibles* by Joan Carroll Cruz or *Mysteries Marvels Miracles in the Lives of the Saints*, by Joan Carroll Cruz. You can call upon these saints (and others) for assistance since their incorruptible bodies showed that they achieved a stage of accomplishment on the spiritual path. By no means is available help limited to just those saints who demonstrated miracles.

Whenever anyone achieves an incorruptible body that doesn't

decay after death, it proves that they succeeded in their Qi and channel cultivation (and thus attained a subtle deva body). Otherwise their body would have immediately decomposed upon death. If miracles are also attributed to that individual, it is further proof of spiritual attainments since miracles can only be achieved by someone who attains a purified independent Qi body. All the masters who attain this keep quiet about the achievement for obvious reasons.

In short, all sorts of assistance for your body and life is available from the spiritual denizens of sacred locations and temples or shrines as well as from living and deceased saints and sages of various religions (help is non-denominational), but you have to do most of the cultivation work on your body and mind yourself. You have to put tremendous hours into the cultivation practice of purifying your Qi and channels that can be accomplished through a variety of spiritual exercises.

Since this is a common requirement for all spiritual practitioners, the aspirants of every religion should freely borrow these practices from one another including from different spiritual traditions. At their core they are non-denominational common practices free of religion and should always be viewed that way.

The foundational cultivation exercises for any type of higher spiritual attainments would be various visualization practices on internal parts of your body (to move your Qi there), pranayama breath work techniques, mantra techniques and inner nei-gong practices that move the Qi within body parts. These techniques, and others, are taught in this book. Nyasa Yoga falls into these practices.

In Vajrayana Buddhism (as well as in Chinese Taoism and Indian Kaula Tantric Yoga paths), one should know that sexual practices to internally move your Qi are also permitted to help you open your Qi and channels, but to be qualified you need to do a tremendous amount of prior hard work and proficiency at these special visualization, breathing (pranayama) and nei-gong practices. In particular, the white skeleton visualization, mantra practice, and *kumbhaka* pranayama are the prerequisites for any type of sexual cultivation practices because without that foundation your efforts will be useless.

CHAPTER 3
THE FIVE PURIFIED BODIES

The reason there is a spiritual emphasis on the different parts of your body is because they must all be transformed on the spiritual path. Every atom and cell of your body must be washed with Qi *for years* to open up all the channels and create an independent deva body.

If you want to succeed on any path of spiritual practice you must cultivate your coarse physical body of bones and flesh through a pathway that purifies its prana and *nadis* (Qi and Qi) channels, and this is normally called kundalini cultivation. This washing of your body via Yang Qi will purify your underlying subtle Qi body, which is like an invisible scaffolding permeating every atom, cell and tissue of your physical body. Once you sufficiently purify or transform your inner Qi body, which takes at least twelve years after an initial Kundalini Awakening, it can then leave your physical shell at will.

Your inner subtle Qi body is basically an etheric energy duplicate of your physical body that leaves during out-of-the-body experiences and upon death. It is a perfect body double composed of Qi/prana, which is an energy more subtle than the material body, and thus it cannot be seen or measured. Because it is made of Qi it has all the powers related to those energies that appear miraculous to humans, whose bodies exist on a lower plane of material condensation.

As of yet, science cannot sense or measure Qi energies at all. Hence, even though we all possess a subtle inner energy body duplicate, since it is not composed of particles modern science does not yet recognize its existence. Qi also has higher energy substance derivatives called Shen, Clear Light and so forth. You can think of them as more subtle forms of matter that are less dense than our own, but still condensed forms of energy. Thus they belong to different spiritual planes of existence.

Through spiritual practice our inner subtle body or etheric double can become an independent deva body, also called an astral body, deity body or *yin-shen*, that can leave your physical shell whenever you want to roam or do things in the world. Attaining this body is the equivalent to becoming a junior-level spiritual master.

Buddhism calls the subtle body the "will-born" body because with its attainment you can, *at will*, put on and take off the external body as if it were a cloak and use your subtle body for experiencing the astral world. This is the Buddhist stage of the Srotapanaa, or "stream entrant," which is the first level of the Arhats. When you can consciously separate the inner subtle body from the physical shell, this makes you feel a greater distinction from being the gross body, but your root nature is not the subtle body either. The root nature of the universe is an ultimate substance/essence or ground energy level.

As Meher Baba and Shakyamuni Buddha explained, upon attaining the subtle deva body achievement you will consider yourself to be this subtle body, which will then become the center of all your activities. Therefore you will now have two bodies you can occupy – a physical and subtle. A new mode of life will then open up along with new powers and possibilities. You will still live in your physical body but your new life will be centered in this higher subtle body until you cultivate another body yet higher, the Causal or Mental body made of Shen that is derived from cultivating the body of Qi. Then you will simultaneously possess three bodies, each capable of doing different things independently of the others.

Upon attaining this Causal body the same process of purification will repeat itself. You will appear to others as existing in the sheaths of the physical or subtle body while actually living in that Causal body, but you can also use your lower bodies to do independent things like extra appendages. For instance, you can use your Causal body to give someone a series of thoughts while using the Qi of your subtle body to be independently working on an individual's Qi to help open up its Qi channels.

When you achieve the next higher body composed of Clear Light (Later Heavenly Qi/Prana) you will then take that as the new center of your life while still appearing to others in the lower bodies, and onwards it goes. With each new body you identify with it as your life vessel, but you maintain a connection with all your lower bodes and use them independently.

While the physical body of form can be considered a solidification of energy, the subtle body of Qi or prana belongs to the realm of energy. Being composed of energy, the subtle body's capabilities are therefore free of the limitations that apply to the human realm. This body can increase or decrease in size, travel incredible distances at will, and become heavier or lighter with thought. It can exhibit a variety of superpowers, as mentioned in Yoga texts, that are actually ordinary powers to subtle plane inhabitants. When a human being believes he has developed superpowers those powers are actually due to these beings and not himself.

The subtle body can see, hear and smell many things inaccessible to the physical body and perform many actions – all of which are achieved by means of energy – that seem miraculous to beings who only possess physical forms. In this body, consciousness is continuously linked with energy and continuously vibrates with energy. The miracles it can perform, such as with healing, all have to do with Qi or energy.

The next spiritual transition upwards is from the subtle body to the Causal body, Mental body, Mantra body or purified illusory body, which is an advance toward a yet higher or purer state of being. Within this body made of Shen, consciousness is no longer fettered by the domination of either the physical body or energy. However, even with this body and its concomitant purity of consciousness, the individual mind or ego-shell cannot attain to the higher realm of Clear Light that constitutes initial enlightenment (*nirvana* with remainder). The Causal body attainment, as high as it is, still does not belong to the level of enlightenment. That body is also not to be considered the ultimate self-nature, but many people become fixated at this stage due to the vast number of superpowers that now become possible in this higher sphere.

One of the most difficult tasks on the road of spiritual cultivation is to go from the Causal body to the Supra-Causal Clear Light body of initial enlightenment, which is difficult because the mind has to be annihilated through the mind itself. To do so you must continue doing all the spiritual practices that you used to attain the subtle body. This requires *both mind and body cultivation.*

If you think that spiritual cultivation is just a matter of meditation alone while ignoring inner energy work – which is a mistaken notion taken up by Zen students who don't know better – you will not achieve the states of dhyana or the body attainments necessary as the foundation for the Tao. You cannot attain dhyana unless you transform the body by opening up its Qi channels, which means cultivating the subtle body attainment. For a higher level of dhyana you need to open up the energy channels within the subtle body and from within it attain a Causal body, and so on it goes.

This whole sequence of spiritual progress – the true spiritual path – either starts upon your arrival in heaven where you become free of religion because you learn the universal truth or upon earth when you start cultivating any of the Yoga roads to these achievements. This path is clearly taught in Buddhism, Hinduism, Taoism, Sufism, Yoga, etcetera. Nyasa Yoga practice is one of those practice road vehicles.

Without a deva body the way you normally arrive at heaven is twofold. As a human you can die and go to heaven (which is just experiencing our world in the higher subtle state of etheric energy) or be reborn in heaven to parents who are already devas.

Death happens to humans when the soul or subtle body (made of Qi) *permanently* excretes the lower physical body shell that encases it. The same applies for any higher body. Your inner subtle body of Qi permanently leaves behind its previous encasing and then lives a life in the subtle sphere independent of the lower physical nature. Religions usually say that your soul or spirit leaves and "goes to heaven," and there are plenty of near-death experiences where people have reported this.

Only an accomplished master can achieve the state where their inner Qi body can leave and then re-enter their body at will. This inner Qi body of a master (their deva or subtle body) is created through the fire of Yoga. Some individuals who achieve this then leave the physical world for good. Others with compassion stay and teach the spiritual path while simultaneously trying to cultivate yet higher spiritual bodies until they attain Complete and Perfect Enlightenment.

To an ordinary individual a spiritual master looks perfectly normal, but they are actually centered in their higher bodies while living in the world wearing their human body like a cloak and using it to interact with people. All higher bodies have the yoga siddhi powers of *anima* (the ability to shrink in size), *mahima* (the ability to expand in size), *garima* (ability to become heavier), *laghima* (ability to become almost weightless), *prapti* (ability to travel to all places and pass through denser matter), *prakamya* (absolute lordship) and *vastva* (power to subjugate others through possession) whereas the physical body does not have these powers at all.

Everything phenomenal in the universe is impermanent and thus destined to perish, including any higher subtle bodies. All bodies composed of energy, even though these are higher subtle essences, have a limited life span which means that life in heaven is also temporary even though normally longer than an earthly life span. After death, whether or not you remain long in a Qi body to "enjoy Heaven" and whether or not you quickly reincarnate again upon the death of that Qi body, it all depends upon how well you cultivated your inner Qi body during life and whilst in Heaven. It is also a function of merit.

The rule of longevity is that subtle, purified or refined essences age slower and retain their cohesion longer than less subtle, coarser elements. They last longer, and so your life in a higher realm lasts longer depending on your merit and how well you cultivated. Since the degree of your cultivation and life span are correlated to how purified your subtle body becomes, if you want to live longer you must always cultivate the path of spiritual practice.

This is not a unique lesson but a common teaching from Buddhism, Vajrayana, Hinduism, Chinese Taoism, Western Alchemy, and the Yoga schools. Most spiritual traditions will tell you that longer and longer life spans are enjoyed by those with greater and greater spiritual attainments since they cultivate their Qi and channels (prana and *nadis*) to attain higher bodies, and so now you know why.

THE FIRST FIVE HIGHER BODIES

To understand the nature of a Qi body we need to first review some basics of Jing, Qi, Shen, Later Heavenly Qi (Emptiness or Clear Light) and Original/Primordial Heavenly Qi. These are the known stages of the refinement of matter that masters talk about. They are energetic substances possible to be extruded from one another due to the practices of spiritual cultivation. If you eventually achieve a body composed of one of these substances then it indicates an advanced degree of physical purification on the road to self-realization.

Once you achieve an independent Qi body, which is the first milestone of physical attainments on the spiritual trail, you can then begin to start cultivating the ultimate Reward body. The final Enjoyment or Reward body is a perfected *sambhogakaya* body used by those having attained Complete Enlightenment. This is a body composed of a very subtle, refined fundamental energy that is called Original (Primordial or Early) Heavenly Qi. In yoga schools this compositional substance is called a fundamental wind or prana.

Despite its high stage, this attainment first starts with this human body of ours and requires a long process of purification, transformation or refinement in order to produce the first step that is the independent subtle body. Our solid material bodies of flesh and blood are composed of Jing, meaning that they arise from the mixture of an egg with semen, but they also have Qi within them. QI has Shen within it, Shen has Later Heavenly (or Clear Light) Qi within it, and Clear Light energy has Primordial Heavenly Qi within it. They are all simultaneously there even within a body of flesh. You should therefore think of the material body of Jing, or form, as solidified energy because it can be cultivated to produce higher states.

Human beings think in terms of the mundane physical body, but once they attain a Qi (subtle, astral, deva, deity, etheric) body they think in terms of energy. Those whose bodies are composed of Qi (devas, angels, protect gods, dakis and dakinis, spirits, etc.) perform many energy feats for human beings to help them. When you say that "a miracle came from God" it usually came from a deva exercising his or her powers.

The transition from the subtle plane to the Causal, conceptual plane of energy constitutes a further advance in the ranks of cultivation achievements. Therefore beings who achieve what is called the Causal, Mental, Mantra, Wisdom or purified illusory body made of Shen (Spirit) are at a stage higher and have more capabilities than devas who have bodies composed of Qi. With this Causal body attainment your consciousness is no longer fettered by the domination of the body or energy but is imprisoned by thoughts; it is mind-ridden. Nevertheless, this body made of Shen lasts longer than bodies composed of Qi and Jing.

The Buddhist sutras and Hinduism clearly teach that sentient beings who live in successively higher heavenly realms have longer and longer life spans so once again you can surmise that those who attain this body will live longer than devas.

Those who reach initial enlightenment (*nirvana* with remaining dependency), and therefore achieve Dharma bodies composed of Later Heavenly Prana (Qi) or Clear Light Prana (Qi) have much longer life spans longer than those beings who have bodies composed of Jing, Qi or Shen. They also have more capabilities as well. As you would expect, those who attain the *sambhogakaya* Reward body required for Perfect and Complete Enlightenment have bodies composed of Primordial Heavenly Prana (Original Heavenly Qi) and the longest life spans of all compared to beings having bodies composed of Later Heavenly Qi, Shen, Qi and Jing.

And so on it goes in terms of bodies, for while spiritual teachings usually stop at the stage of Perfect and Complete Enlightenment whose Enjoyment body is composed of Primordial Heavenly Prana, there are probably an infinite number of stages past this. After all, who can ever say with certainty that their body is composed of the most Primordial First Essence, the primordial absolute substratum that is responsible for all subsequent cosmic energy and matter? How would you know that you could not purify it even further and reach a yet higher stage of attainment? Nearly all spiritual teachings for the human realm are for certain reasons limited to discussing just these five levels.

As with Qi, Shen and the higher Pranas, the ultimate, absolute, fundamental or Primal Essence or energy substratum, whatever it is, must be within us but be so subtle in nature that no one can detect what it is. We only need some way to cultivate and refine that foundational essence out from its lower evolutes to enjoy a physical form composed of that purer essence. Then one can live a yet longer life made of that substance.

Many masters work furiously to generate a body at this level as soon as possible. Every body generated through cultivation must rise from within a body of the lower level substance, and the lowest level is the impure human body that can first give rise to the deva body of subtle Qi. Hence you must work very hard to purify your physical body to affect your inner Qi body of subtle energy. The way to do so is through devoted spiritual energy yoga practices such as Nyasa Yoga. It is through the road of spiritual practices that you can attain all five bodies that are commonly mentioned in most spiritual traditions. Are those five bodies really mentioned? Yes!

For instance, the sage **Sri Siddharameshwar Maharaj** (Vedanta) taught that we have the Physical, Subtle, Causal, Supra-Causal and Para-atman bodies. These correspond to bodies made of the five essences previously mentioned. You are encouraged to read his books.

Taoism talks about the five bodies being made of Jing, Qi, Shen, Later Heavenly Qi and Primordial Heavenly Qi. It states that the stages of the spiritual path are that "Jing transforms into Qi, Qi into Shen, Shen into Emptiness, and you have to abandon even Emptiness to return to the Tao."

This means that when the Jing body transforms you can attain a Qi body, when the Qi body transforms (is purified) you can attain a Shen or Causal body out of it, when the Shen body purifies you can attain Emptiness (which corresponds to the Supra-Causal or Dharma body), and you have to go past this stage to get the highest body whose corresponding mental continuum is "considered" the Tao, or original nature. The Supra-Causal or Emptiness attainment corresponds to the Clear Light body or Dharma body of Later Heavenly Qi (Prana) while the Tao/Immanence body that is (supposedly) one with the original nature is composed of Primordial Heavenly Qi (Prana), and is akin to the perfect *sambhogakaya* Enjoyment Body of Buddhism.

Taoism, as well as several other ancient spiritual traditions such as the **Greek and Medieval Mystery Schools**, also promotes the concept of five elements transforming into one another to denote the five bodies. Thus you have the earth (Physical body), water (Subtle body), fire (Causal or Mental body), wind (Supra-Causal body) and space (Primordial Heavenly Qi body) elements that transform into one another. In Taoism, with each new body attainment you become a different type of "Taoist Immortal," which are stages of accomplishment that can be matched with the Buddhist Arhat stages of attainment.

In the *Diamond Sutra*, **Shakyamuni Buddha** clearly pointed to the five bodies by talking about the Human eye, Deva eye, Wisdom eye, Dharma eye and Buddha eye. These eyes belong to the same five bodies we have been discussing – the Human body (corresponding to the form skandha/aggregate), Deva body (Subtle body corresponding to the sensation skandha), Mental body (Causal body corresponding to the conception skandha), Dharma body (initial *nirvana* with remainder enlightenment body of Later Heavenly Prana), and Buddha body (the perfect *sambhogakaya* body composed of Primordial Heavenly Prana).

When Buddhism talks about your physical actions, verbal actions (speech), mental actions, willful resolutions, and then subtle knowledge or sublime wisdom it is also referring to the Physical body, Subtle body, Causal body, Supra-Causal body and perfected *sambhogakaya*. Naturally these are also the form skandha, sensation skandha, conception skandha, volition skandha, and consciousness skandha by other names.

The *alaya* consciousness of Buddhism, which is the immediate (but not final) source of matter and mind, corresponds to the stage of initial enlightenment that an Arhat achieves. This corresponds to the composite volition skandha that encompasses the predispositional forces (elements) of both mind and matter. You attain these stages of realization by cultivating the Supra-Causal body, but it is not yet Complete Enlightenment.

Christianity talks about the stages of the Body, Soul, Spirit, Kingdom of Heaven, and union with the Father or ultimate one. This sequence refers to five bodies composed of the same higher essences previously discussed. In this case you should note that Christianity calls the most primal essence (original nature) the "Father" while Hinduism calls It "Shiva" and Islam calls It "Allah."

Vajrayana or Tantric Buddhism talks about the Physical body, Impure illusory body (subtle or deva body), Purified illusory body, Wisdom light (Clear light) or Dharma body and then Buddha body, which is the perfect *sambhogakaya* Enjoyment/Reward body made of very subtle fundamental wind. There are many different names used by Vajrayana Buddhism and Dzogchen to signify these attainment stages, so the terminology used here may be different than what you normally encounter. For instance, Buddhism also matches the five bodies and skandhas with the Buddhas Akshobya, Ratnasambhava, Amitabha, Amoghasiddhi and Vairocana.

Sadguru Sadafal Deoji Maharaj of the **Vihangham Yoga**

tradition (a **Nath Siddha** tradition) also clearly states that we can cultivate higher bodies. Starting from our Gross body we can also attain a Subtle body, Causal body, Prime Causal body, and Superconsciousness body. In the Nath tradition the technical names are a *Sthula deha, Sukshma deha, Karana deha, Mahakaran deha*, and *Hansa deha*, which are the same five bodies that everyone else mentions.

Ramalinga, of the **Tamil Siddha and Nath Yoga** traditions, talks about the stages of cultivation achievement starting with the unripe Physical body and then proceeding to a purified Qi body, body of Vibrations, Wisdom Light body and then Body of Immanence. These five bodies are the *Stuhla deha, Suddha deha, Mantra deha, Jnana deha* (*Divya deha* or body of light, *Kailaya deha*), and Body of Immanence. Even though the *Suddha deha* is just the subtle body of Qi we normally achieve by cultivating spiritual practices, because this body is higher than our physical nature he calls it a "perfected body."

In **Druze** (which is a Unitarian religion that combines aspects from Islam, Judaism, Christianity, Gnosticism, Neoplatonism, Pythagoreanism, and Hinduism) we have the five limits, which represent the five spheres of existence. We then have the Physical body as well as the Universal Soul sphere representing the Subtle body, the Logos/Word sphere representing the Mental Plane or Causal body, the Cause/Precedent Sphere relating to the *alaya* consciousness of Buddhism (and thus the Supra-Causal body composed of Later Heavenly Prana), and the Immanence sphere representing the Primordial Heavenly Prana body necessary for Complete and Perfect Enlightenment.

The **Sufi Meher Baba** talks about us having a Gross body, Subtle body, Mental body, Universal body and Shiva-Atma or Paramatma body. He also talks about the ranks of spiritual attainment being the rahrav (or wayfarer) that is the ordinary individual; wali (friend of God) or advanced yogi who is someone that attains the first or second dhyana; the pir, sant or perfect yogi who is someone that attains the third dhyana; and the Sadguru or Mahayogi who gains *Wasla* or divine union, which is the enlightenment of the fourth dhyana. In his terminology the Beyond-Beyond state of *Wara-ul-Wara* or *Ghaib-ul-Ghaib*, which is the state of Complete and Perfect Enlightenment, is the *Paramatm* state. These stages also match with the different body attainments.

The *Taittiriya Upanishad* and **Advaita Vedanta sage Shankara** spoke of the five sheaths covering our True Self being the *annamaya kosha* (foodstuff body), *pranayama kosha* (energy or Qi body made of Prana), *manomaya kosha* (mind-stuff sheath or Causal body), *vijnanamaya kosha* (wisdom sheath) and *anandamaya kosha* (bliss sheath). The five *koshas* also correspond to the five bodies of the spiritual path. If you cultivate the five body attainments you are also cultivating the five koshas. Many scholars mistake the *vijnanamaya kosha* (wisdom sheath) and *anandamaya kosha* (bliss sheath) as pre-enlightenment koshas, but this is incorrect. Most of the information about this is meant to mislead people on purpose. The *vijnanamaya kosha* corresponds to the enlightenment of the Arhat (a Supra-Causal body attainment) and *anandamaya kosha* refers to the Immanence body attainment of Perfect and Complete Enlightenment, namely a perfect *sambhogakaya.*

The great Indian sage **Goraksnath** talks about there being five stages to the self-unfoldment of the Divine Shakti, or five stages of her self-manifestation. This, too, ends up corresponding to five bodies that can traverse or enjoy five different realms of being and all act independently.

Islam also has a Sufi philosophy of emanation or Divine Descent that mentions five realms of being. These correspond to the five bodies. According to this scheme the First, Original or Primordial level of existence is Allah, an incorporeal existence that is the original nature. This is *Alam-i-HaHoot*, the Realm of He-ness (Is-ness). It is the primordial Divine Essence prior to manifestation that exists as Alonehood (*Ahdiyat*). According to Sufism, *Ahdiyat* is primordially pure and incapable of being conceived; this essence exists and cannot be exemplified with anything. It is at the primordial level of non-Creation and somehow everything emanates from It despite its absolute purity or aloneness. Non-Moslems call this the True Self, True Reality, Anama (Nameless Origin), Buddha nature, Parabrahman, Nirguna Brahman (Brahman without attributes), Shiva, Father, original nature or fundamental essence.

From the First (Allah) or Real emanates the existence of a second. This is an utterly incorporeal substance called *Alam-i-YaHoot* (the Realm of First Manifestation) that is an existence dependent on the first which *appears* different from its own essence (Allah) and yet is not a separate entity. It is *Wahid-ul-wujud*, or Unitary Existence.

In Hinduism this is Saguna Brahman while according to Goraksnath this is Nija-Sakti that is pure, eternal, and imperceptible. Consciousness schools relate this sphere of energy to an undisturbed state of consciousness simply in order to make correspondences that prompt you to cultivate emptiness. In Buddhism this first emanate or manifestation level corresponds to the substance of the *sambhogakaya*. Thus the Immanence body is composed of the refined energy/substance of this sphere/plane of existence.

In Islam *Alam-i-HaHoot* is said to have no attributes and yet the first manifestation of *Alam-i-YaHoot* is by definition an attribute. To explain it one must say that the attributes of God are neither other than God nor identical with Him. They are *appearances* and thus seem different or apart from Him but they cannot be other than Him since they are Him in essence.

Something somehow appears from the original essence without attributes, but no one knows how since the original essence cannot change. Since It cannot change It cannot give birth to anything. Furthermore, that which somehow appears cannot be different from the original essence and yet because there is an appearance (where previously there was none) it must be different in form or quality from that which originally has no attributes, and yet is the same thing.

To explain this, Hinduism says that Saguna Brahman appears from Nirguna Brahman. Even so, Shakti (the Primal Illusion or entire realm of manifestation) and Shiva (the original nature) are essentially the same. Shiva (the original Nature or Parabrahman) and Shakti permeate one another, are the same as one another, or non-different.

Buddhism also explains this saying that that all things related to *nirvana* and *samsara* are interdependent. Furthermore, it says that in the twelve links of interdependent origination karmic formations somehow appear from the original nature, and uses the word "ignorance" to explain that we don't know how karmic formations first appear. How can something emanate or diffuse out of an ultimate energy state or substance that is perfectly pure, free of impurities and never alters? No one knows, just as no one knows in quantum mechanics how a wave can become a particle and a particle can become a wave. Nevertheless, in time the "karmic formations" somehow form, develop or evolve into the universe including sentient life capable of consciousness because of its structure. You cannot take the Old Testament Bible seriously and consider that this process simply took a matter of days.

Continuing, *Alam-i-YaHoot* is the first step of Divine descent or emanation called *Noor-e-Mohammed* (the "Light of Mohammed"). Thus it is a "second" in the sense that the First, the *Alam-i-HaHoot*, was always pre-existing. You can also call it the "first emanation" instead of the "second existence." As stated, to Hinduism this is Saguna Brahman (Brahman with attributes) as opposed to Nirguna Brahman (Brahman without attributes). This is also Shakti, the partner of Parabrahman that never changes.

The whole universe and its creation are latent or hidden in *Noor-e-Mohammed* (Shakti) since it is their foundational substrate in terms of energy with attributes, but at this level of emanation the material universe is not yet in manifestation since that level of condensation has not yet happened. In Taoism this equates to the Earlier (Primordial or Original) Heavenly Prana and in the vernacular of consciousness Buddhism equates this with the realm of neither thought nor no-thought since this transcends the Later Heavenly Prana realm of the Supra-Causal body along with the *alaya* consciousness and it states of movement and non-movement.

In terms of consciousness, the *alaya* consciousness can be broken into two realms – a moving aspect of manifestation (that you can experience by cultivating the samadhi of infinite consciousness) and its unmoving aspect (that you can experience by cultivating the samadhi of infinite nothingness), which you can also consider an unmanifest state. For Goraksnath these two are Para-Sakti (which is unmanifest, indivisible and inscrutable) and Apara-Sakti (which corresponds to emanation, expansion, and active consciousness) that are the evolutes of Nija-Shakti which is itself the first evolute of Anama (the original nature).

Some Sufis, rather than properly referring to this as an energy plane, colloquially say that the second existence of *Alam-i-YaHoot* "is like awareness" and can know of its own existence, so the descriptive schemes of Ibn Sina and al-Farabi call it the "first intellect." This is actually the level of energy that Buddhism refers to as the consciousness skandha and Goraksnath says it is akin to an undisturbed state of consciousness. This level of energy being transcends all lower realms of sentient beings having consciousness. When Hinduism says that the whole universe is consciousness this is really referring to the energy substrate at this level *that isn't actually consciousness* but just an energy substrate that needs a body and life to become "consciousness" or "intellect."

The big problem with most spiritual schools is that they framed everything in terms of levels of consciousness in order to get people to cultivate meditation, namely empty and clear states of mind that don't cling to thoughts. However, the real truth is that you develop a spirit body composed out of a new plane of material more subtle than the last, and your mind/consciousness within that body is just as ordinary as it is in this plane although a little more empty, calm or pure because of all the work done in opening up cranial Qi channels during the generation process. For instance, if the Qi channels open in your brain then the energy flow within it will be more efficient. Your mind will accordingly be calmer and more quiet. However, you never really find the fundamental essence of the mind/consciousness, but just develop a body composed of the substance that corresponds to finer and finer levels of energy, and you identify one of these ultimately fine energy levels as the fundamental mind simply to motivate people to cultivate.

The Sufi idea is that from the acts of conception of the "first intellect" plane - its own cognitive acts - the other existences arise. In the *Surangama Sutra*, Shakyamuni Buddha also said that all the worlds and existences arise/form due to thoughts that produce karma or consequences. They arise due to the interdependence of cause and effect that links thoughts and actions with results. In other words, other existents arise due to previous existents. Al-Suhrawardi, in his Sufi philosophy of Illuminationism, also explains this by saying that it is through complex interaction that the various realms gives rise to one another and mundane reality. Taoism calls this transformation.

From the second existence of *Alam-i-YaHoot* (which is the first emanation), another non-corporeal emanation comes, which is the third plane of existence. This is called *Alam-i-LaHoot*, the Realm of Absolute Unity. It is also called the soul of Mohammed as well as *Rooh-e-Qudsi* (the Divine Soul). The other religions call this the realm of universal consciousness, cosmic consciousness or the *alaya* consciousness. It is a world of Unity – a purely incorporeal, purely spiritual, purely non-material realm that is transcendent to denser matter. Thus it corresponds to the Clear Light stage of Later Heavenly Prana, which is the Supra-Causal realm that eventually gives birth to all of denser created matter.

This is a composite sphere and in Buddhism this is also called the volition skandha that encompasses the roots of both matter and mind. Few in Buddhism know that the volition skandha, which represents components of both mind and material forces, is at the same level as the *alaya* consciousness that is the root of matter and mind. Properly speaking, despite the mistake in many texts, the consciousness skandha is actually one step higher than the individual's volition skandha and the "cosmic unity" level of the *alaya* consciousness.

In Islam the *alaya* consciousness attainment is the stage of *wahdiyat* or conscious Oneness (Oneness in Manyness). At this level of unity, an individual can become conscious of Oneness-in-many. Anyone who reaches the initial *nirvanic* stage of enlightenment calls this realm Oneness or Unity since you can know all minds. The substance of your body attainment is a refined stage of energy that transcends all the lower realms, thus permeating everything, and this fact leads to special abilities in terms of knowing about the happenings of lower realms. In short, everything corresponds across traditions once again. Up to this sphere of emanation, the stages of *HaHoot, YaHoot* and *LaHoot* are all above material creation.

The fourth level of emanation is then *Alam-i-Jabrut* (the Realm of Power), which is a bridge to the lower realms and thus the Causal sphere. This is equivalent to the conception skandha in Buddhism. In Islam this is also *Mumtan-ul-wujud* or the Mental sphere.

The fifth level of emanation is the *Alam-e-Malakut* (Realm of Intelligence) that corresponds to the Subtle plane and is responsible for the souls of animals and plants. This Islam also calls this *Mumkin-ul-wujud*, the world of angels and spirits. Obviously this is the realm you enter upon death, or attaining the subtle deva body, which corresponds to the sensation skandha of Buddhism. The emotions of lust, greed, etc. are felt within the subtle body, as are animal passions.

The *Alam-i-Nasut* (Realm of Physical Bodies) corresponds to the realm of matter and material bodies. This is also *Wajib-ul-wujud* (Necessary Existence), which is everything relating to gross corporeal existence. Thus you can see that even in Islam we have the five bodies, realms or spheres just like in other religions.

The Vedanta sage **Sri Nisargadatta** also said, "The person merges into the witness, the witness into awareness, awareness into pure being which becomes the real Self." This too corresponds to these five stages of spiritual advancement – person (Physical body), witness (Subtle body), awareness (Mental, Mantra or Causal body), Pure Being (Dharma body, Clear Light body or Later Heavenly Prana body), and real Self (Primordial Heavenly Prana body). In Vedanta, Parabrahman is the real Self or original nature.

Explaining the transformations of consciousness at the advanced stages of achievement, Nisargadatta also said, "When the 'I am myself' goes, the 'I am all' comes. When the 'I am all' goes, 'I am' comes. When even 'I am' goes, reality alone is." Within this sequence, the "I am all' stage (which is sometimes called cosmic or universal consciousness) corresponds to initial enlightenment, which is the unity stage of the *alaya* consciousness. It corresponds to *nirvana* with remainder (initial enlightenment), the achievement of the Later Heaven body (the Clear Light body or Dharma body) whose substance transcends the entire physical plane.

People who first attain enlightenment commonly describe it by saying that they are everything ("I am all") because their body substance is at a higher plane of existence (energy) that now transcends all of lower material creation yet permeates it all. Because the thoughts and consciousness of sentient beings in lower realms is due to energies they now transcend, in terms of consciousness the adept can now readily know all these thoughts through special means. Thus they attain "union with God," "cosmic consciousness," "universal consciousness," "unity consciousness," "super consciousness," or the *alaya* consciousness. This is why Mahavira, the founder of Jainism, said that the Self attaining omniscience had access to infinite knowledge, perfect perception, infinite bliss and infinite energy.

In Buddhist terminology, when you achieve the samadhi of infinite nothingness, this is when you surpass the stage of "I am all" that corresponds to the samadhi of infinite consciousness. All thoughts drop away in the samadhi of infinite nothingness. This samadhi, which is absent of thought, enables you to develop the Original Heaven Prana body whose concomitant realm of unmanifest consciousness (supposedly) corresponds to the realization of True Reality.

This nomenclature is all just skillful means since there are probably higher stages still. Therefore the Primordial Heavenly Qi attainment is not yet the proper correspondent to the foundational, ultimate state of True Reality, but every spiritual tradition speaks only about these initial five stages of attainment.

Buddhism also talks about the ten Bodhisattva bhumis, which are also stages of accomplishment on the cultivation trail. Each set of two bhumis refers to a body-mind attainment level, but the bhumis normally only run to ten stages of the cultivation path. Thus we only have five bodies. However, if we go to a set of thirteen bhumis, as is also possible within Buddhism, we introduce an extra body-mind attainment past the typical tenth bhumi normally taken as complete enlightenment. In some Vajrayana traditions even more bhumis are discussed that correspond to yet higher attainments.

You don't need to talk about anything higher than the first five bodies because it is hard enough to get even this far. Furthermore, most spiritual schools talk about consciousness rather than body attainments although there is a one-to-one correspondence of body composition (plane of energy) and the attendant/concomitant clarity of consciousness for a body of that composition. For instance, without a body there is no such thing as consciousness or knowing so with every stage of attainment there must still be a body in order for there still to be a life or existent being. However, the body must be of a sufficient purity to be able to support a mental continuum of that level of dhyana. Only a new type of body can do this for each of the dhyana attainments.

The point that "your real Self is not a body" simply refers to the fact that everything, absolutely everything originates from a fundamental nature/essence/energy that through some type of development, effusion, production or manifestation process (rather than a Big Bang) eventually produces the universe and all its contents through a long period of evolutionary cause and effect interactions. Therefore that original essence or Energy is the real True Self. That is the fundamental nature of your self, so that is the fundamental self-nature.

The original essence or fundamental nature is your True Self so you are It, you are Brahman. You are just a biochemical machine that somehow evolved from this long process of emanation and evolutionary transformation and subsequently developed the ability to spin thoughts (consciousness) to "know," but what you really are is that original primordial energy nature out of which you ultimately evolved. That is your true Self. Life, as an independent sentient being, is something that apparently exists but not permanently, and it is not independent but rather interdependent with everything else. It is part of a whole and thus dependent on everything else for its own existence.

There is no such thing as a bodiless existence state, namely a state where you still exist by having consciousness but without a body. Buddhist teaching on this ability are just fictitious skillful means meant to help you cultivate a higher degree of emptiness and mental attachment so that you can cultivate a yet higher body vessel on the spiritual path. When Buddhist or Hindu teachers talk about having an infinite body in discussing the Formless Realms of existence, this is also a fib to help you make progress in letting go and cultivating an "empty mind" that is detached from the thoughts you have. As to having an infinite body, which is borderless, this is impossible.

The point to take home is that you can talk about the spiritual path in terms of consciousness stages/realms or body attainments. You can also talk about it in terms of skandhas and powers (due to different body/realm attainments). Normally most spiritual schools only talk about consciousness attainments, which are usually denoted as degrees of "mental emptiness" or pristine clarity. This has been the historical norm because it is the easiest and best way to encourage people to practice meditation, namely by phrasing everything in terms of consciousness states that have correlates with an "empty mind." However, those attainments are always matched with body attainments because they can only be achieved by higher stage bodies even though this remains unspoken.

You simply cannot attain a higher stage of dhyana unless you cultivate a spiritual body of higher refinement (higher energy). Most schools don't tell this practitioners because they don't want to discourage them, so they hint at this by saying that you need purification/transformation of your Qi and channels to attain dhyana.

The quotes from sages like Sri Nisargadatta talk about the consciousness aspect of cultivation achievements whereas the body enjoyment attainments - stages of *sambhogakaya* achievement - are rarely discussed except in Buddhist texts or in the works of Meher Baba or Ramalinga Swamigal. After you finally attain the subtle Qi or deva body, you will be introduced to such teachings for how to cultivate the higher bodies necessary for the spiritual path. Essentially those teachings are to repeat the cultivation yoga you did to attain the subtle body in the first place, which include the exercises within this book.

THE FOUR BODIES PERSPECTIVE OF INCOMPLETE *NIRVANA* WITH REMAINDER

Some spiritual schools only talk about the first four bodies and leave out any references to the fifth body composed of the very subtle fundamental energy ("wind") called Primordial Heavenly Prana. As stated, this is the stage of the perfect *sambhogakaya* whose mental continuum corresponds to Complete and Perfect Enlightenment. It is hard enough to get to the *nirvana* stage of enlightenment, which would be the Dharma body, Supra-Causal body or fourth body of Later Heavenly Prana (whose mental continuum is the universal *alaya* consciousness). Therefore they only mention the three bodies leading up to this clear light and wisdom achievement rather than the next step of attaining the Perfect and Complete Enlightenment stage of Buddhahood, or No More Learning. After all, attaining the *alaya* consciousness, or initial *nirvana* enlightenment, is equivalent to the stage of unity or "union with God" mentioned in many religions.

To go beyond this and reach Perfect and Complete Enlightenment you must first be able to attain proficiency in a state entirely absent of thoughts, which is called the "samadhi of nothingness" in Buddhism. Other spiritual schools describe this thoughtless nothingness state as an absolute vacuum state of consciousness. This is because without thoughts, including the I-thought, the entire world and all experience disappears during this temporary experience. Hence there is no experience at all, a nothingness or vacuum of experience where the world disappears.

Although there is no thought, this corresponds to Sri Nisargadatta's stage of Pure Being as well as Sadguru Sadafal Deoji Maharaj's intermediate state of "being conscious" (*Kaivalya*) prior to superconsciousness (*Hansa deha*), which means Complete and Perfect Enlightenment. Only by achieving the samadhi of infinite nothingness can the higher essence of Primordial Heavenly Prana separate out from the Later Heavenly Prana body to form the purified *sambhogakaya* Enjoyment Body.

As stated, naturally there are probably higher stages (essences) still but no cultivation teachings, except for some rare Vajrayana Tantras, talks about the higher stages past what we provisionally call Perfect and Complete Enlightenment. Only the higher bodhisattva bhumis cataloged by Vajrayana Buddhism approach this topic. Upon reaching the tenth bhumi you attain the first *real* spiritual empowerment, and then yet higher cultivation teachings are given for the beings at that level so that they can cultivate further.

If we talk about the Taoist nomenclature of Jing, Qi, Shen and Later Heavenly Prana (very subtle fundamental wind/energy) in terms of planes or spheres of existence, we can match this with the **four dhyana heavens** catalogued by Buddhism. The dhyana accomplishments correspond to stages an aspirant goes through in rising from the mundane sphere to the subtle sphere, from the subtle sphere to the mental sphere, and from the mental sphere to the state of freedom.

Each dhyana corresponds to a different stage of **arhatship**, or progress stage towards "*nirvana* with remainder" enlightenment. Only the stage of Complete and Perfect Enlightenment is *nirvana* without remainder, *nirvana* without any remaining dependency. Each of the four dhyana equates with a different type of body composition (Qi, Shen, Clear Light) although the first and second dhyana attainments both correspond to a body of (impure and purer) Qi.

According to Buddhist teachings, the first dhyana (subtle body or deva body attainees) practitioners, called Srotapanna or Stream-enterer Arhats, obtain access to the higher deva realms called the Brahma heavens. The second dhyana practitioners, called Sakradagami Arhats (Once-returners), have a higher level subtle body attainment and can reach the Radiance heavens. The third dhyana (Causal body or Mental body) attainees are called Anagami Arhats (Non-returners) and can reach the third dhyana Glory heavens. One shouldn't pay too much attention to descriptions of these heavens, but simply take them as higher energy realms or planes of existence.

The fourth dhyana attainees are enlightened and therefore called full Arhats. They possess a Clear Light or Dharma body composed of Later Heavenly Qi and have access to even higher heavenly realms called Pure Abodes that the lower Arhats cannot reach. The full Arhats achieve "*nirvana* with remainder" upon enlightenment and do not shed the remainder until they achieve the fifth body. When they achieve it then the attainment is called "*nirvana* without remainder," No More Learning, or Perfect and Complete Enlightenment. At that stage they are then called Great Golden Arhats.

For **Confucianism**, Mencius explained these stages saying that there are the Faith, Beauty, Grandness, Sage and then Divineness stages of spiritual attainment. These correspond to the first, second, third and fourth dhyana attainments along with Perfect and Complete Enlightenment. Once again, even Confucianism recognizes the five stages of spiritual achievement.

In **Judaism** we also have the *Asiyah* (World of Action), *Yetzirah* (World of Formation), *Beriah* (World of Creation), and *Atilut* (World of Emanation) that also correspond to the realms of Jing, Qi, Shen and Later Heavenly Qi.

We also have the Matter, Soul, Nous (the intelligible), and the One stages of **Platonism** that correspond to the Human body (Jing), Subtle body (Qi), Causal body (Shen) and Supra-Causal (Later Heavenly Qi) bodies as well.

The **Sufi Al-Suhrawardi** (The Master of Illumination) also taught an emanationist cosmology using the analogy of a "Philosophy of Illumination." According to this schema, all creation is a successive outflow from the Supreme Light of Lights (*Nur al-Anwar*), and it unfolds in a descending order of ever-diminishing intensity. This basically means that various spheres of being or existence somehow emanate from an original nature, and each is different from the next in terms of coarseness/refinement or density although all the energy realms interpenetrate.

In this sequence there are Matter, the Soul, Intellect and a fourth realm named the *'alam al-khayal* that is continuous with the whole of reality. Thus we have the Human Body, Subtle body (Soul), Causal or Mental body (Shen), and Supra-Causal (or Dharma) body that is a Clear Light (Later Heavenly Qi) body matching with the *alaya* consciousness of cosmic unity.

As previously pointed out, these four essences mentioned across all the various spiritual traditions actually refer to the first, second, third and fourth dhyana attainments of Buddhism. They are followed by the "*nirvana* without remainder" attainment that corresponds to Perfect and Complete Enlightenment - the stage of No More Learning that is Perfect Buddhahood.

In Buddhism the four milestone achievements of the four dhyana, since each corresponds to a different body attainment that then ignores the previously attained lower bodies, are explained as freeing oneself from the form, sensation, conception and volition skandhas. When you break free of the form skandha or physical body it is because you attain a deva body of subtle Qi, which equates to the realm of the sensation skandha. When you break free of the sensation skandha it is because you attain a Causal or Mental body of a higher type of energy churned out of the subtle body, which then equates to the realm of the conception skandha and third dhyana. When you attain a Dharma or Supra-Causal body out of the Mental/Causal body then you have broken free of the conception skandha and have reached the realm of the volition skandha (and the enlightenment of the fourth dhyana), and so on it goes. Zen texts are misleading on these matters because anyone who attains the Supra-Causal body naturally knows they are enlightened, as does their master. You don't have to be tested on knowing that you have generated this extra body.

The volition skandha is matched with Later Heavenly Qi (initial *nirvana* enlightenment) and the consciousness skandha with Primordial Heavenly Qi, which is the body substance of a Perfect Buddha. Primordial Heavenly Qi transcends the substance, energy level or manifestation level of the *alaya* consciousness; the *alaya* consciousness is not the primordial consciousness skandha. The volition skandha, which encompasses the deep impulses of consciousness *and* the forces of matter, actually corresponds to the *alaya* consciousness.

For those of us just wishing to go to Heaven without these higher aspirations, please remember that these bodies, substances or essences are the spiritual path that people in Heaven are cultivating. Once there, heavenly denizens do not want to come back down as humans again through reincarnation and so everyone is cultivating spiritual practices to achieve higher spiritual bodies. This results in higher realms of enjoyment or rebirth, longer lives and greater abilities. Buddhism clearly tells us that a significantly higher spiritual body cuts off rebirth in the lower realms forever. Only after achieving enlightenment, which corresponds to a body composed of Later Heavenly Qi (which transcends all the lower realms composed of Jing, Qi and Shen) can you escape the lower realms forever.

The question then arises, what are devas doing as spiritual practice? Many things, including helping humans in their ordinary affairs by influencing their thoughts and activities, but personally they are trying to generate merit and cultivate their Qi to a higher stage of purity so that they can attain the next higher body. In terms of Buddhist explanations, the Desire Realm devas want to reach higher heavenly attainments, which requires a yet higher stage of Qi purification. Devas can use their body made of Qi (prana) to cultivate both the first and second dhyana, but for the third dhyana they need to generate a new body vessel (a Causal body) composed of Shen.

Every time you refine your Qi sufficiently – opening up the channels within a higher body and refining its energy so that a yet higher body can emerge – you can eventually generate a body of yet higher, purer substances that can leave it. This is why you cultivate your prana, *nadis* and chakras on the path. Then you will live, so-to-speak, within that body as your main life vehicle while retaining your lower shells.

No one at the lower levels can see these higher bodies so people are normally unaware of your attainments. They might be able to sense that something is different about you, but have no way to explain it or put their fingers on it. The thing they will most often say is that you don't seem to be attached to anything (of this world because you identify with a higher world where everything is better) and at times you don't seem to totally be here. That's because you reside in a higher body that is doing something elsewhere but still using the human body as an appendage.

As previously explained, the flip side of body cultivation - which refers to consciousness rather than essences - is to say that people are trying to mentally cultivate a higher stage of mental purity or "emptiness." Most all schools talk about pristine consciousness, pristine awareness, emptiness, no-thought and empty mind but this is the flip side to the body attainments. They don't emphasize the body attainments because they don't want people to get attached to form, but spiritual cultivation is a mind-body affair. Both mind *and body* must be cultivated on the spiritual path; an over-emphasis on mind will cause individuals to neglect inner energy cultivation for years, which is to their disadvantage while an over-emphasis on life-force (Qi or prana) cultivation will not enable anyone to cultivate higher bodies due to the natural clinging involved with nei-gong efforts.

Physical bodies on every plane of existence are composed of essences/substances, and the concomitant (naturally accompanying) consciousness for a body has the same energy nature as that body's substances for that plane. A consciousness or mind needs a physical body vessel to support its existence. If you attain a higher level body vessel then its concomitant purity of consciousness (degree of pristine awareness) will correspond to the greater purity and refinement of that biophysical mechanism. At the level of the perfected *sambhogakaya*, the concomitant empty or unmanifest state of consciousness is considered to be the original nature but this is just a way of speaking rather than the truth.

To achieve a more pristine consciousness you therefore need a body composed of purer essences whose energy channels (especially those within the brain) have far less entanglements, knots or blockages since obstructions produce errant energy flows that give rise to random thoughts rather than empty clarity. In short, *you need to cultivate both mind and body on the spiritual trail* if you want to attain the higher heavenly realms of being, which can be talked about in terms of "Pure Abodes" or the first, second, third and fourth dhyana.

In spiritual cultivation we can say you are trying to cultivate a more subtle or purer state of consciousness that is largely free of random, wandering, meandering thoughts. With each stage your mind/consciousness becomes more clear, calm and quiet until it seems perfectly empty, crystal clear and pristinely aware. Only a purer body of cleansed energy channels can allow this to come about. Therefore instead of saying you are trying to cultivate a higher consciousness we can also say that you are trying to cultivate a purer body whose energy and channels support a higher level of purity of consciousness.

To go up the spiritual ladder, devas themselves (which includes our ancestors who have passed away and not yet reincarnated) need to cultivate higher stages of spiritual attainment. These correspond to more subtle spiritual bodies made of more refined essences. This is the true spiritual path – you can talk about it in terms of bodies (essences or substances or spheres of manifestation or planes of being) or consciousness. This is one of the purposes of religious spiritual practice but few people seem to understand this.

These facts explain why the Vajrayana school of Buddhism calls the deva body (subtle body) an *impure* illusory body, namely a body of impure Qi. Once the Qi (prana) of this impure deva body becomes purified a deva can then, at will, generate a higher *purified* illusory body out of this lower shell, namely a Causal or Mantra body, just as our subtle body can leave the shell of our physical nature. In other words, the stage of impure Qi is followed by a stage of purer energy, called Shen. A body composed of Shen can eventually generate a Supra-Causal body composed of Clear Light energy or Later Heavenly Qi from within it, and so on it goes …

According to Vajrayana teachings only the purity of a Shen body can achieve the next stage of enlightenment since it is the precursor stage. In some schools they call the Arhat's enlightenment body the pure illusory body and in other schools the Clear Light body.

To make things clear and avoid the confusion that normally accompanies Vajrayana teachings of Esoteric Buddhism and Dzogchen, we will call the pure illusory body the stage before achieving a Clear Light body of Later Heavenly Qi, which Vedanta calls the Supra-Causal body and Buddhism calls the Dharma body. These various terms from many different traditions make the common teachings much easier to understand. The names of the bodies and their substances do not matter. What matters is that you understand that there is a progression of higher bodies you must cultivate, and with each new body the stage of consciousness is somehow *better*. It is somehow more pure, clean, empty, pristine or pure.

Every time you achieve a new body you break away from, depart from, "extinguish," ignore, or leave behind the old body, which Buddhism calls an aggregate or skandha or sheath. The previous body still exists as long as you live, but you then live centered in the higher body and identify with it while retaining the existence of each lower body (as an appendage) until its karma is exhausted. The body attainment you want to shoot for at a minimum is the one that corresponds to enlightenment, which is composed of a very subtle fundamental wind, energy, Qi or Prana of material creation we call Later Heavenly Qi. Your mental continuum at that point is one of an Arhat.

The higher your spiritual body, the higher the plane of existence or spiritual realms you can reach, which are called "Pure Lands" in Buddhism and "Heavens" in other religions. Advanced spiritual bodies can freely travel the spiritual realms, and have various powers of mastery over the energies of the lower realms they transcend. This is why various masters, gurus, prophets, saints or sages – depending upon how many bodies they have achieved - are known to have miraculous powers that work on various levels. As humans we can manipulate matter, but a deva can manipulate Qi (and matter with training), a higher deva can manipulate a more purified level of energy that we call Shen, and so on. Buddhas can also manipulate the minds of sentient beings, but "manipulate" means affecting them in a positive fashion.

Because they look normal to us but are actually living centered in the shells of their highest spiritual bodies (while their lower body shells remain alive), masters on earth can perform spiritual feats at subtle energy levels. Devas, spirits or angels are just one step higher than us and so they share in some of these miraculous capabilities that involve Qi or Shen, and thus they can affect our thoughts.

Someone who has attained an independent subtle body of Qi then lives in the subtle plane that is all around us and receives sense impressions through his subtle senses. The person is then subtle-conscious, and while registering the sensations of the physical world can detach from them. This is why masters at times seem uninterested in what is around them or non-present when you try to hold a conversation. They often seem empty because their higher body is not there. They can be talking to you and using their higher body to visit your home to see what is on your desk, or enter your brain to see your memories, and in this way they can know things that they normally could never know.

A human master who attains a body of Shen, which is the next higher level of more purified Qi, is conscious of their mental Causal body composed of that substance. Thus they pay less attention to their Qi body and human body while still using them too. Outwardly such a master appears as an ordinary gross-conscious human having all the same desires, thoughts and emotions as we do but they are actually living vividly in a higher sphere, plane or realm called the Causal or Mental plane, although tethered to their lower bodies that they can use for different tasks.

Basically, the higher your stage of spiritual achievement, the more refined, subtle or purified the substance of the body you live in. You basically discard your lower aggregates – though beings at those levels don't know it – and live in a higher body and higher plane while keeping alive the lower shells and using them as they see fit. This can be understood through the *Surangama Sutra* of Buddhism (see *Meditation Case Studies*) and many of Meher Baba's publications. Sri Siddharameshwar Maharaj (see *The Master Key to Self-Realization*) also did a great job in discussing the various bodies of the spiritual path.

As discussed, there are well-defined stages of spiritual attainment commonly recognized by all the major religions because *these are the common, shared attainment stages of the spiritual path*. These stages, bodies and realms are real, they definitively mark different levels of attainment as to the higher and lower, they provide access to different levels of being, and they are common, non-denominational attainments. Each higher stage of this attainment sequence represents a more refined stage of mind and body purification than the lower stages.

All the genuine spiritual traditions match regarding these teachings because anyone who cultivates any genuine state of attainment - starting with the subtle body that gains you access to the heavens - discovers that these substances and realms do indeed exist. That's why the saints and sages of different religions end up speaking of the same things but simply call them by different names.

If we talk about these planes in terms of evolutionary emanations from an original nature, we have the universal religious idea that everything originates from one original essence. No one can say how the purest original essence - which is absent of any type of attribute, form, substance, impulse or movement and exists solely in Itself as Itself - somehow gave birth to the first evolute or effusion, so Buddhism says we just don't know how things have originated from It. Shakyamuni Buddha calls our lack of understanding "Ignorance" since it is impossible for something to be born from something that doesn't change, so we can only speculate about the process of generation that has formed the cosmic realms.

Jainism also says that you cannot create something out of nothing, arguing that all constituents in the universe must therefore have always existed in primordial form (which must be the True Self, true self-nature, original nature or fundamental essence) and they must certainly follow natural laws in how they transform and evolve into subsequently denser evolutes. Taoism calls this "transformation," Buddhism calls it "cause and effect," while

Confucianism calls this "change" and Islam calls this "complex interaction" but no one can talk definitively about the first movement or Primal Cause for all these subsequent transformations. Perhaps in other far older realms the inhabitants have extensively investigated this and come up with the proper science and physics.

"Ignorance" means we don't know something, so that is the proper way to describe how the manifest universe came about out of something so pure that it doesn't change its nature and therefore never alters. With the way things are, all we can therefore do is cultivate to as high as possible in the universe and sequentially find different spheres or planes of existence that are higher and more subtle stages of energy. In each realm we will be given teachings for how to get to the next level and leave the lower spheres forever.

Along the way we must also choose our career in the unending cosmos, and these are represented by the Bodhisattva vows of the Mahayana path in Buddhism. Many beings who have made it to the high stages have vowed not to attain complete extinction of the ego and all cessation of suffering until all beings in the universe are equally liberated by reaching enlightenment. This basically means they will keep enlightening beings forever since the universe lasts forever. That is the career they have chosen, and it is a path that involves vows of compassion.

In other words, the road of spiritual practice does not just involve cultivating consciousness but bodies composed of very purified substances that are absent of the coarser elements found in lower level bodies. Those bodies, due to less obstructions and impurities in their channels, which affect disturbances in consciousness, have more purified degrees of consciousness. Furthermore, the higher your stage of spiritual attainment, the better your Reward or Enjoyment body, and the more spiritual powers you can have and realms you can visit. This is another meaning of the various stages of the spiritual path.

STAGES OF CULTIVATION

For us, the trick is not to get worried about all these higher bodies that you can attain through the process of spiritual cultivation. You just start cultivating, do your best, and see what happens as explained in my *Meditation Case Studies*. This short explanation only provides the general schema or roadmap of the cultivation trail.

The trick is to just get started at this entire process using the best or most efficient cultivation practices other than just attending religious services. Just get started and see how far you can get because the cumulative results are carried over to your Qi body upon death, and one can continue cultivating in Heaven from there.

If you are lucky to attain the subtle (deva) body of Qi while alive, Buddhism calls this "entering the stream," which is the first stage of an enlightened Arhat called a Srotapanna (stream-entrant or stream-winner). If your spiritual practices are insufficient so that you don't achieve the stage of entering the stream while alive, when you die your purified inner Qi body will still assure you a place in Heaven and you can continue to cultivate and succeed from there. This whole pathway, however, can be finished entirely while as a human, but the first step always begins with cultivating your mind, merit and your Qi and Qi channels.

To summarize, if you sufficiently cultivate your Qi and energy channels then you will achieve the inner subtle body attainment – an independent body of Qi that can enter and leave your physical body at will. If you don't achieve this body due to your practices, you will at least transform the Qi and channels (*nadis* and chakras) of your physical nature enough that you can live longer with a healthier constitution, have a much clearer mind, can change your fortune and will go to Heaven upon death. Lower realms, due to a predominance of Yin Qi rather than the Yang Qi of spiritual practices, correspond to lower levels of being such as ghosts and hells that are the reward of people who do evil ("Yin") deeds in life.

In other words, success at the Yoga of spiritual practice means at the minimum going to Heaven; greater success at spiritual practice means arising in a deva body whereas *really succeeding* means achieving the Later Heavenly Qi body and *nirvanic* enlightenment. If you don't achieve the milestone of "entering the stream" but still cultivate, your reward will be to live longer and healthier, to be reborn in Heaven, and to cultivate a clearer mind that can help you change your fortune for the better.

When we look at a human body we can say it has an equal balance of Yin and Yang energies, but they are not clearly differentiated such that you can always feel these two forms of Qi unless you cultivate. This is because Qi channels are normally obstructed and entangled and your internal energy flows are therefore unbalanced and uneven. For the subtle body to emerge, however, the Qi first must become purified and clearly differentiated into Yin and Yang natures. Sometimes this is described by saying that you cultivate pure Yang Qi, which will enable the subtle body to emerge, but the truth is that you have to cultivate both Yin and Yang Qi. You cannot cultivate just Yang Qi alone just as you cannot just cultivate ascending Qi in the body, for it must also descend. "Cultivating Yang Qi" just means cultivating the next higher stage of purity than the physical body, namely the Qi in general that forms the subtle body. For the higher Causal body the Qi/prana/energy must be purified even more.

The famous master Ramalinga Swamigal (Vallalar) says that the subtle body is the "house of kundalini" (another name for Yang Qi) because you attain it when the physical body is "burned out through the fire of Yoga." He also explained, as everyone else does, that you achieve the subtle body when the aspirant's body of impure elements has been transformed into purer elements. Once again, this is just another synonym for prana/Qi cultivation.

Taoism calls any human who attains this an "Earth Immortal," which is roughly equivalent to the first dhyana attainment of Buddhism. As stated, this *yin-shen*, subtle body, deva body, astral body, or impure illusory body attainment is also equivalent to purifying the sensation skandha of Buddhism since your emotions and feelings are felt within your inner Qi vehicle. In some schools this is described as the "plane of souls for animals" since we feel all our emotions in the subtle body.

The next higher spiritual attainment in Taoism is the "Spirit Immortal." This is the Shen stage of Taoism, purified illusory body of Vajrayana, Mantra *deha* of the Tamil Siddhas, or Causal body of Hinduism. It is achieved through purifying that Qi subtle body even more until a new body is generated from within it that is free of all the lower Qi elements that still pollute its nature. Devas, for instance, are also cultivating to rid their own Qi bodies of gross impurities to attain this body.

This Shen body, Causal body, Mantra body, Mental body or purified illusory body - which is more refined, transfigured and transphysical than the lower Qi body of devas or our own physical body of matter - has many more supernatural capabilities than these lower bodies. A master at this level, which is roughly equal to the third dhyana attainment of Buddhism, can raise the dead to life and create new forms in new worlds.

The next higher stage of attainment is the "Celestial Immortal" stage of Taoism that corresponds to the fourth dhyana of Buddhism. This is the Arhat level of achievement that equates with initial *nirvana* enlightenment. The mind at this attainment level is often compared to the transparent, substanceless, clear nature of light, which is why it is termed the "clear light" stage of attainment.

Someone who finally generates the Clear Light or Later Heavenly Qi body that corresponds to this level can freely travel all the celestial realms, and because it is superior to all the subsequent denser (less pure) realms created as evolute consequences of this energy level, it has access to all the minds of humans and lower beings since their bodies and minds are composed of lower essences. Remember, there are higher bodies still!

Buddhism doesn't like to talk about bodies in its explanations but instead uses consciousness. Therefore it says that this is not Perfect and Complete Enlightenment but will explain using reasons like "because at this stage the Arhat will still have residual impressions of a separate self and thus retains remainders." Such teachings follow the pattern of the *Lotus Sutra*, which teaches masters to use skillful means to entice people out of a burning house, and once out rewards them with great gifts and the truth.

Because consciousness explanations are a better vehicle for encouraging people, they usually take preference over body/form teachings in the world's religions. After all, with body teachings you know perfectly well if you succeed at cultivating a deva body or not, but with consciousness teachings about emptiness you don't really know where you stand in terms of spiritual progress. Hence you keep working hard even though there is no chance of attainment. With consciousness/empty mind teachings you will always be cultivating harder to develop an "empty mind."

Why all this repetition of the same explanations over and ovr again? These stages must be repeated because too much ignorance and confusion exists in the world's spiritual schools since most traditions do not emphasize these attainments. Zen books are particularly misleading in regard to body attainments and the necessity of cultivating your Qi and channels. Only after hearing these matters many times will you see that the same teachings are found across countless traditions, which should give you confidence and faith in the path, and this emphasis will clear up the spiritual path in its entirety.

In comparing a Qi body to the ordinary human body you already know that the subtle body is more purified or refined (less dense) than a physical body and will last longer, which is why devas live longer than humans. A master who cultivates a subtle deva body will also live longer in Heaven than humans who die and "go to Heaven" because a master's Qi has undergone a higher stage of purification refinement due to his spiritual efforts of cultivation. Therefore, if you want to live longer in Heaven as a deva, now is the time to get started at cultivating spiritual practices *while living* since that will transform and purify your energies. You can use any path you want to do so – Christianity, Judaism, Buddhism, Hinduism, Sufism, Shinto, Taoism, Yoga and so on – but you absolutely must cultivate some type of spiritual practice. People have succeeded from nearly every spiritual tradition when they used the correct cultivation methods. The more successful you are at your spiritual efforts, the better will be your Qi and the higher will be your stage of spiritual attainments.

Remember that becoming able to eject your inner Qi body from its physical casing at will (and not due to some weakened physical state or an accident that causes a near death experience) is not the ultimate spiritual attainment, nor is that body your ultimate soul vehicle, but just one of the initial milestones on the spiritual path. It is only a tiny step towards enlightenment. Nevertheless this is called the beginning of the *sambhogakaya* attainment in Buddhism, or ultimate Reward Body you earn from cultivation efforts.

Nyasa Yoga gives you a path for cultivating a subtle Qi body or body of prana, which corresponds to the first dhyana attainment of Buddhism, by cultivating the Qi and channels (*nadis* and chakras) of your present physical body in special ways that concentrate on individual pieces. Next you must link everything together as one whole and try to feel the Qi of your entire body as a single unit. Whenever you concentrate on purifying the Qi and channels in a certain region of the body, that is a derivative form of basic Nyasa practice. For instance, one can consider the famous white skeleton visualization method of Buddhism a Nyasa practice (but without a mantra) since it starts with visualizing pieces of the body and ends in affecting your entire inner body of Qi as one whole.

The way to cultivate your Qi sufficiently enough to produce a subtle body is to start with the normal virtuous ways of most religions such as devotion, performing kind deeds, and practicing ethics and generosity. These practices open up your Qi channels naturally and gently. An extensive amount of Yoga stretching and bodywork (or martial arts) will also open up your Qi channels especially if used along with visualization and pranayama. You can attain a deva/deity body through this road if you also have a spiritual master and undergo many Nyasa-like nei-gong practices.

The gist of it is that if you want higher spiritual attainments then it requires that you cultivate your energy channels through meditation and various types of yogic exercises. The best results will come from a wide variety of qi-gong and nei-gong exercises that include mantra, meditation, and inner Nyasa practice. You must repeat the same type of work for every new body you want to attain as well. Each new body gets you one step higher on the scale of progress towards a perfect *sambhogakaya* and Complete Enlightenment, or Perfect Buddhahood.

ROADS OF PRACTICE

There are many ways to cultivate your Qi and many other roads of spiritual practice you can employ, but for simplicity's sake we will use Shakyamuni's categories of ten large roads of practice. This includes concentrating on Buddhas (other enlightened beings and their teachings); studying and following cultivation teachings (Dharma); relying on others who have attained enlightenment (Sangha); strictly following certain rules of discipline (*sila*); practicing charity, generosity and virtuous ways; following certain practices that normally lead to Heaven; breathing and breath work practices (including pranayama, qi-gong and nei-gong); mental peace and resting practices (including vipassana meditation); special body cultivation practices (such as Yoga and martial arts); and practices that deal with death and dying. Nyasa practice, since it is a nei-gong exercise, falls into the categories of body and breath work cultivation.

In *Look Younger, Live Longer* I revealed the ten auxiliary roads of practice that can help you with the task of cultivating your Qi and channels so that you attain health and longevity. These supplemental avenues of spiritual cultivation can also help you transform your inner Qi body as well. This includes eating special foods, herbs and minerals; cultivating your Qi and breathing practices; cultivating your saliva and hormones; absorbing the energies of the sun and moon (or planets); practicing mantra and meditation; cultivating certain sexual practices that involve discipline; and matching yourself with earthly and heavenly energies.

In Chinese Taoism, the approach to opening your Qi channels involves meditation along with a combination of Qi supplementation (augmentation) and maintenance (continuance) strategies. The basic principle is to accumulate and retain your Qi so that the increasing quantity of Qi will eventually open up your channels due to the available forces.

Yoga practices (asanas) are also used to help transform and purify your body, meaning that the physical stretching can untangle knots in your muscle fibers and thus help to open up the Qi channels within them. If you combine this with pranayama, mantra and visualization then the results will be spectacular. A famous Russian stretching method also is to go to a decent stretch of a muscle, flex the muscle being stretched, hold your breath to increase the intensity of the flex, and then release the breath and the flex at the same time.

You essentially need certain types of Yoga and spiritual practices to open your Qi channels, and among the best are stretching exercises along with mantra, visualization and *kumbhaka* pranayama efforts to force Qi through your Qi channels. Unfortunately people who are spreading yoga today are largely missing the *kumbhaka* pranayama, visualization and mantra aspects of practice. Mantra practice not only helps vibrate open Qi channels or calms your mind so that your Qi can rise naturally, but has the added benefit of asking for help from higher powers to lend assistance for the task of spiritual cultivation. *Kumbhaka* breath retention – where you hold your breath inside and then forcefully expel it when you can't hold it any longer - helps force Qi through your channels to open them and clear them of obstructions. Visualization will also help because wherever your mind goes your Qi will follow. If you focus your mind on a region of your body then your Qi will go there, thus bringing Qi life force energy to the region to open up all the Qi channels in the vicinity.

Once you bring Qi to an area inside your body, two options are then available. You can (1) try to guide it or, (2) just let go of the feelings and watch-observe-know-witness the energy sensations without altering or nudging the process in any way. This is the practice of "anapana," which lets your Qi energy, once released or stimulated, do whatever it wants to do to open up your channels naturally. All you do is follow your breath, meaning follow your Qi/prana movements by knowing them without getting attached to them. However, sometimes when you feel blockages you should push/nudge your Qi in an attempt to smoothen out the flow in that region. I explained this in *Internal Martial Arts Nei-gong*. Afterwards you then detach from mental entanglements and start witnessing once again without attaching to the sensations arising. You want the surging or coursing of Qi currents in the body, when they arise, to feel unblocked and smooth.

Effective spiritual practices work towards eventually opening up *all* of your body's millions of Qi channels so that you can eventually enjoy an independent spiritual life. You eventually attain the initial deva body composed of subtle Qi by first activating the vital Qi energy of your physical body. It will then purify your Qi channels by pushing through the duplicate underlying Qi structure of your physical body. At the minimum, transforming your Qi and channels will win you a place in Heaven when your physical body gives out while if very successful you can arise during this life time with a deva body made of Qi.

That is the initial spiritual path in a nutshell – it is just a path of Yoga that has been made complicated by the dharma teachings of every school that tend to mislead you by overly complicating matters. To succeed you must cultivate gong-fu, and if you are not a virtuous, ethical person then the Buddhas will not help you succeed in generating a deva body that lives very long. They'll help you cultivate your Qi but you'll have to put in extra effort yourself to make up for the lack of virtue..

If you don't cultivate, the underlying subtle Qi structure that scaffolds your physical body will simply be your body that "goes to Heaven" upon your death. It will last longer or not in heaven depending upon whether or not you cultivated in life, so do so. Since it is still unpurified as regards higher (more subtle) forms of energy, as a living vehicle within Heaven it won't last forever and upon death in that Qi realm you will eventually come back down again to be reborn as a human once more, or as a deva again if you cultivated hard and accumulated enough merit.

Cultivating your Yang Qi to make this all possible happens to a greater or lesser extent upon any road of genuine spiritual practice. Even normal religious devotion causes your Yang Qi to arise within you and start to open up your Qi channels. This is yet another reason why saints have always encouraged good deeds, acts of merit, kindness, charity and good behavior. If you are this type of person they will readily help you cultivate a subtle body while alive. Just this path of virtuous behavior by itself is also a form of Qi and channel cultivation. Additionally, if you are not a virtuous person then the Buddhas and devas will not help you as much with your cultivation efforts. They will certainly help you, but you'll have to carry more of the burden yourself due to selfishness of behavior on your part.

Unfortunately, most people don't know about the more efficient yogic practices to cultivate your Qi directly, such as Nyasa Yoga practice, but simply follow the normal course of religion that produces an inferior passage to Heaven. It is now time to introduce many of these techniques to help you achieve the end result of cultivating some stage of a superior deva body.

CHAPTER 4
"ONE UNIT" WHOLE BODY
CULTIVATION METHODS

Nyasa practice is a cultivation exercise that involves concentrating on body parts (to grab and stimulate their Qi) together with mantra recitation. Relying on the fact that your thoughts and Qi (prana) are linked, you try to grab/feel the Qi of separate component pieces of the body, lingering on each in turn. During that stay you should either send energy to the body part; stir up the energy within that body part; imagine heavenly energy going into that body part; visualize changing its color or texture; imagine placing a symbol, letter or deity on that body part; or recite mantras from within the area in order to activate/energize the prana (Qi) in the region and send it through the *nadis* (Qi channels) in that area. Other cultivation methods can be tried as well.

This focus on the energy within a body part will both activate/stimulate the Qi/prana in its immediate surroundings as well as bring additional Qi to that area since Qi responds to your thoughts and comes to where you place your attention in your body. Your Qi/prana will always follow the movements of your thoughts so if you think of a body part and try to feel it, or mentally change its color (which means you have to mentally grab it first and then somehow imagine that you are changing it in some way that produces a Qi response) you will energize the area. You will bring Qi to the location or simply stimulate that area's Qi.

Your concentrated focus on a spot will accumulate Qi in that region, or move the Qi already within that area, which is what you try to do with Nyasa practice because of the effect this produces in opening up Qi channels (*nadis*). As Qi the moves within a body region due to your focus and concentration, its movement will open up the channels and pathways within that location. This is how you can cultivate all your body parts in turn.

Thus, Nyasa Yoga practice is simply a way to use sound (mantra), light (visualization), sensations (feelings) and concentration (thought) to open up the *nadis* (Qi channels) in a selected portion of your body. It is therefore a type of energy Yoga. As you finish concentrating on one section of your body, which is usually just a single body part, you then proceed to another region until you do your entire body in sequence.

There are many types of Nyasa practice, with some being very complex and elaborate. Usually practitioners are taught to recite a different mantra for each body part they touch, and try to feel or stir up a Qi vibration in that part of the body by using the mantra "spoken as if from that location." You can also use your own efforts to move the Qi, but most practitioners don't know that they are also supposed to feel, grip, excite, stimulate or move the Qi of that part to help their Qi open up the channels in the region. They are simply told that they are to touch various parts of the body while chanting specific mantra sounds "to invoke the presence of the deity" inside their body.

To just touch a body part and recite a mantra is wrong; you must try to feel the body part and move its Qi when you do this. That is what will transform the Qi and channels in a region, and is the entire point of the practice. This turns Nyasa Yoga into a form of nei-gong inner energy work. If you simply touch an area and recite a mantra there you are asking that a deva or deity will use their own efforts to open the channels in that region. They are busy people. Are you worthy of that effort?

WHITE SKELETON VISUALIZATION

Several famous cultivation techniques related to Nyasa Yoga are the white skeleton visualization practice of Shakyamuni Buddha and the fire skeleton visualization practice of Mahavira, the founder of Jainism.

The white skeleton visualization involves individually visualizing all the bones of your body as shining with a bright silvery light, or like sunshine, which is energizing to your Qi. Since your skeleton stretches throughout your entire body and your muscles are draped upon it, it runs parallel to the flow of the major Qi channels within your body. All your muscles run along its course, so by concentrating on your skeleton you will bring Qi to all those muscles as well as your bones. This will help to open up your Qi channels everywhere.

Here is how it works ...

If, through focus and concentration, you bring your attention to a bone, imagining that it is shining with a bright light (while trying to feel it), you will bring Qi to that bone and its surrounding tissues. That energization, stimulation or activation of Qi will open up the Qi channels in the tissues and vicinity along the length of the bone (basically the bones and muscle fibers encompassing the size of the visualization area), and this is the purpose of the practice.

When doing the practice you must not keep the visualization in your head but actually feel your bones at the same time in order to bring Qi to them, otherwise you will find that you are visualizing an image that does not connect with the actual body parts. If your mind does not connect with your body parts you will only be cultivating mental concentration rather than the transformation of your physical nature. In Nyasa Yoga you avoid the problem by touching a body part a a reminder so that you focus on it.

The white skeleton visualization can be done either sitting or lying flat on your back, though sitting in a meditation posture is best. There are over thirty different variations of the practice that will energize your Qi so that it starts opening your Qi channels, so we will just discuss the basic principles. If you understand the basic principles and what you are trying to accomplish with this visualization practice then you can create all sorts of other variations.

To practice, in whatever position you have chosen you should first take a couple of deep breaths and release any tension you feel in your body. Make yourself comfortable for the sadhana.

Next, starting from your left big toe, begin to visualize that you no longer have flesh on the left foot and that your left big toe bones shine with a dazzling white light. First visualize the two bones of your left big toe shining with a bright white light, then all of the other toe bones on your left foot (there are three bones per toe). Try to feel the bones when you do this because you want to send Qi to the channels in this region. You can even be looking at your feet when you perform the visualization to make sure you are visualizing bones within your feet and actually feel them. Always try to feel the Qi within the bones you visualize rather than simply keep images within the brain that do not connect with the body.

When you are done, maintain that vision/feeling of the left toe bones and switch sides to start visualizing the bones of your right big toe shining with a dazzling white light, and then progress to all of the toes of your right foot shining brightly. As with your left foot, you stop when you are simultaneously visualizing (and feeling) all the bones of your toes in your foot.

Continuing, switch back to your left foot and visualize all of the other remaining bones within this foot, and then all of the remaining bones in your right foot. Now the bones of both feet should be shining with a bright white light.

Next, visualize your left ankle and then right ankle bones shining with a dazzling bright light. All the bones in your feet (tarsals, metatarsals and phalanges) should now be simultaneously seen in inner vision as shining with a bright white light. Try to feel the energy in the feet and along the bones; if the feet get warm it means that your practice is working because your Qi is starting to open up your Qi channels in this area. If you need to, look at your ankles in order to send Qi to this region as you visualize the bones within your flesh. You can also spin the Qi along the bones, in whatever fashion you feel is necessary, to jump start the opening of channels in these regions.

Proceeding higher, start visualizing both of your left lower-leg bones (the tibia and fibula) and then your right lower-leg bones as shining with sunshine-like light. Remember to look at your legs if necessary so that your visualization of the bones inside your flesh actually connects with the actual bones, and try always to feel the energy of those bones, such as by feeling their shape, as you visualize them shining with light. This is one of the fastest ways to open your Qi channels and transform your physical nature. You can also spin your Qi along the lengths of the bones as well, and in advanced practices you can combine this with Taoist (and martial arts) bone marrow washing practices.

Continue upwards like this visualizing that all the flesh is being stripped off your bones and all the exposed bones are shining with a bright white light. Feel the energy as you do this because the practice will bring energy to each body part in turn. This might not happen for weeks but it will eventually happen in time. Also, practice being joyful and happy when doing this visualization, offering the flesh away as a kind of offering, because both the emotion of joy and offering will raise the Yang Qi of your entire body. You can also practice being exhilarated or ecstatic to raise your Qi energy when you do this too. The idea is to generate the feelings of joy since this usually excites or stimulates your Qi in a positive uplifting sense.

With standard Nyasa practice you would simply be touching each body part in turn and reciting a mantra on each part as you touch it. Here you visualize each bone in turn and hold the cumulative visualization of all the previously shining bones as you add more. Eventually you will be visualizing an entire skeleton shining within your body. Even if you have to finish the practice quickly, try to get to a stage where you are cultivating all the Qi of your body as a whole of connected parts.

This is how you cultivate all the Qi of your body starting with the feet, which are the most difficult area in the body to cultivate. Later, when you attain proficiency at the basic practice, you can also add mantras and other variations as you visualize each bone. This brings the method closer to traditional Nyasa practice.

As stated, another higher method is to visualize each bone shining with a bright light while cultivating an attitude of extreme joy, and spinning the Qi around and within the bones and surrounding tissues, as done in Taoism and many Yoga schools. This is one of the quickest ways to cultivate your Qi and channels.

Normally Nyasa practice simply involves reciting a mantra on each body part, which directs your attention and energy to the region. In this case we are substituting a visualization effort of each body part, while internally feeling it, for the mantra. The visualization uses bright light and the emotion of joy to raise the Yang Qi of each part when doing this cultivation practice.

Any efforts you bring to a region to stimulate its Qi – such as visualization, pranayama, concentration on the sensations and mantra – will help to open up the Qi channels in that region. Thus Nyasa practice is a means of cultivating your Qi and Qi channels in all your muscle fibers as does visualization practice when performed correctly. Since Qi channels will eventually open when you consistently apply this practice, we can also call it a purification technique for transforming your entire physical body. Similarly, we can call it a method for building the strength of your inner Qi body. You can call it a method of transforming or opening Qi channels and purifying your Qi as well.

To finish the white skeleton visualization practice, gradually work your way up your body and continue visualizing that your body is just a set of shiny white/silvery bones without flesh and try to feel any sensations of energy or warmth in those regions. In time you will certainly feel warm at certain areas within your body because of the influx and activation of your Qi.

In visualizing your bones one by one, once you go up through your hips and spine (spinal vertebra) to reach your neck, make sure to go down both arms to your hands and fingers. It is difficult to cultivate the fingers and fingertips, which is why many masters who use the rainbow body technique to turn their body into energy, shrinking it in the process, often leave behind pieces of their fingernails. This usually indicates that they were not able to fully cultivate this difficult area of the body, so make sure you don't skip the hands and fingers during your practice.

After your hands and fingers, eventually you will reach the head and can end the sadhana with a visualization of your skull bones shining with a bright white light. Then you throw all these visualizations away and rest your mind in emptiness.

At the initial stages of this practice it is not important that you correctly visualize each individual bone of your body with extreme accuracy, though that is an excellent exercise in concentration. *What is important is that you send Qi throughout the extent of your entire body, using your bones as the general structural map that will guide you.* Later you can work at visualizing your bones perfectly.

If you wonder which are the most important bones, initially it would be the spinal vertebrae from the pelvis into the head because you especially want to open up your spinal Qi channels at the earliest stages of cultivation. Most every cultivation school has practices for opening up the Qi channels within your spine, so you can practice sending energy up and down the length of the spine, and spinning it in various winding or oscillatory ways along its length, in order to open up this pathway of nerves. The Kriya Yoga tradition and

Taoism have excellent methods to do this.

Another important point is to practice being happy or joyful when performing these visualizations because these emotions will tend to generate Yang Qi. Positive emotions generate Yang Qi within your body while negative emotions (depression, fright, anxiety, shame, guilt or grief) give rise to sensations of Yin Qi within you.

A variation on this basic technique you should know about is that some people imagine their bones *within their flesh* shining brightly while the standard technique is to imagine that you have no flesh on your bones at all and are just a skeleton. This helps you detach from the view of being a body, but to cultivate your Qi channels you can use whichever method seems best.

In other variations, you can imagine that immediately around the bright whiteness of your bones is a yellow aura that changes into a bright red color which permeates the rest of the meat/flesh surrounding your bones. When you stare at a bright red fire this is what you normally see – a white hot core center surrounded by a yellowish aura that changes to a red flame. You can use this image to cultivate the Qi channels within your bones all the way through to your flesh.

Another alternative is to imagine that your body's flesh is the color red all the way through except for the very bright white shining bones. You can look at you arms or calves, for instance, and try to imagine that the flesh is red but the bones within are shining with a bright white light. You should try to feel their shape as well or recite a mantra (such as "Hreem") along their length when you do this. This is an exercise you can do throughout the day for either the entire body or single body parts. Some people concentrate with intensity on a different body part every day.

While you are supposed to practice being enthusiastic and joyful during these visualizations, which generates Yang Qi, a classic preliminary to these visualizations is to imagine that your body passes through several repulsive stages before the flesh is stripped away. In this version of practice, you progressively visualize (and try to feel) that your body becomes (1) a swollen corpse, (2) discolored bluish corpse, (3) festering corpse, (4) fissured corpse, (5) gnawed corpse, (6-7) dismembered or hacked and scattered corpse, (8) bleeding corpse, (9) worm-eaten corpse, and then you perform the white bone visualization.

Once you understand that you have the ability through visualization to move your Qi due to the inherent linkage of mind and body (since your thoughts and Qi are connected), you can understand how visualizing that your body passes through these stages can cultivate both your Yin Qi and Yang Qi energies to greater states of purity. Many such derivative methods are available.

Once the visualization of your entire skeleton is complete, try to maintain a complete visualization that your entire body is just a set of white bones shining brightly until you feel that your Qi has become evenly distributed in a balanced manner everywhere.

Whenever you feel any sensations that arise in your body just note them but don't grasp onto them or cling to them. That's called witnessing practice, and since this involves Qi sensations it is a special type of witnessing practice called anapana. Also, try to maintain a joyful state of mind as you perform this entire visualization routine because as stated, joy gives rise to positive energies, and thus gives rise to the Yang Qi necessary for opening your Qi channels. If you just do this exercise in a sterile frame of mind you decrease the possible benefits because you cut down on the volume of Yang Qi that should be produced at that time.

After you visualize your entire body as a set of brightly shining white bones, visualize that they *all* become dust that is blown away and the only thing left remaining is empty space that you cannot hold onto.

In other words, where your shining white bones once were, now there is nothing but empty space. You are just a bodiless existence that has consciousness. Ignore the energy feelings that arise while experiencing this empty mental state of non-clinging because if you interfere with those energy flows you will thwart the efforts of your Qi to open up the Qi channels within your flesh.

Remaining like this, aware of your feelings and witnessing them but without interfering with them or trying to move those energies, is the best way to perform anapana practice. You first stir up or stimulate the energies in your body through visualization, mantra and nei-gong or qi-gong type efforts, and then once energized you simply let go and with detachment witness as the energies start to move everywhere.

MAHAVIRA'S BODY PURIFICATION SADHANA

A similar whole body technique for cultivating your Qi was introduced by Mahavira, the founder of Jainism.

For this visualization method, you imagine that there is a large bright red lotus flower inside you at the level of your navel, pointing upwards, that is burning with red flames. You must imagine that these fiery flames joyously stimulate the energy everywhere in your body to arouse it. It is important to visualize that the flames extend upwards so that *they even protrude out the center of your head.*

The reason you must visualize the flames protruding out of the top of your head is because by concentrating on a point outside of your body this will help to draw Qi upwards, and thus this visualization will draw your Qi through the two branches of your spinal nerves that separate in the brain and reach to the top of the head.

These left and right nerve bundles that branch out from the spine are symbolized as horns (or antlers) in most cultural traditions. The horns of Moses, horns of Yamantaka, horns of Isis holding a sun above her head, two pointed ears of an owl, and antlers on gods with animal heads (such as stags) and so on are symbols of these two spinal branches that must be opened by the ascending Qi within your body.

At the level of your heart, you must imagine an inverted lotus flower that is also bright red in color. Thus you have a red lotus flower in your belly with a red fire (sometimes the color gold is substituted) blazing upwards, and a red lotus flower at the level of the heart that is turned upside down.

For Mahavira's visualization, you imagine that the flames flow between these two lotus flowers, making the trunk of your body energized with Qi, and it then extends or energizes your entire body turning it bright red with color. Luminescent red from head to toe and full of Yang Qi (fire) energy, you soak in the energetic feelings that result from this visualization, feeling the energy everywhere, and then imagine that your entire body eventually turns into glowing red embers.

After you visualize your entire body as filled with this fire energy and turning into glowing embers, imagine that a strong wind blows off all the embers and ashes and then a heavy rain falls from above washing all the ashes away. This is like the final phase of the white skeleton visualization where you imagine that the body turns into dust that blows away to reveal emptiness. For Mahavira's method, imagine that what is left after the ashes blow away is a crystal clear, transparently pure soul (body) that is seated at your spot.

When this is achieved, next let go of all the imagining and rest your mind in empty space (just as you did for the white skeleton visualization). Ignore everything just as you normally do in anapana practice; you don't blank out things and prevent them from arising, but by being empty space you let everything arise within you without attachment since you don't have a body. Be at peace and let your Qi arise.

The last point to this visualization is to practice being euphoric, elated, happy, joyful or thrilled when doing this exercise because as previously explained these emotions will help you generate Yang Qi during the process. You want to stir up your Qi with a positive fervor and feel the energy moving everywhere inside you.

For instance, the emotional fervor of bhakti practices cultivates ecstasy in Christianity and Hinduism. This is useful precisely because the emotional rapture and ecstasy help move your Qi for cultivation purposes. They are not holy states in themselves due to spiritual development. They are just a way to whip up joyous emotions in a positive way to ignite or activate the Yang Qi of your body so that you start opening up Qi channels and start creating a subtle body. That is how they become spiritual practices when used in conjunction with other spiritual exercises such as nei-gong practices that smoothen your Qi all over. Otherwise they are just useless emotional fervor.

There are other fire practices to help transform the physical body other than Mahavira's method. For instance, in the *Vijnanabhairava* there is a method of imagining that your body is being burned by the fire of kundalini – the power of Kalagni Rudra the universal destroyer - rising from the big toe of the right foot. To do this practice you imagine that the kundalini fire and heat arises from the right foot's big toe and extends everywhere within your body, turning it red hot with kundalini fire. For this practice you must also recite the mantra "Om Raksarayaum tanum dahayami namah." Another mantra you can use to help activate your kundalini is "Om Ah Hung Ha Lah Tah Ray."

There is also a derivative of the fire *kasina* practice of

Buddhaghosa within the *Visuddhimagga*, an ancient meditation text, that cultivates both your mind and Qi. With this practice you hold in your mind the fiery image of the sun or a fire while visualizing a flame within your abdomen that slowly gets bigger until your whole body is in flames, everything gets burned away, and you are left with no body and an empty state of mind. This washing of oneself using fire is the fire *kasina*.

Buddhaghosa also instructed meditators to sit in front of a body of clear water with their eyes almost closed. They were to observe the water without much interest and then to gradually forget their body and mind to become unified with the water. "Becoming one with water," which would help purify their Qi channels, was the water *kasina*. Sometimes you are to feel the water within your body (via imagination) so as to open your Qi channels since the visualization is supposed to move your Qi, and other times you should just forget the body completely.

Practitioners could also find a wall and while facing it visualize that it became empty, and extend that emptiness to their body. This was the earth *kasina* concentration practice. Lastly, they could go to a mountain top and observe the empty sky of endless space, extend that emptiness to their body and then merge with the universe. This was the space *kasina* that helps you cultivate an empty mind.

VAJRAYOGINI PRACTICE

Yet another visualization technique is to vividly imagine, while also stirring up sensations every way you can, that your body becomes luminescent red with vibrant vigorous energy, or you become entirely flames, or you are bathing in a sea of fire. Red fire energy is traditionally used across nearly every spiritual tradition to represent Yang Qi, just as seen in pictures of the Tibetan deity Vajrayogini. Vajrayogini is therefore a related visualization *yidam*.

Vajrayana (the Tantric or Esoteric school of Buddhism that specifically focuses on Qi practice to transform and purify your subtle body) explains that you identify your body with that of the *yidam* deity - such as Vajrayogini, Chakrasamvara, Kalachakra, Hevajra, Guhyasamaja and Yamantaka, Hayagriva, Kalachakra, Kurukulla, Tara, Vajrakilaya, etcetera - for the purposes of spiritual "transformation," but it doesn't tell you that this simply means nei-gong Qi practice to stimulate your Qi so that it becomes energized and opens all your energy channels. Whenever anyone concentrates on a religious deity, including within Vajrayana practices and Hindu deity visualization, various enlightened Buddhas and devas for that locale will try to help the practitioner make progress in their spiritual cultivation.

Once you accomplish this visualization by making it stable in your mind or by feeling the energy evenly spread all over, you then release the visualization and let your mind rest in emptiness without attaching to any of the Qi sensations that arise within you.

In a Vajrayogini visualization you imagine that your body becomes filled with the fiery red energy of the deity, while trying to be joyful and enthusiastic, and typically you simultaneously recite a mantra (at many locations throughout your body) requesting aid in the practice. As usual, the purpose is to cultivate/purify your Qi and channels. The possible mantras include the following (you try each one by reciting it many times during a day and see how well your Qi changes; after trying them all use the one you like best):

Om Vajrayogini Hum Phat
Om Vajrayogini Hum Phat Soha
Om Vajrayogini Hum Phat Ah
Om Vajrayogini Hum Phat Oh
Om Vajrayogini Hum Phat Eee
Om Vajrayogini Hum Phat Lah
Om Vajrayogini Hum Phat Hum
Om Vajrayogini Hum Phat Hee
Om Vajrayogini Hum Phat Hah
Om Vajrayogini Hum Phat Hey
Om Vajrayogini Hum Phat Bah
Om Vajrayogini Hum Phat Too

Each mantra requests Qi assistance (for purifying your Qi and opening your channels) from a different family of enlightened Buddhas and masters responding to the Vajrayogini mantra. The families are actually a bit competitive in trying to outdo one another in helping you make progress. You have to see which one works best for you and then stay with that mantra for some time to get the best results. Don't waste the efforts of spiritual beings trying to help you.

If you start doing this practice then continue doing so for at least 30 days in order to make progress.

You can recite one of the mantras (just use one for a session) without attaching it to any particular body part, or you can sequentially place it upon (recite it as if from within so as to move your internal Qi) different body parts while also visualizing them shining with bright red energy. If you use it for each major body part – the head, trunk, arms and legs – you must end up activating the Qi of your body as a whole.

Both men and woman can visualize that they are the female Buddha Vajrayogini. In fact, men often perform this visualization practice - imagining that their Qi changes and they become the female Vajrayogini - in order to purify their Yin Qi energy because both Yin and Yang Qi are needed in cultivation and both must be purified.

This, of course, is just using your imagination to cultivate your Qi. Many imagination-based methods are used in the world's religions to cultivate your Qi and transform your body for samadhi-dhyana attainments, which really means body attainments. For instance, the instructions for deity yoga are that you should imagine with strong visualization that you exist in the form of an external deity body, sometimes projected in front of you. These are just nonsense instructions for the uninitiated to build concentration powers.

What you are really supposed to do is feel the Qi inside your body for every body part you visualize of your physical body becoming a deity. In other words, feel the Qi in every part of your body to open up all the channel pathways in that part, including those within atomic bonds. Deity yoga is a practice for transforming your physical body's Qi and channels instead of creating some strange new astral deity shape that is an independent form hanging in space.

Deity yoga is supposed to be an internal nei-gong practice. It is not a practice that develops a deva body in the form of some strange looking (non-existent) deity. However, that was the type of practice instruction that worked best thousands of years ago, and now it is time for better instructions to come out. If modern people do not learn the true purpose and path of cultivation practice they will ignore it entirely. Instead they will spend hours working on their muscles at the gym instead of engaging in inner Qi practice, start implanting electronic devices within it, or pursue all sorts of extreme

68

thrills and distracting high tech gadget novelties that miss the spiritual path entirely.

Visualizing yourself as being a deity external to your physical body is just concentration practice, which has its own benefits (See *Visualization Power* by Bill Bodri). When you do this practice, enlightened Buddhas and their deva students will be using their own Qi energies to work on opening the energy channels of your physical body, but the visualization practice doesn't actually produce an external deity body at all; you can only cultivate the Qi of your physical body! Even when you visualize an external deity body in space you will paradoxically feel the Qi of your own body – in fact the same parts being visualized – being worked on inside you because of helpful spiritual powers.

The rule is to always link any mental visualizations with feelings/sensations in your physical body to transform the Qi and Qi channels within your body, otherwise you will lose years of practice effort. Therefore it is best to visualize your own body becoming transformed rather than creating an independent body in space. Many times you will find yourself visualizing some body part *transforming in your mind*, but you cannot seem to connect that mental visualization with the Qi of the relevant body part you are focusing on, which then makes your practice effort less effective. If you visualize the Qi channels opening in your cerebellum and work on that region, for instance, you should always try to feel the Qi movements in the anatomically correct position you are visualizing.

Vajrayana Buddhism and various Yoga schools offer different cultivation methods where the instructions are actually scientific nonsense. For instance, there are concentration practices for counting drops or visualizing drops melting within channels, visualizing red or white bodhicitta, and exercises like visualizing the fire element melting into the water element of the body and so forth. These are all just concentration (visualization) exercises because they do not correspond to any truly existent biophysical processes, so they are nonsense because these visualized processes and phenomena don't really exist. They are just visualization-concentration exercises that masters invented ages ago.

When you finally attain the deva body of subtle Qi (also known as the "will-born body" in Buddhism, *yin-shen* in Taoism or impure illusory body in Vajrayana) and escape the physical shell to speak with all the heavenly residents around you, you will find out that most of these exercises – and lengthy treatises by masters on drops and elements melting into one another and so on - are a crock of nonsense. They are what Buddhism in the *Lotus Sutra* calls "skillful means" – a skillful way to get people to practice and progress even though false, but which lead to a wondrous result even though fictitious. What you were really doing was practicing concentration with your visualization efforts, and higher beings were working on opening up your channels at that time. That's the secret behind these techniques.

The supernatural visions one receives during such practices are just illusions created and projected by Buddhas and devas into your brain, otherwise you wouldn't be able to see anything at all. They *do not* correspond to any real phenomena occurring but are just used as a motivational mechanism to help inspire you to keep working hard and do some of the more difficult concentration exercises and cultivation methods.

Many religions use the same cheating methods of false visions and wrong explanations in order to help lead practitioners forwards to cultivating their Qi, otherwise who would work so hard at the effort since it takes many years of continuous practice? Once a method catches hold within a tradition and becomes popular, all the Buddhas and devas within the tradition start to master the relevant vision projections to keep cheating people in order to help move them forward.

In the *Lotus Sutra* of Buddhism this is called skillful means – cheating people in order to lead them out of a burning house. However, don't think this type of supernatural misdirection is only used in the eastern spiritual traditions because this deceptive method of projecting false (illusory) visions or "mara delusions" is used by the devas (angels) in Christianity, Judaism, Islam and all other religions, too, as they try to help spiritual practitioners open up their Qi channels. Only those practitioners who work hard enough, because they have been inspired by such deceptions, can actually generate the subtle body and become an Arhat spiritual master.

In any case, visualizing that you become like the red-colored Vajrayogini, become Vajrayogini, receive help from Vajrayogini, become one with Vajrayogini, sexually unite with Vajrayogini, or even the act of reverently paying homage to Vajrayogini are many of the different ways to cultivate your Qi. All religions use such methods, though in different forms, to help practitioners attain the deva body and become saints of those traditions.

When you read of priests who greatly venerated the Blessed Mother Mary of Jesus, or Hindu masters who practiced venerating Kali, Gauri or Lalita Tripura Sundari in India, you can understand that they were actually doing the very same thing - cultivating to purify the Qi of their bodies and requesting help from female masters to do so.

It is easy for women to cultivate their Yang Qi via certain manly activities (hence the female heroes such as Athena one could emulate) without anyone noticing, but sometimes men cultivating their Yin Qi perform strange actions that are not publicly acceptable (ex. Ramakrishna, Papaji, Hercules, Thor, Arjuna, etc. wore women's clothes while imagining that they were women in order to cultivate their Yin Qi). However, men do not become homosexual, practice homosexuality or fall into homoeroticism during such exercises. They simply cultivate their Yin Qi at this time.

To cultivate their Yang Qi, women can and should also at times visualize that their body becomes male and that they are a male Buddha (for instance a red male Buddha like Amitayus), which is an effort symbolized by the many Hindu goddesses who at times became warriors who killed demons. This sort of imagination practice will stimulate the Yang Qi in their body, and various efforts along these lines have been practiced by many female cultivation masters who attained realization. Men and women who wish to practice these routes need a very wise enlightened master to do so.

THE SOMA DUCK EGG VISUALIZATION

Another visualization, which is related to the prior three, is the Duck Egg or Soma Cream visualization taught by Japanese Mountain Master Hakuyu to Hakuin Ekaku, who later became one of Japan's most famous Zen masters. The story behind the transmission of this technique is rather interesting.

As a Zen student, Hakuin had worked strenuously at his meditation efforts and thereby activated the Yang Qi of his body. He had worked hard enough to initiate a kundalini awakening and as the kundalini energy was freely running about inside him opening up all his Qi channels, he felt terrible energy imbalances that he had no way to cure. No physician he consulted or meditation technique he used seemed to be able to help cure him of his ailments since this was, after all, a powerful internal energy affair that involved the activation of all his internal energies. Thus he went into the mountains seeking Master Hakuyu for a remedy. Master Hakuyu explained his problem and taught him this special nei-gong visualization technique for harmonizing his body's internal Qi energies.

As with the previous techniques, the Soma Cream visualization can also be used to cultivate your body in its entirety by filling your body with harmonizing Qi that helps to open up your Qi channels. In this case Master Hakuyu taught the method to Hakuin in order to help him smoothen out his unbalanced Qi energies, but it is also a method for purifying your Qi and opening your Qi channels as well.

The method Master Hakuyu transmitted is to "Imagine that a lump of soft butter, pure in colour and fragrance and the size and shape of a duck egg, is suddenly placed on the top of your head. As it begins to slowly melt, it imparts an exquisite sensation, moistening and saturating your head within and without. It continues to ooze down, moistening your shoulders, elbows, and chest; permeating lungs, diaphragm, liver, stomach, and bowels; moving down the spine through the hips, pelvis, and buttocks.

"At that point, all the congestions that have accumulated within the five organs and six viscera, all the aches and pains in the abdomen and other affected parts, will follow the heart as it sinks downward into the lower body. As it does, you will distinctly hear a sound like that of water trickling from a higher to a lower place. It will move lower down through the lower body, suffusing the legs with beneficial warmth, until it reaches the soles of the feet, where it stops.

"The student should then repeat the contemplation. As his vital energy flows downward, it gradually fills the lower region of the body, suffusing it with penetrating warmth, making him feel as if he were sitting up to his navel in a hot bath filled with a decoction of rare and fragrant medicinal herbs that have been gathered and infused by a skilled physician.

"Inasmuch as all things are created by the mind, when you engage in this contemplation, the nose will actually smell the marvellous scent of pure, soft butter; your body will feel the exquisite sensation of its melting touch. Your body and mind will be in perfect peace and harmony. You will feel better and enjoy greater health than you did as a youth of twenty or thirty. At this time, all the undesirable accumulations in your vital organs and viscera will melt away. Stomach and bowels will function perfectly. Before you know it, your skin will glow with health. If you continue to practise the contemplation with diligence, there is no illness that cannot be cured, no virtue that cannot be acquired, no level of sagehood that cannot be reached, no religious practice that cannot be mastered. Whether such results appear swiftly or slowly depends only upon how scrupulously you apply yourself.

"I was a sickly youth, in much worse shape than you are now. I experienced ten times the suffering you have endured. The doctors finally gave up on me. I explored hundreds of cures on my own, but none of them brought me any relief. I turned to the gods for help. Prayed to the deities of both Heaven and earth, begging them for their subtle, imperceptible assistance. I was marvellously blessed. They extended me their support and protection. I came upon this wonderful method of soft-butter contem-plation. My joy knew no bounds. I immediately set about practising it with total and single-minded determination. Before even a month was out, my troubles had almost totally vanished. Since that time, I've never been the least bit bothered by any complaint, physical or mental."[1]

SHINGON FIRE CEREMONY

Related to these methods are the practices of the Japanese Shingon Fire ceremony. These are also related to Vedic fire ceremonies and fire purification ceremonies of Zoroastrianism in terms of what they are meant to help you accomplish.

Most all fire ceremonies – including Vedic fire ceremonies held by Brahman priests - symbolize the fact that the Yang Qi (kundalini) of your body, represented by the fire, rises within your body due to spiritual cultivation and then cleans out all your Qi channels. The ceremonies themselves absolutely do not purify your body in any way, shape or form but are just a symbol of kundalini cultivation and purification. They were invented as a ceremonial reminder that you

[1] *Wild Ivy: The Spiritual Autobiography of Zen Master Hakuin*, trans. Norman Waddell (Boston: Shambhala Publications, 1999), pp. 105-107.

should be cultivating spiritual practice to make your kundalini arise as this is true spiritual practice and the most important thing in life. During a fire ceremony you can stare at the fire and imagine that the energy (or fire element within your own body) becomes stimulated, starts stirring, and moves everywhere to purify your Qi and channels.

In the Shingon Fire ceremony, participants sit around a blazing fire built within a small square frame, which symbolizes your pelvis (the pelvic girdle). Specifically, a four-sided fire pit symbolizes the root chakra, namely the bottommost muscles in the pelvis that make the form of a square as well as the energy in this locked-up region. The pelvis is the region where Qi channels are blocked from the constant discipline of holding back energies for this is the region we taught not to use in pissing, shitting or fucking whenever we want. Therefore we dam up the energies in this region, which tends to lock up kundalini energies in the pelvis and waist.

To practice correctly during fire ceremonies, you stare at the flames while feeling the energy arise within you and coursing through your body, especially ascending up the spine. It is common to recite the Mantra of Light ("Om amogha vairocana mahamudra manipadma jvala pravarttaya hum" or in Japanese "On abokya beiroshano makabodara mani handoma jimbara harabaritaya un") during a Shingon Fire Ceremony, *which can also be recited during any other fire gatherings or fire ceremonies regardless of the religion.* In fact, it can be recited without a fire ceremony since it just alerts enlightened Buddhas to the fact that someone is a spiritual cultivator and needs help with their Qi and Qi channel purification! The Agni fire mantras of India usually serve the same purpose.

Having bodies composed of the Supra-Causal energy level equates with what is colloquially called cosmic or unity consciousness (*alaya* consciousness). This is the level where it is said that a practitioner "permeates" the being of all souls, meaning that the energy of that sphere is the fundamental substrate of all lower spheres. By possessing a body composed of the transcending energy/substance level that is the clear, transparent substratum of all lower bodies (and thus "souls"), enlightened beings at this level are somehow able to hear mantras they identify as their own and will respond in kind with appropriate help as they can.

A person with this higher body attainment, which various sutras and other religious texts identify as an "infinite consciousness" attainment, is said to be able to experience himself in everything of a lower nature. His universal (*alaya*) mind is said to be able to include all minds in its scope (its reach depends upon his stage of cultivation). This is just a way of speaking. With practice someone with a body at this level can learn to hear when someone anywhere calls his name. He can learn to hear all mantras, all requests for help, knows when anyone performs his mudra, knows when anyone views a sculpture or painting he wishes to respond to, knows when people read a particular sutra or passage in a book, and knows when anyone thinks of him or any particular topic he is interested in. Knowing the minds of all beings, and taking their troubles as his own, he experiences all their suffering and if the compassion is high enough, takes upon himself the desire to relieve beings of their suffering since he knows them to be his own forms. This explanation is not perfect without errors, but serves to explain some of the Buddhist teachings about higher body attainments.

The Yoga practices of Mula Bandha used to stretch the muscles in the pelvis can help open up the Qi channels in this area, which makes it easier for the pelvic Qi to ascend up the spine. Another way of saying it is that Mula Bandha and the related Yoga exercises for the pelvic muscles will release any energy trapped within this area, allowing it to then be used for spiritual cultivation. Mula Bandha is something that everyone should practice, especially men who must learn ejaculatory control on the path of spiritual cultivation.

Since it hard to stretch the pelvic muscles the older you get, it is better to begin stretching them when you are young, especially before twelve years of age (puberty). That is something parents should encourage in their children. Yoga, leg splits, forward toe-touching bends, the pigeon pose, and certain martial arts exercises will certainly loosen and stretch the muscles in the pelvis, making them more flexible. This opens the Qi channels around the perineum so that the energy flows in this region will be smoother and cause fewer irritations than what would normally arise for somebody who didn't stretch those muscles. Increased flexibility due to stretching these muscles leads to far less sexual pressures and thus, less loss of Jing and Qi. That, in itself, is a benefit to spiritual cultivation.

Puberty is a time when children start to become sexually aware so it is best to help children stretch these muscles as much as possible before the onset of puberty and the initiation of sexual activities.

After these muscles have been stretched, Qi (vital energy) can proceed through the muscle channels without irritation, and with less irritation there is then less sexual desire and subsequent activities such as masturbation.

While we have just discussed the region of the root chakra, Qi also has difficulties penetrating through the sacral chakra region (and then upwards through the spine) because there are many ligaments and tendons surrounding the sacrum. However, by stretching the legs, waist and hips in various fashions this will tremendously help to open up the channels in the pelvic floor and sacrum to speed your spiritual cultivation efforts.

In particular, you must make efforts to stretch the deep perineal muscles, ischiocavernosus muscles, levitator ani, ileococcygeous muscles, gluteus maximus and other pelvic muscles to help your spiritual cultivation efforts. Some practitioners simultaneously imagine their Qi at the base of the sexual organs and at the sacrum and try to draw the energy between these two points, but they have to be careful not to stimulate and then give into sexual desire when they do this.

It also helps to obtain a diagram of the pelvic floor and then visualize a square within the pelvic floor muscles in order to pull Qi through these muscles. The pelvic floor muscles, when viewed from below, resemble a square (with a diagonal partition), which is why Tibetan stupas have a square base and why the root chakra has four sides.

GENERAL PRINCIPLES

All of these practices can be used to open up the Qi channels and energy connections between the atoms within your body that form a large matrix or body double composed of Qi. The basic idea is that you can use visualization as one type of energization or stimulation mechanism for your Qi (since it moves your Qi). The process call also be further amplified by emotional states of joy and fervor. Once you stimulate your Qi enough that you get it moving and can feel it, try to increase the size of the body region you are concentrating on until you can feel your Qi everywhere.

Once you reach a state of harmonious fullness, you should then let go of stimulating the sensation of the Qi moving inside you (which might sometimes feel uncomfortable as it encounters friction when opening up channels) and rest in an "empty mental state" that lets everything mentally arise without your interfering with the process.

Space has many things within it, so resting your mind so as to be "empty like space" does not mean blanking out thoughts, stopping them or suppressing them to somehow, in that way, be like space. It means acting like a bodiless witness who just witnesses, observes or watches everything that is happening, but because he has no body he does not attach to anything that is occurring. This is the basis of anapana practice for observing your Qi, and the true meaning of cultivating an empty mind. You let everything arise but without the concept of being a body although you are always a body for without a body there can be no such thing as consciousness. Consciousness can only arise within a body vessel whose structure permits it to arise.

First stir up or push your Qi everywhere, then let it settle into a state of harmony and balance (that you help produce by pushing it appropriately to smooth it out when and where necessary) and then let go and practice the witnessing of anapana.

Thoughts always arise within an empty mind, but "being empty" means you don't attach to them, but just let them rise and fall, come and depart, appear and then disappear without clinging to them or interfering with them. You are like an infinite bodiless observer, like space, and so they all happen within you.

Just as the planets move about in their orbits without your need to hold them back or push them in any way, in "being empty like space" you just let go of whatever energy or thoughts arise that do arise, and know them without clinging or altering them in any way.

This is alternatively called non-clinging, non-attachment, detachment, dispassion, independence, freedom from thought, observation, knowing, awareness, witnessing, anapana or presence practice.

In this way, you will give your body and Qi the fullest play possible so that your Qi channels can open naturally from the Qi that has just been amply stimulated.

CHAPTER 5
THE *MAHAVAIROCANA SUTRA*
AND *YOGA YAJNAVALKYA*

There is a Tantric Buddhist scripture – *The Mahavairocana Sutra* (*Vairocanabhisambodhi Sutra*), which is also called *Mahavairocana's Enlightenment, Supernatural Transformations, and Empowerment*. It contains one of the earliest examples of Nyasa practice for individual body parts although few know this fact.

In "The Allocation of the Letters" chapter of this sutra, the Buddha Vairocana is talking to the Bodhisattva Vajrapani explaining how to cultivate various sections, pieces or segments of your body. The way to do this is to think of a portion of your body, such as an arm or leg, and next try to feel energy within it while reciting a mantra as if from that area. This follows the principles we have just discussed. It helps if you actually look at the area you tend to affect.

Many people think that in tantric Buddhist practice (which simply means you are working to cultivate your body's vital energies) you are supposed to visualize the body part clearly in your mind and generate yourself as some imaginary deity that is outside of your body. This is incorrect as that is only an exercise in concentration (visualization) rather than internal Qi transformation. These were instructions given ages ago to throw off practitioners who didn't have a teacher for the correct technique.

The correct technique is to stimulate Qi within an area of your body in order to open up all the channels in the vicinity, and thus you try to push, activate, or stir up the energies and sensations in that region. If you try to send energy to that area, feel that area, stretch that area, change the color of that area, or recite a mantra from that area, etc. then any practice that you do which helps excite, arouse, energize, vivify, vitalize, fortify and localize the feeling of Qi in that region will help to activate Qi in that area and open up its Qi channels. When used in conjunction with mantras for each body part, that, in essence, is Nyasa practice.

The *Mahavairocana Sutra* is universally applicable to practitioners of all schools and encouraged as a practice vehicle for both men and women. You do not need a special initiation, consecration, empowerment or permission to practice this Nyasa method although with all kundalini or nei-gong Qi methods a wise teacher is recommended.

All that an initiation, consecration, empowerment, blessing or permission really means is that you make a connection with an enlightened teacher (who has attained a Later Heavenly Prana body whose substance transcends your own and thus can affect your Qi whenever he/she uses his own energies) to help you with your Qi and Qi channel cultivation. By attending such an "empowerment" you simply make known that you are doing these efforts and are tagged for help and guidance by a teacher.

RAM/RAH AND VAM/VAH

The *Mahavairocana Sutra* contains a very simple nei-gong practice that uses the two sounds Rah and Vah, which you are taught to recite in the upper and lower parts of your body, or on the right and left sides respectively. The sound Ram could also be used in place of Rah, and Vam can be substituted for Vah. These are actually the preferred sounds to be reciting rather than Rah or Vah.

In Vedic culture, Ram is the *bija*, or root seed sound, for the right side of the body and Vam is the *bija* mantra (sound) for the left side of the body. Ram stands for the fire element and Vam for the water element. The right side is considered Yang, fiery or solar in nature while the left side is considered Yin, watery or lunar in nature. These are just convenient associations but not really truths.

If you mentally repeat Ram while breathing through your right nostril it will increase the fiery nature of your Qi, which you should try to feel on your entire right side when you do so, and repeating

Vam when breathing through the left nostril will increase the cooling nature of your Qi. When reciting Vam and concentrating on the left side of the body you should try to feel cooling Qi everywhere, too. According to Vedic teachings, the sounds Lam and Ham can also be used to affect your Qi, too, but in a different fashion.

As regards the instructions from the *Mahavairocana Sutra,* when reciting the Rah/Ram sound you should try to feel it in your entire chest centered in the region of the heart while imagining that your entire upper body is red in color and (energized by being) on fire. The whole purpose of the fire visualization is, as previously explained, to activate your Qi. You should try to feel the Qi in that entire region at the same time you do this, and while not specifically mentioned you should try to generate the feelings of happiness, joy or exhilaration at the same time to also help move/excite your Qi during the practice.

When reciting the Vah/Vam sound, you should try to feel it in the entire lower abdomen of your body below the rib cage down to the perineum. Ancient books aren't so precise or specific so they will suggest you recite it as if from the center of your body at the level of the navel although you should try to vibrate, stimulate or energize this entire abdominal region. This is basically the abdomen or lower belly called the *dantian* in Chinese.

At the same time you should imagine that the entire lower half of your body (including your legs and feet), starting from this area, is blue or white in color, which are the traditional visualization colors for cooling water. While the *Mahavairocana Sutra* suggests using the color white (representing smoothness, purity, lightness and coolness), sometimes a better choice is to imagine that the lower part of the body is blue in color since this better represents the water element.

Just as you can experiment with the sounds used for this type of practice and the location where you feel the sounds, you can experiment with various combinations of colors and other visualization techniques to make it more effective. The important point is to transform your Qi channels by opening them via Qi stimulation, so if you discover some more effective technique then use it.

Put briefly, you should imagine that the upper part of your body is made of red fire while reciting Rah or Ram, and visualize that the lower part is cooling, liquid blue water while reciting Vah or Vam.

You also evoke appropriate images and sensations in your mind when imaginarily "transforming" your lower body into water as you do the practice. Of course it is impossible to turn your body into fire or water; you are simply using imagination to stir up a specific type of Qi through this practice, namely you are trying to differentiate the Yin Qi and Yang Qi from one another and clean out their appropriate Qi channels. This is why you can later imagine that the lower part of your body is hot, energetic, vigorous fire while the upper half is cooling water, and then do the same switcheroo for the left and right or front and back sides of your body.

Hence, after this basic "top-fire bottom-water" visualization-sensation-mantra practice, you can then do the same thing by creating dualistic opposite visualizations involving the left and right sides of the body – reciting Rah/Ram from the right side of your body imagining it is the fire element while reciting Vah or Vam from the left side of your body imagining it is the water element. Then switch sides with Rah/Ram on the left and Lah/Vam on the right. You can, during a different practice session, work on the back (red, fire, Rah/Ram) and front (blue, water, Vah/Vam) sides of your body as well. This will invigorate or stimulate the Qi everywhere, which will lead to the opening of your Qi channels. The rule is: moving Qi/prana opens up Qi channels (*nadis*).

Since this practice will stir up your energy this means sexual desire is sure to rise, so when this happens do not give in to sexual impulses (and thereby lose your Qi and Jing through ejaculation) but focus on breathing practices or stretching exercises to smoothen out the uncomfortable imbalances.

Sometimes cutting down on your food intake, which weakens people, can help lower the problem of sexual desire during cultivation (since your energy is lower) and thereby helps to avoid a man's subsequent loss of Jing and Qi through ejaculation which usually follows when sexual desire arises.

For women, it is not detrimental to orgasm during sex even after doing cultivation methods like this that stir up your vital energy. A woman's physiology is different than a male's and so there is very little loss of energy that cannot be quickly replenished after orgasm. Therefore a woman need never fear orgasm during sex or block a coming orgasm because she feels she shouldn't lose energy due to cultivation concerns. This worry is wrong and unfounded.

During any type of sexual relations both partners should try to feel maximum joy during their activities in order to help excite and move their Qi through their channels. In this way the method can become sexual cultivation of Qi and Qi channels rather than just sex. The mantra "Ohm Ah Hung Lah Rah Tah So" is often used by those practicing sexual cultivation and pursuing the opening of Qi channels through that technique.

Some tantric schools use the emotions of anger (wrath) or pride to stimulate Yang Qi on the upper part of their bodies to open the channels, but another tantric (and Vajrayana method) is that you can also use sexual desire, bravery or courage, reverence for a higher power, longing, joy and love or kindness to cultivate the movement of your Yang Qi in order to open up channels.

The Buddhist practice of cultivating the four immeasurables also helps cultivate your Qi for higher body attainments. You can also try to engender the necessary Yang Qi by cultivating infinite (immeasurable) emotions of amazement, thrill, awe, inspiration as well as feelings of transcendence or spirituality. You can also cultivate an infinite feeling of being triumphant, strong, energetic, joyful, animated, fiery, filled with dance, amused or heroic.

The idea is to imagine or project that you have an aura of this emotion that is infinite in size and to become that emotion while letting the emotive energy move the cells of your body within you. You use that emotion to stir your Qi/prana. One can also try to project that emotion into the external environment by self-generating it inside oneself and then amplifying it as much as possible as it is projected outwards.

The positive emotions of love and joy during sex, which is itself a physical activity that moves internal energies that open your channels, can together be combined into sexual cultivation for the spiritual progress of Qi cultivation. Unfortunately, it is difficult for qualified partners to find one another and for men to learn sufficient ejaculation control for this method.

NYASA PRACTICE WITHIN THE *MAHAVAIROCANA SUTRA*

The text of the *Mahavairocana Sutra* also contains a Nyasa practice, which involves speaking certain sounds (mantras) as if from certain areas of the body. As with traditional Nyasa Yoga practice, you can also touch that particular body part at the same time you recite the mantra, visualize a corresponding Sanskrit letter (or something else) on that body segment, imagine that body segment changes color while feeling the sensation of Qi within it, and so on when focusing on a region. All these alternatives have the same purpose of trying to move the Qi within an area in order to open up its Qi channels.

The particular Nyasa teaching within the *Mahavairocana Sutra* appears as a dialogue between the Buddha Vairocana and the Bodhisattva Vajrapani that runs as follow:

> Next, Vajrapani, you should listen attentively as to how to arrange the letter gateways as taught by the Buddhas.

> The letter Ka is placed below the throat;
> The letter Kha is placed on the palate;
> The letter Ga is identified with the neck;
> The letter Gha is placed inside the throat;
> The letter Ca is placed at the root of the tongue;
> The letter Cha is identified with the entire tongue;
> The letter Ja is identified with the tip of the tongue;
> The letter Jha is placed where the tongue arises;
> The letter Ta is identified with the legs;
> The letter Tha is identified with the thighs;
> The letter Da is identified with the hips and waist;
> The letter Dha is identified with the buttocks;
> The letter Ta is the anus;
> The letter Tha should be known as the abdomen;
> The letter Da is identified with the two hands;
> The letter Dha is called the armpits;
> The letter Pa is identified with the back;
> The letter Pha should be known as the chest;
> The letter Ba is identified with both upper arms;
> The letter Bha is identified with the lower arms;
> The letter Ma resides in the heart;
> The letter Ya is the genitals;
> The letter Ra is called the eyes;
> The letter La is identified with the forehead;

I and Ī are the two corners of the eye;
U and Ū are identified with both lips;
E and Ai are identified with both ears;
O and Au are identified with both cheeks;
The letter Am is the letter of bodhi;
and the letter Ah is parinirvana.

If a yogin knows this entire method, the practitioner will accomplish enlightenment. The assets of an omniscient one will always be in his heart. The world will call him "omniscient."

You can find the full *Mahavairocana Sutra* within the *Mahavairocana-Sutra* (Chikyo Yamamoto) and the Numata Institute publication *The Vairocanabhisambodhi Sutra* (Rolf Giebel). This is actually a Nyasa practice where you are supposed to recite the sound while concentrating on the corresponding body part until you can feel the Qi in the region. The point is that Buddhism contains Nyasa Yoga just as does Hinduism.

Running through the entire course of sounds and body part correspondences will activate the Qi all over your body, and is an internal energy (nei-gong) practice used to help you purify your Qi and Qi channels. This is a preliminary form of help so that you can cultivate your subtle energies and eventually attain the deva body that equates with breaking free of the form skandha. This is normally described in Buddhism as helping you achieve the first dhyana attainment.

YOGA YAJNAVALKYA

The *Yoga Yajnavalkya* contains many Kundalini Yoga practices just like the *Mahavairocana Sutra*. Most people know little about the *Yoga Yajnavalkya*, which is a Hindu yoga text written as a dialogue between the sage Yajnavalkya and Garji Vachaknavi, the daughter of the sage Vachaknu who was herself a renowned expounder of the Vedas.

The *Yoga Yajnavalkya* contains some of the materials found in Patanjali's *Yoga Sutras*, but also additional material on cultivating kundalini energy (Yang Qi) because Yajnavalkya had mastered the art of Kundalini Yoga. You can certainly use the exercises within it, in conjunction with other Yoga books, to cultivate your Qi and channels. It is an excellent companion to Nyasa Yoga.

Nyasa practice is used to slowly generate Qi cleansing of channels in body segments, which is something that the *Yoga Yajnavalkya* employs for five large body sections rather than many individual body parts. In Nyasa Yoga you think of a particular segment, touch it and recite a mantra as if from it in order to help open up the channels in that body segment. This does nothing "magical" in terms of purification or transformation, which is why you have to employ your own efforts at moving internal energy to stimulate your Qi and channels in the region. This practice just schedules your efforts of pushing or trying to activate Qi in individual body parts.

Nonetheless through this practice of purifying your Qi and channels everywhere you aim at eventually purifying all the parts of your body. The final success of Qi cultivation for humans is that you can generate an independent deva body that can leave your physical sheath to come and go as you please (without anyone knowing it), and then using that body you have to practice similar techniques to separate out the next higher level of refined Qi *from within it* to generate the next higher stage body.

In the past the spiritual traditions did not talk about this openly. They only referred to spiritual results in terms of "purifying consciousness" (such as achieving the empty, very empty, great empty or all-empty subtle states of consciousness that correspond to the four dhyana and different subtle bodies) or achieving deeper, higher, emptier, more peaceful or holier states of mind. If they focused on energy exercises then devas would become involved and cause many problems for practitioners who lacked a spiritual master. It is not that people cannot handle the typical energy transformations of a kundalini arousal. It is that they cannot handle the problems caused by devas involved with the process, as explained in *Meditation Case Studies*.

Nonetheless, kundalini or Qi transformation is paramount for any efforts at "mental purification" because it opens up all the Qi channels of your brain (and body) through which the vital energy flows when generating your thoughts. If the channels don't open in your brain you will always have neurons firing randomly and be subject to an excessive level of wandering, meandering random thoughts that prevent mental peace and clarity. With each new body, the level of mental peace is deeper because the Qi channels are smoother, more open and the mind becomes more clear. With each new body it becomes easier to forget the sensation of being a body because the channels become so purified and refined. This is why masters speak of "infinite consciousness" for if you lose the edge sensations of being a body in your consciousness (because your channels have been opened completely) it will seem as if consciousness is always empty, and thus infinite.

In the *Yoga Yajnavalkya* there is a Kundalini Yoga spiritual exercise similar to the Ram-Vam Qi cultivation technique taught within the *Mahavairocana Sutra*. This exercise, however, segments the body into five parts rather than two parts.

In this Kundalini Yoga exercise, from your feet to your knees is considered the region of the earth element. From the knees to the anus is considered the region of the water element. From the anus to the heart is considered the region of the fire element. From the center of the heart to the region of the eyebrows is considered the region of the air element. From the center of the eyebrows to the top of the head is considered the region of the space element.

According to Yajnavalkya's practice instructions, when focusing on the region of the body from the feet to the knees you should recite the mantra Lam (or Lah) and try to feel the vibration within the body throughout that section. You can also visualize Brahma at the same time if you like. Other options include visualizing/imagining (while feeling them) that your feet become luminescent or change color.

For cultivating the Qi in the region from the knees to the perineum you should recite the sound Vam (or Vah), which is attributed to the water element just as in the *Mahavairocana Sutra*. You should also try to feel a vibration of Qi throughout that section while reciting because the purpose of the mantra is to help move your Qi to open Qi channels. You can also visualize the Hindu lion-faced Buddha Narayan at the same time you do this. Other options include imagining (while feeling them) that this section of the body (or the entire hips all the way to the feet) becomes cool, blue water.

To cultivate the Qi in the chest and heart region into the head you recite Ram (or Rah), which is the same sound used in the *Mahavairocana Sutra*. Once again, you also try to feel the Qi throughout that section of your body (or the vibration made by the sound) because the purpose of the mantra is to help move your Qi to open your energy channels.

Depending upon how you phonetically recite them, the sounds ending with -am or -em (Ram, Lam, Vam, etc.) usually stimulate vibrations more easily while –ah sounds (Vah, Lah, Rah, etc.) are typically more forceful and projectile in nature. However, for every individual this is different. The syllables ending with the –ang, –eng or –ung sounds (Rang, Lang, Vang, etc.) also have a different effect on stimulating your Qi as well. Mantras usually end in a sound that is translated as Hum, Hung, Ho, or Hun. Each of these alternatives has a different effect on your Qi/prana. Therefore, the rule is to use which sound works best at moving your own Qi when reciting mantras and thus it is often permissible to change mantras (after using the original for awhile) in order to get a better result.

You should always try various sound alternatives like this when practicing various cultivation techniques because there is no one right way to do most methods, just *what works best for you* in helping you transform your Qi and channels. What you want is progress, not the perfect pronunciation of a mantra! The important point is to use a sound to move your Qi rather than to think that a particular sound is holy or magical. If a different sound seems to work better then try using it for awhile.

While performing Yajnavalkya's Kundalini Yoga practice on the fire element you can also visualize Rudra or imagine that this section of the body (or the entire hips all the way to the feet) becomes reddish (the fire element) in the ways mentioned previously. Whatever works best in energizing your Qi is the method to use rather than to blindly cling to an ancient text book of instructions and try valiantly to follow its instructions to the letter. Try to discover improvements because none of these things is locked in stone. All these methods were invented by people who experimented on themselves and then left what they found as guidelines for others. Once you have the wisdom to understand a technique you can try various alternative to transform your Qi and channels.

To cultivate the Qi in the region of the head starting from the center of the eyebrows to the top of the head (inside the brain), Yajnavalkya says to recite Yam (or Yah). You can also recite Yam as if from the center of the brain since this is one of the regions you are ultimately trying to affect. Eventually all the Qi channels in the brain must be opened, which is a feat you can hasten by using diffusion tensor imaging (DTI) diagrams of cranial nerves (from the internet) to guide qi-gong and nei-gong efforts. When working on the head and brain, additionally you can also visualize a figure of Ardhamarisvara, which is a co-joint male-female figure of Shiva and Parvati that symbolizes the two halves of your brain stem (and brain) that you are trying to cultivate with this technique.

The last visualization corresponds to space, which means that you let go of any of the feelings you have generated through the prior practices, and let your mind rest empty as if it is boundless space (as if your consciousness is space that accepts everything arising within it without moving or attaching to anything). You don't have to chase away any thoughts but just let go of everything that arises within your mind, which is by nature empty of content like space. This is basically detaching from the Qi in one body and then centering yourself in the more subtle Qi of a yet higher body, thus cultivating it. The cultivation of infinite space is actually cultivating the Causal body.

For instance, if you detach from the sensations that appear in your mind, which correspond to Qi movements in your inner subtle body that you constantly cling to, by transcending those sensations with detachment you center yourself in the Qi of the Causal or Mental body, and thus start to cultivate its higher degree of Qi refinement.

Another of the Qi channel purification practices within the *Yoga Yajnavalkya* involves pranayama instead of mantra. For this practice you inhale air into your chest and abdomen and hold it while focusing on your (1) navel, (2) the tip of your nose and (3) big toes. This focus of concentration, while doing *kumbhaka* breath retention practices, will force open particular Qi channel routes to those areas. Because this exercise helps to open your Qi channels, this is why the *Yoga Yajnavalkya* is considered a tantric Yoga or Kundalini Yoga text.

As the *Yoga Yajnavalkya* explains and shows through its various techniques, cultivating your Qi (which it calls prana) will cause your channels to open. This is a gradual process that might cause perspiration, trembling or make your body feel other sensations just as the *Hatha Yoga Pradipika* mentions.

One of the best sensations is to feel a lightness in the body because your Qi circulation has become smooth and balanced through this process. This is what you want to feel at the end of all energy work. First you stir up your Qi, activating or stimulating it to help it arise and open up your channels. Then you must try to reach a level of balance and harmony of that energy within your body, and remain in that state practicing anapana (just stay centered as a bodiless witness of the sensations that arise). Emptiness meditation always ends such body-based energy practices.

Therefore, at the end of all the inner energy work techniques, from every school and tradition, you try to smoothen out your Qi and then rest in that resultant state of balance and harmony while "cultivating emptiness," which means mental freedom from attaching to the thoughts that arise. Just let the energy do whatever it wants to do and let whatever thoughts arise that arise, but don't follow them with entanglement. Just witness everything that arises in your mind like an independent third person observer. This means that you reside in a state of bliss (the body feels pleasant because your Qi is balanced) while observing any mental constructs that arise within your consciousness, but you never cling to them.

If a couple engages in sex, for instance, this will stir their energies while they simultaneously feel emotions of joy, love and excitement. If you use this activity to excite your Qi all over, and use the energies evoked to help open up restrictions in your body, you will then elevate sex into a spiritual practice. While a woman is free to orgasm without detriment, a man who loses his energies through ejaculation will no longer have them available to open up his Qi channels, so the best time to stop is when both partners feel blissful and comfortable all over. Then they can rest in each other's arms and practice the witnessing meditation practice just mentioned.

CHAPTER 6
NYASA YOGA PRACTICE

Nyasa means "to place" or to "take the mind to a point." In Nyasa practice you ordinarily touch a part of your body at the same time as pronouncing a mantra and visualizing a deity, letter or some other image at that touch point. In other words, you touch a series of specific locations on your body while "placing" a mantra on that body part. This actually means you try to bring Qi or prana to that area. When you bring your focus to that point you should also try to feel that area. In India, Nyasa practice is considered an important tantric rite for transforming or purifying your body, but only if you end up "washing" the area with Qi/prana so as to open up the local Qi channels (*nadis*).

Nyasa is often practiced before or during certain pujas (religious ceremonies) because it is meant to help purify the practitioner's body. That only happens if it is used as a form of inner Qi practice, or nei-gong, and lacking this instruction most users fall far short of achieving any benefits.

In Buddhist Vajrayana, Nyasa Yoga is similar to the practice of concentrating on the *bindus* or points of the body (*marma* points or acupuncture points) and reciting mantras at those locations in order to open those areas. However, in this case Nyasa is done with entire limbs and regions of the body such as the teeth, side of the face, lower leg, upper arm, ankle and so on. When you recite mantras at *bindu* points you are also supposed to enlarge/widen the area of focus to encompass the whole Qi of the surrounding section and stimulate the localized Qi, but most practitioners are unaware of this. You cannot just recite a mantra on a spot and expect something miraculous to happen. You must try to bring Qi to that area to wash open its Qi channels for the Yoga to have any effect.

In other words, in Nyasa practice you touch various parts of your body and seize or feel the Qi of that area with your consciousness. You also recite a mantra as if invoking a higher power to help you open up the channels in the vicinity. You append the mantra's vibration upon the spot to stir a Qi vibration within the area. You want to consecutively stimulate the Qi in every part of the body and use the Nyasa sequence as a roadmap of which areas to work on in turn. It helps if you also grab that area using visualization as is done with the white skeleton visualization practice.

You shouldn't just touch a body part, recite a mantra and then run through the whole Nyasa quickly. Since you are trying to transform the Qi/prana of your body, each time you do a Nyasa it should require some definite practice time as this is a step-by-step nei-gong practice. Just touching a body part while reciting a mantra is not some magical way to open Qi channels or gain divine protection. You must linger upon an area and concentrate on it to move its Qi.

Whereas the white skeleton visualization simply proceeds from bone to bone, Nyasa Yoga practice proceeds from body segment to body segment, and the focus on an area is always accompanied by reciting a mantra (sometimes feeling it from that location) as well as by visualization effort of some kind, which also brings Qi to the region.

Nyasa practice is said to "divinize" the body of the practitioner, which simply means you are supposed to use it for internal Qi cultivation and the final result, if successful, is a divine spirit body - a subtle energy deva body made of Qi. Colloquially it is alternatively said that Nyasa practice "infuses the life of the sponsoring deity into the body by associating mantras with every part of the body and the whole of it." Once again, this is just a fancy way of saying that you use it for Qi cultivation. If you just recite a mantra and touch a spot of your body, this does nothing at all, which few people understand. You must turn this into a method of Qi/prana cultivation.

Some people describe Nyasa saying that it allows you to "recognize divinities within your body." Another explanation says it results in the perfection of your organs, senses and mind and leads to "bodily enlightenment," which means the bodily perfection of your channels being purified and a subtle body being generated. Reading between all these explanations, you can readily infer the meaning that you can use the routine to infuse or energize your body with spiritual energy, meaning Qi. Either the energy comes from without (a deity or higher spiritual being) or from within because you activate it yourself.

Basically, Nyasa Yoga is supposed to stimulate the body's Qi/prana, which is your own latent spiritual energy, vital energy or life force. If possible, you try to generate and then lead your Qi from place to place to open those sections of your body. However, Hinduism typically describes it as a purification practice for invoking the support of a deity in spiritual cultivation efforts, and sometimes uses it to request a "shield of divine protection." According to traditional explanations, it invokes in the body-mind of the aspirant various forces and energies from Divinity. Once again, the meaning of this "shield" and divine energies is that you generate an inner deva body of subtle energy through this practice *together with other cultivation exercises*, for this practice is far from sufficient by itself to do so.

The truth is that everything in tantric purification, since you are at the beginner stages of the spiritual path, primarily has to do with your Qi cultivation, namely the purification of your Qi and Qi channels so that you can attain the deva body, or first dhyana attainment; Qi cultivation can only take you that far and no further. If a "spiritual" activity isn't affecting your Qi in a positive fashion then on the cultivation road it is pretty much useless other than for generating merit. Buddhas, masters and deities can lend their own Qi to your purification efforts, but the effect will be minimal unless you work hard yourself. Therefore you have to do most of the coarse dredging of your Qi channels yourself through very tiresome, troublesome practices like stretching, pranayama and internal energy work (nei-gong) as reported.

While Nyasa is the practice of bringing your consciousness to a certain body location, it is the various means of stimulating, activating or moving your Qi – such as through touching, visualization, mantra, stretching, feeling the Qi at the spot – that is important for opening up all the Qi channels in that vicinity. If you put any supernatural explanations of "protection" aside, that is its only true purpose. Since the net result of transforming all your Qi channels is indeed a Qi-substance deva body that can leave the physical frame at will, we can correctly say that it "divinizes" your body, but only if you practice it correctly.

People tend to quickly and unthinkingly run through Nyasa as a type of purification ritual without knowing these principles of what it is meant to accomplish, and thus they do it incorrectly without achieving any real benefits. For the best results you need to stay on each spot to cultivate the Qi of that area. When you recite the mantra from that location, you should linger and try to feel a full vibration in that region.

Just quickly touching a spot and saying a mantra will do nothing for you at all, which is why the white skeleton visualization has you focus on each individual bone for a long enough time that you can visualize it shining with bright energy. An even higher method is to visualize a bone shining with a bright light and spinning the Qi around its location in all sorts of ways, which will shave years off your practice. That will energize the Qi around it, which is what you also try to do with Nyasa practice for the part that you touch. In fact, you actually don't need to touch any location with your finger but simply focus upon it with concentration to stimulate the energy. When you can feel the energy, then you can pass on to the next location in the sequence.

You don't even need to abide by the original sequence specified in a Nyasa because if you understand what it is doing then you can design your own Nyasa sequence and inner Qi cultivation technique. Any particular Nyasa Yoga regimen is simply a method, created by some guru or master, to help you get started. Other alternatives are available.

At the end of each practice session you must – as with the White Skeleton visualization, Vajrayogini practice, Mahavira practice, Master Hakuyu's method or other nei-gong and internal energy work methods – diffuse the energies throughout your body so that your body feels harmonious. Indian schools usually poetically describe this by saying something like, "He becomes permeated by the energy losing himself in the divine Self." Actually, you just evenly distribute the Qi you have activated over your body and then ignore those feelings (called "bliss" even though they don't necessarily feel "blissful") after they seem to become full and balanced. Then you rest in that state and cultivate emptiness or samadhi.

That is the purpose of the practice.

Because Nyasa is used to evoke and then properly distribute your Qi, Shakti or prana over your human frame, Yoga asana practices and Pilates exercises (stretching), when combined with concentrated energy work on those body parts being stretched, would also help you achieve the objective of cultivating your Qi and channels. This is the essential principle and rational basis of all this and similar Tantric practices.

TYPES OF NYASA

Now there are many kinds of Nyasa practice, which extend to the very complex and elaborate. The more popular ones include Matrika Nyasa, Pitha Nyasa, Rashi Nyasa, Nakshatra Nyasa, Kara Nyasa, Anga Nyasa, Jiva Nyasa, Lipi Nyasa, Rishi Nyasa, Shadamga Nyasa (Hridayadi Shadamga Nyasa), Kara (hand) Nyasa, and Sadanga Nyasa.

Some Nyasas are associated with particular deities since it is colloquially said that a Nyasa will divinize the practitioner with the deity's powers or energies. For example, Bala has a Nyasa practice for women and men. Ganesh has a Nyasa Yoga practice as well. Kali, as another example, has hundreds of related Nyasa practices. These Kali Nyasa routines are particularly appropriate for cultivating both your Yin Qi and Yang Qi.

Nyasa can also be connected with other phenomena since all you are doing is iterating through that list of phenomena while touching different parts of your body. That list can therefore include the letters of the alphabet, a list of deities or even astronomical phenomena; the list has nothing to do with anything actually happening in the cosmos.

Thus, in the Mahashodha Nyasa the practitioner places planets, constellations, sacred sites and other cosmological elements on her or his body. There is also a very extended Jvalamukhi Nyasa which relates to human breathing and the position of the chakras within the body.

In some cases the *bija* sounds or mantra of the Nyasa are specifically designed to affect the Qi in the region pointed to, but when this is not the case it is simply the power of a deity (who comes due to the calling of the mantra) to move your Qi, or your own forceful efforts at energization, that are the important thing rather than the particular sounds. In most cases you should just try to move the Qi yourself and not think of any such thing as supernatural intervention. Nonetheless, typically a Buddha and his/her deva students take on responsibility for anyone reciting their Nyasa and they come to help ardent practitioners.

MATRIKA NYASA

The popular Matrika Nyasa involves the fifty letters (phonemes) of the Sanskrit alphabet, which are placed on specific zones of the body to "infuse it with energy." As this is done, a practitioner is required to use various hand gestures (mudras) while reciting the letters. The letters are prefixed with "Om" and suffixed with "Namah" so that their pronunciation effectively becomes a mantra.

The way that Matrika Nyasa and all others work is that the mantras are like a phone call to enlightened beings devoted to *that* Nyasa who, upon hearing it being used, then, in turn, lend their energy to your own efforts at Qi channel cultivation. This is why it is said that the Nyasa sounds "install the spirit (Qi or Prana)" of the relevant (sponsoring) deity into the body. If you superficially jump from one body part to the next then little will be accomplished, but if you linger and do some energy work at the location by trying to arouse and hold the Qi at the spot then the results will be substantial.

As stated, Nyasa practice requires several minutes of concentrated work to move the Qi throughout all the body locations listed for each Nyasa. You should mantra not just once but several times on each body spot, while trying to affect the Qi with qi-gong style methods, and then work the whole body in steps.

When reciting the letter you should try to feel the vibration of each sound being established on that particular part of your body or the vibration of Qi in that region. This is very important because essentially *Nyasa Yoga is Qi and Qi channel (prana and nadi) practice.* If you aren't making any consciousness effort to move the Qi in that location then it is the same as doing nothing at all, and you are wasting your time at the Nyasa Yoga.

These fifty Sanskrit letters, or *matrika*, are traditionally considered the sound creators of the entire universe (which of course isn't true). The *matrika* are said to represent a complete description of reality from the highest to lowest level of emanation and thus are typically used as seed mantras in Hindu culture. As energy work one can therefore recite the entire Sanskrit alphabet, starting at the top of the head, by appending each letter to different parts of the body, going downwards, while directing your Qi (prana) and attention to each mantra location along the way. The matrika can serve as a step-by-step guide for getting the job done, but the truth is that the *matrika* are just Sanskrit vocabulary sounds, and are neither the fundamental building blocks of the universe or holy vibrations.

Most of the mantra regions selected in cultivation practices correspond to the *marma*, acupuncture or striking points used in Yoga, Ayurveda, martial arts and Traditional Chinese Medicine, but they are actually zones and regions that can extend to several inches in size rather than just points. Nyasa practice is meant to affect a larger region than a traditional *marma* or acupuncture point, and some even relate to certain acupuncture meridians or *nadis* that are said to have sensitive spots or apertures at these locations.

Another mystical (but mistaken) explanation associated with Nyasa is that the mantra-bodies of deities are composed of the *matrika* or phonemes of the Sanskrit alphabet. That is, the sounds of the Sanskrit alphabet represent different energies that form various parts of deities and through this Nyasa practice those parts are built up within the practitioner. In performing the Nyasa, by reciting the mantras one is then building up a body of sound.

This is just an excellent fib that encourages practitioners to do nei-gong work on all the different parts of their bodies to cultivate the subtle energy that eventually becomes the deva body. Unfortunately, most religious people are unclear about this and fall into superstitious or supernatural ideas about the effectiveness of a Nyasa practice.

For Nyasa practice, a practitioner usually places his hand or finger on different parts of his body, uttering distinctly at the same time the appropriate *matrika* sound for that part. When the practitioner feels that all their Qi has been stimulated through the recitation of the mantra sounds, they should smooth out the Qi of their body afterwards at the practice conclusion.

For some Nyasa you are supposed to contemplate a Deity while performing the Nyasa practice. For these practices, when the practitioner feels that the nature, energy or disposition of the Deity has come upon him (that is, if the Nyasa has a sponsoring deity such as Kali or Ganesh) the practitioner is supposed to identify themselves with the Deity they contemplate and then spread the presence of the Deity's energy all over their body.

It is said that when a Nyasa practitioner finally feels that the *bhava* (nature, disposition) of the Deity has come upon him – which means that your Qi is finally being stimulated by your forceful exertions – then Nyasa has become a great auxiliary to your spiritual cultivation. In cultivating your Qi it has ennobled you. Reciting a Deity's mantras, *bijas* or syllables is therefore poetically compared to wearing jewels on different parts of the body. The *bijas* or sounds are like jewels which the cultivator places on the different body parts. However, this is so only if the practitioner uses those sounds to push, move, or stimulate the Qi around whatever region they touch.

In short, Nyasa practice is just a way of using sounds to cultivate the Qi in the individual parts of your body so that you open and purify your Qi channels. Every bit of Qi cultivation helps on the spiritual trail until you generate the deva/deity body through all this work. Nyasa practice is not effective enough by itself to help you generate an independent subtle deva body of refined Qi, but was a cultivation practice developed by ancient sages to help assist in the overall larger task of full body Qi purification.

Don't ever worry about the correct pronunciation of the sounds for a Nyasa Yoga technique. When performing such a practice, just do your best. Some people are too worried saying, "This isn't the exact pronunciation so it won't work" when the big thing is work at Qi and channel practice of any sort – the effort you make to move your Qi - and not the exact pronunciation of the syllables. Close enough is good enough since the syllables will not produce any special vibratory effects tuned to individual body parts anyway. People just associate the sounds with the planets, constellations, letters and so forth to create a long list rather than the fact that there is an actual connection between those sounds/energies and body parts.

Remember that there will be no physical effects from just reciting a mantra and touching parts of your body. However, if you take some extra steps and use this as a form of Qi cultivation – by trying to feel the sensation in that area by sending energy to it yourself - then there are indeed profound physical effects possible, which is the whole purpose of the practice. When reciting each mantra sound you should focus your attention on the particular joints or body parts that they indicate to get the best results.

Understanding those principles, here are the sounds (the pronunciation marks are absent in order not to frighten people away from trying the mantras) and body parts for a derivative of **Matrika Nyasa** practice:

Am – Top of Head
Am – Forehead
Im – Right eye
Im – Left eye
Um – Right ear
Um – Left ear
Rm – Right nostril
Rm – Left nostril
Lm – Right cheek
Lm – Left cheek
Em – Upper lip
Aim – Lower lip
Om – Upper teeth
Aum – Lower teeth
Am – Upper palate
Ah – Lower Palate

Kam – Right shoulder
Kham – Right elbow
Gam – Right wrist
Gham – The base of the right fingers
Nam – Right fingers tips

Cam – Left shoulder
Cham – Left elbow
Jam – Left wrist
Jham – The base of the left fingers
Nam – Left finger tips

Tam – Right leg (and hip)
Tham – Right knee
Dam – Right ankle

Dham – The base of the right toes
Nam – Tips of the right toes

Tam – Left leg (and hip)
Tham – Left knee
Dam – Left ankle
Dham – The base of the left toes
Nam – Tips of left toes

Pam – Right abdomen (side of the trunk)
Pham – Left abdomen (side of the trunk)
Bam – Lower back
Bham – Navel
Mam – Whole belly (lower abdomen)

Yam – Heart and Blood plasma
Ram – Blood
Lam – All Muscles
Vam – Fat tissues
Sam – All Bones (Skeleton)
Sam – All Nerves
Sam – Reproductive tissues
Ham – Qi (Prana)

Sam – Area from the heart to right hand
Sam – Area from the heart to left hand
Sam – Area from the heart to right foot
Ham – Area from the heart to left foot
Lam – Area from the heart to navel
Ksham – Area from the navel to the top of head.

Yet another derivative is to combine the *matrika* sounds with the Shakti mantra *bija* "Hrim" to bring about a different energetic result. This Nyasa would be performed/recited as follows:

Hrim Am – Top of head
Hrim Am – Front of head
Hrim Im – Right eye
Hrim Im – Left eye

Hrim Um – Right ear
Hrim Um – Left ear
Hrim Rm – Right nostril
Hrim Rm – Left nostril
Hrim Lm – Right cheek
Hrim Lm – Left cheek
Hrim Em – Upper lip
Hrim Aim – Lower lip
Hrim Om – Upper teeth
Hrim Aum – Lower teeth
Hrim Am – Upper palate
Hrim Ah – Lower Palate

Hrim Kam – Right shoulder
Hrim Kham – Right elbow
Hrim Gam – Right wrist
Hrim Gham – The base of the right fingers
Hrim Nam – Right fingers tips

Hrim Cam – Left shoulder
Hrim Cham – Left elbow
Hrim Jam – Left wrist
Hrim Jham – The base of the left fingers
Hrim Nam – Left arm to finger tips

Hrim Tam – Right leg (and hip)
Hrim Tham – Right knee
Hrim Dam – Right ankle
Hrim Dham – The base of the right toes
Hrim Nam – Tips of the right toes

Hrim Tam – Left leg (and hip)
Hrim Tham – Left knee
Hrim Dam – Left ankle
Hrim Dham – The base of the left toes
Hrim Nam – Tips of left toes

Hrim Pam – Right abdomen (side of the trunk)
Hrim Pham – Left abdomen (side of the trunk)

Hrim Bam – Lower back
Hrim Bham – Navel
Hrim Mam – Whole belly (lower abdomen)

Hrim Yam – Heart and Blood plasma
Hrim Ram - Blood
Hrim Lam – All Muscles
Hrim Vam – Fat tissues
Hrim Sam – All Bones (Skeleton)
Hrim Sam – All Nerves
Hrim Sam – Reproductive tissues
Hrim Ham – Qi (Prana)

Hrim Sam – Area from the heart to right hand
Hrim Sam – Area from the heart to left hand
Hrim Sam – Area from the heart to right foot
Hrim Ham – Area from the heart to left foot
Hrim Lam – Area from the heart to navel
Hrim Ksham – Area from the navel to the top of head.

PITHA NYASA

In Pitha Nyasa the Pitha are used in place of the *matrika* during the practice. The Pitha (Peetha) are a list of sacred centers in India representing great spiritual energy that you can identify with locations in the body.

The Pitha Nyasa runs as follow ("Aim" is pronounced "Aym"):

Aim Hrim Shrim Am obeisance to Kamarupa – Head
Aim Hrim Shrim Am Varanasi - Circle of face
Aim Hrim Shrim Im Nepala - Right eye
Aim Hrim Shrim Im Paundrardhana - Left eye
Aim Hrim Shrim Um Purasthira Kashmira - Right ear
Aim Hrim Shrim Um Kanyakubja - Left ear
Aim Hrim Shrim Rm Purnashaila - Right nostril
Aim Hrim Shrim Rm Arbudachala - Left nostril
Aim Hrim Shrim Lm Amritakeshvara - Right cheek
Aim Hrim Shrim Lm Ekamraya - Left cheek
Aim Hrim Shrim Em Trisrotasi - Upper lip

Aim Hrim Shrim Aim Kamakoti - Lower lip
Aim Hrim Shrim Om Kailasa - Upper teeth
Aim Hrim Shrim Aum Bhrigunagara - Lower teeth
Aim Hrim Shrim Am Kedara - Tongue tip
Aim Hrim Shrim Ah Chandra Puskarini – Throat
Aim Hrim Shrim Kam Shripura - Right shoulder joint
Aim Hrim Shrim Kham Omkara - Right elbow
Aim Hrim Shrim Gam Jalandhara - Right wrist
Aim Hrim Shrim Gham Malaya - Right hand finger root
Aim Hrim Shrim Nam Kulantaka - Right hand finger tips
Aim Hrim Shrim Cham Devikota - Left shoulder joint
Aim Hrim Shrim Ccham Gokarna - Left elbow
Aim Hrim Shrim Jam Maruteshvara - Left wrist
Aim Hrim Shrim Jham Attahasa - Left hand finger root
Aim Hrim Shrim Nam Viraja - Left hand finger tips
Aim Hrim Shrim Tam Rajageha - Right leg joint
Aim Hrim Shrim Tham Mahapatha - Right knee
Aim Hrim Shrim Dam Kolapura - Right ankle
Aim Hrim Shrim Dham Elapura - Right sole of foot
Aim Hrim Shrim Nam Koleshvara - Right foot toes
Aim Hrim Shrim Tam Jayantika - Left leg joint
Aim Hrim Shrim Tham Ujjayini - Left knee
Aim Hrim Shrim Dam Chitra - Left ankle
Aim Hrim Shrim Dham Kshirika - Left sole of foot
Aim Hrim Shrim Nam Hastinapura - Left foot toes
Aim Hrim Shrim Pam Uddisha - Right side of the body
Aim Hrim Shrim Pham Prayag - Left side of the body
Aim Hrim Shrim Bam Shashtisha – Back
Aim Hrim Shrim Bham Mayapuri – Navel
Aim Hrim Shrim Mam Jalesha – Belly
Aim Hrim Shrim Yam Malaya – Heart
Aim Hrim Shrim Ram Shri Shaila - Right shoulder
Aim Hrim Shrim Lam Meru - Back of neck
Aim Hrim Shrim Vam Girivara - Left shoulder
Aim Hrim Shrim Sham Mahendra - Heart to right hand palm
Aim Hrim Shrim Sham Vamana - Heart to left hand palm
Aim Hrim Shrim Sam Hiranyapura - Heart to right foot sole
Aim Hrim Shrim Ham Mahalakshmi Pura - Heart to left foot sole
Aim Hrim Shrim Lam Oddiyana - Heart to genitals

Aim Hrim Shrim Ksham obeisance to Chayachatra - Heart to top of
head.

GANESH NYASA

The Ganesh Nyasa is "sponsored by" the enlightened being
Ganesh, who is impersonated by many enlightened masters
(Buddhism calls them Buddhas) who answer the many requests to
Ganesh for help. You might try to visualize or simply think of
Ganesh while performing the Nyasa, but the rules of practice remain
the same whether or not you do this. The Nyasa runs as follows:

Aim Hrim Shrim Am - Head
Aim Hrim Shrim Am - Forehead
Aim Hrim Shrim Im - Right eye
Aim Hrim Shrim Im - Left eye
Aim Hrim Shrim Um - Right ear
Aim Hrim Shrim Um - Left ear
Aim Hrim Shrim Rm - Right nostril
Aim Hrim Shrim Rm - Left nostril
Aim Hrim Shrim Lm - Right cheek
Aim Hrim Shrim Lm - Left cheek
Aim Hrim Shrim Em - Upper lip
Aim Hrim Shrim Aim - Lower lip
Aim Hrim Shrim Om - Upper teeth
Aim Hrim Shrim Aum - Lower teeth
Aim Hrim Shrim Am - Tongue
Aim Hrim Shrim Ah - Throat
Aim Hrim Shrim Kam - Right shoulder
Aim Hrim Shrim Kham - Right elbow
Aim Hrim Shrim Gam - Right wrist
Aim Hrim Shrim Gham - Base of right fingers
Aim Hrim Shrim Nam - Right finger tips
Aim Hrim Shrim Cam - Left shoulder
Aim Hrim Shrim Cham - Left elbow
Aim Hrim Shrim Jam - Left wrist
Aim Hrim Shrim Jham - Left root of fingers
Aim Hrim Shrim Nam - Left finger tips
Aim Hrim Shrim Tam - Right thigh

Aim Hrim Shrim Tham - Right knee
Aim Hrim Shrim Dam - Right ankle
Aim Hrim Shrim Dham - Right foot
Aim Hrim Shrim Nam - Right toes
Aim Hrim Shrim Tam - Left thigh
Aim Hrim Shrim Tham - Left knee
Aim Hrim Shrim Dam - Left ankle
Aim Hrim Shrim Dham - Left foot
Aim Hrim Shrim Nam - Left toes
Aim Hrim Shrim Pam - Right side of the Body
Aim Hrim Shrim Pham - Left side of the Body
Aim Hrim Shrim Bam - Back
Aim Hrim Shrim Bham - Navel
Aim Hrim Shrim Mam - Belly
Aim Hrim Shrim Yam - Heart
Aim Hrim Shrim Ram - Right collar bone
Aim Hrim Shrim Lam - Shoulder hump
Aim Hrim Shrim Vam - Left collar bone
Aim Hrim Shrim Sham - Heart to right palm
Aim Hrim Shrim Sham - Heart to left palm
Aim Hrim Shrim Sam - Heart to right foot
Aim Hrim Shrim Ham - Heart to left foot
Aim Hrim Shrim Lam - Heart to genitals
Aim Hrim Shrim Ksham – Heart.

RASHI (CONSTELLATIONS) NYASA

With the Rashi Nyasa, you are using the fact that there are twelve zodiac signs to cultivate twelve different body parts. Those inclined to astrological research can find other correspondences between a sign (Aries, Taurus, etc.) and body parts, and can then repeat the method using any other physical correspondences they find so as ro work with the Qi of their entire body another way.

The reason you can do this on your own is because the mantra you recite identifies the Nyasa you are using to enlightened beings who have taken a vow (selected on their own as their job) to "protect it," which means help the humans using it to cultivate their Qi. The relevant enlightened beings that help with Qi cultivation will know what to work on when you start to practice a particular Nyasa.

If you go beyond the published Nyasa formula and work extra to also move, activate, stimulate or stir up the Qi in other body segments you are doing extra cultivation work, which is what Buddhas want to happen. Once again, the purpose is that you succeed in Qi cultivation, not that you follow a formula perfectly.

Traditional Vedic astrology says that Aries represents our head; Taurus the neck; Gemini the upper chest, shoulders and arms and hands; Cancer the breasts; Leo the solar plexus; Virgo the navel region; Libra the lower abdomen, kidneys, reproductive system, and lower back; Scorpio the public region, private parts, anus and rectum; Sagittarius the thighs and hips; Capricorn the knees; Aquarius the calves and ankles; and Pisces the feet.

While the Rashi Nyasa pairs mantras with different body parts you can also use it, as explained, on different astrological correspondences as just mentioned:

Aim Hrim Shrim Am Am Im Im obeisance to Aries - Right foot
Aim Hrim Shrim Um Um to Taurus - Right side of penis
Aim Hrim Shrim Rm Rm Lm Lm to Gemini - Right side of belly
Aim Hrim Shrim Em Aim to Cancer - Right side of heart
Aim Hrim Shrim Om Aum to Leo - Right shoulder joint
Aim Hrim Shrim Am Ah Shhm Sham Sam Ham Lam to Virgo - Right side of head
Aim Hrim Shrim Kam Kham Gam Gham Nam to Libra - Left side of head
Aim Hrim Shrim Cham Ccham Jam Jham Nam to Scorpio - Left shoulder joint
Aim Hrim Shrim Tam Tham Dam Dham Nam to Sagittarius - Left side of heart
Aim Hrim Shrim Tam Tham Dam Dham Nam to Capricornus - Left side of belly
Aim Hrim Shrim Pam Pham Bam Bham Mam to Aquarius - Left side of penis
Aim Hrim Shrim Yam Ram Lam Vam Ksham to Pisces - Left foot.

PLANET NYASA

With the Planet Nyasa, you are using the fact that there are nine planets to cultivate nine different body sections. Those inclined to astrological research can find other correspondences between the planets and regions of the body, and use this methodology for other correspondences they find. As stated, the Nyasa simply steps you through the process of cultivating the entire body in parts and the mantras simply alert spiritual beings pledged to that Nyasa to help you with your Qi cultivation. Knowing these principles, you can change things according to circumstances.

Traditional Vedic astrology states that the Sun represents our bone structure, right eye, sight, heart and stomach; the Moon represents our mind, emotions, body fluids, left eye, glands, tonsils, sense of taste, breasts, chest, loins; Mercury represents our skin, sense of smell, memory, intelligence, speech, consciousness, respiratory canal, intestines and throat; Venus represents semen, sense of taste, sexual organs, reproductive system, face, beauty of eyes; Mars represents the muscles, head, testicles and penis, bone marrow, blood pressure, bile, and vigor; Jupiter represents the liver, gall bladder, spleen, fat, sense of sounds and ears; Saturn rules over our tendons, joints and spine, legs, knee, ankles, sense of touch and nerves. Western astrology suggest different correspondences between planets and body parts and organs.

While the Planet Nyasa pairs mantras with different body parts than the traditional astrological correspondences, you should know by now that you can still use it anyway. This Nyasa runs as follows:

Aim Hrim Shrim Am Am Im Im Um Um Rm Rm Lm Lm Em Aim
    Aum Om Am Ah obeisance to the Sun - Heart
Aim Hrim Shrim Yam Ram Lam Vam to the Moon - Centre of brow
Aim Hrim Shrim Kam Kham Gam Gham Nam to Mars - Eyes
Aim Hrim Shrim Cam Cham Jam Jham Nam to Mercury - Ears and
    the brain stem
Aim Hrim Shrim Tam Tham Dam Dham Nam to Jupiter - Throat
Aim Hrim Shrim Tam Tham Dam Dham Nam to Venus - Heart
Aim Hrim Shrim Pam Pham Bam Bham Mam to Saturn - Navel
Aim Hrim Shrim Sham Sham Sam Ham to Rahu - Mouth
Aim Hrim Shrim Lam Ksham to Ketu – Genitals.

In Vedic astrology there are many mantras that call upon the power of the planets for changing your fortune. The Vedic planetary mantras basically ask the Buddhas or enlightened deities representing those energies to help you change your Qi, perfect your body, give you the right thoughts and in that way change your fortune.

Some Vedic astrologers actually achieve the subtle body through the use of these mantras in conjunction with meditation practice and other spiritual exercises. In Taoism and Yoga there are also various methods to absorb the energies of the planets or constellations such as the Sun, Moon, Venus, Big Dipper or Pleiades. One common set of mantras for balancing the energies of the planets, which you can compare with the Nyasa and use in a similar fashion (such as by imagining that you draw the cited planetary energies into your body), is as follows:

Om Sum Suryaya Namah – Sun
Om Bum Budhaya Namah – Mercury
Om Sum Sukraya Namah – Venus
Om Cam Candraya Namah – Moon
Om Kum Kujaya Namah – Mars
Om Brm Brhaspataye Namah – Jupiter
Om Sam Sanaya Namah – Saturn
Om Ram Rahave Namah – Rahu
Om Kem Ketave Namah – Ketu

Yet another set of Tantric mantras for the planets that can be used to cultivate your Qi runs as follows:

Om Hram Hrim Hraum Sah Suryaya Namah – Sun
Om Bram Brim Braum Sah Budhaya Namah – Mercury
Om Dram Drim Draum Sah Sukraya Namah – Venus
Om Sram Srim Sraum Sah Candrata Namah – Moon
Om Kram Krim Kraum Sah Kujaya Namah – Mars
Om Gram Grim Graum Sah Gurave Namah – Jupiter
Om Pram Prim Praum Sah Sanaye Namah – Saturn
Om Bhram Bhrim Bhraum Sah Rahave Namah – Rahu
Om Stram Strim Straum Sah Ketave Namah - Ketu

If, through mantra practice, you harmonize all the Qi of your body, this is the same as "harmonizing all the elements of the body." In other words, since each planet represents a different element of your body (Air, Water, Fire, Water, Earth) as well as different organs and body parts, reciting these planetary mantras to harmonize your Qi is the same as cultivating the energy of the planets. If you finally succeed at "divinizing your body" by becoming able to generate the subtle body, then you have accomplished the practice.

Lastly, there is a little known practice of "Golden Surya" visualization for mastering the fire element of the body. It is said to represent the power of all the Sun King Buddhas throughout the cosmos. This mantra is as follows: "Ohm Ah Var Rah Hum." Those who practice this sadhana first imagine that their body becomes the fire element due to the power of all the suns. At a higher stage of practice after the first visualization is mastered then you imagine that your body becomes golden in color like a Buddha such as Amitofo or Ksitigarba.

The normal progression in tantric practices is to master *red* deity visualization before *golden* visualizations. At the next higher stage of progress (and there are higher levels still corresponding to meditation on being emotions such as infinite compassion or infinite kindness) you imagine being transparent and empty like infinite space.

There are many variations for the basic Golden Surya (Sun King) practice and these are just a few indications.

NAKSHATRA NYASA

With the Nakshatra Nyasa, you are using the fact that there are twelve zodiac signs to cultivate twelve different body parts. In other words, you cultivate the body by breaking it into twelve pieces instead of just two, such as with the Ram/Vam dichotomy. The Nakshatra Nyasa runs as follows:

Aim Hrim Shrim Am Am obeisance to Ashwini - Forehead
Aim Hrim Shrim Im to Bharani - Right eye
Aim Hrim Shrim Im Im Um to Kritika - Left eye
Aim Hrim Shrim Rm Rm Lm Lm to Rohini - Right ear
Aim Hrim Shrim Em to Mrigashira - Left ear
Aim Hrim Shrim Aim to Ardra - Right nostril
Aim Hrim Shrim Om Aum to Punarvasu - Left nostril
Aim Hrim Shrim Kam to Pushya - Throat
Aim Hrim Shrim Kham Gam to Ashlesha - Right shoulder
Aim Hrim Shrim Gham Nam to Magha - Left shoulder

Aim Hrim Shrim Cam to Purva Phalguni - Back
Aim Hrim Shrim Cham Jam to Uttara Phalguni - Right elbow
Aim Hrim Shrim Jham Nam to Hasta - Left elbow
Aim Hrim Shrim Tam Tham to Chitra - Right wrist
Aim Hrim Shrim Dam to Swati - Left wrist
Aim Hrim Shrim Dham Nam to Vishakha - Right hand
Aim Hrim Shrim Tam Tham Dam to Anuradha - Left hand
Aim Hrim Shrim Dham to Jeshtha - Navel
Aim Hrim Shrim Nam Pam Pham to Mula - Pelvis
Aim Hrim Shrim Bam to Purvas Ashadha - Right thigh
Aim Hrim Shrim Bham to Uttara Ashadha - Left thigh
Aim Hrim Shrim Mam to Shravan - Right knee
Aim Hrim Shrim Yam Ram to Dhanishta - Left knee
Aim Hrim Shrim Lam to Shatataraka - Right ankle
Aim Hrim Shrim Vam Sham to Purva Bhadra - Left ankle
Aim Hrim Shrim Sham Sam Ham to Uttara Bhadrapada - Right foot
Aim Hrim Shrim Lam Ksham Am Ah to Revati - Left foot.

Those inclined to research can find other correspondences between the planets and regions of the body, and then use the appropriate Nyasa mantras for any extra correspondences they find. "Use the Nyasa" simply means to use the mantras to step through a sequence of Qi cultivation concentrations on different body parts in turn.

For instance, the traditional Vedic astrological (Jyotish) correspondence between the nakshatras and body parts is Ashwini (top of foot), Bharani (sole of foot), Kritika (head), Rohini (forehead), Mrigashira (eyebrows), Ardra (eyes), Punarvasu (nose), Pushya (face), Ashlesha (ears), Magha (lips/chin), Purva Phalguni (right hand), Uttara Phalguni (left hand), Hasta (fingers), Chitra (neck), Swati (chest), Vishakha (breasts), Anuradha (stomach), Jeshtha (right torso), Mula (left torso), Purva Ashadha (back), Uttara Ashadha (waist), Shravan (genitals), Dhanistha (anus), Satabishak (right thigh), Purva Bhadra (left thigh), Uttara (lower legs), and Revati (ankles). One could use the appropriate Nyasa mantras on any of these logical body parts with the intent to purify the Qi of your body entirely.

OTHER NYASA

There are many other Nyasa and they all follow similar principles. You touch, name/mantra, and visualize a sequence of places in your body. You become conscious of every place in your body in turn, bringing Qi to the area to energize the Qi up within it. *You linger on that area, reciting the mantra several times while there* until you connect with the Qi of the region to move it, and when it is stimulated sufficiently you then move on to the next location in the sequence.

At the end of the whole practice you try to harmonize the excited energy so that blockages to Qi flow within your body (that are revealed through the method) do not bother you. You also want to avoid being stimulated into sexual activities due the energetic stimulation. "Harmonizing your energy" also means that you want to eventually feel the Qi of your whole body as a single coherent unit. You want to feel your Qi everywhere within you. If you imagine that you are wearing a scuba diving wet suit, you would be trying to feel as energy everything contained inside it.

A similar practice is to imagine the body as being an empty shell after you stir up the internal energies everywhere inside it, and to keep smoothing them out (because you might feel internal obstructions) until you can imagine that your body dissolves and no longer exists. This is another way to cultivate your Qi and Qi channels to a state of smooth functioning wherein you can no longer feel the body anymore, and in that bodiless-feeling state (where you can thereby ignore the body) you try to cultivate emptiness/clear consciousness.

Witnessing or observing the energies within you that arise due to meditation is the real anapana practice of Buddhism. However, the missing piece of instruction is that you should actively try to stir up internal energies instead of waiting years for your Qi to start moving. You try to stir up the energy everywhere inside your body through various means called "cultivation" or "spiritual exercises," and then observe where you feel blockages, restrictions or tightness and try to smooth them out so that the Qi passes through those areas.

After you activate the Qi of your body through Nyasa (or any other practice), you then sit quietly in meditation and let it *flow everywhere* without interfering with it. Always follow Nyasa by meditation, otherwise stirring your Qi up but not meditating afterwards will never give your Qi an opportunity to reach a state of flow whose evenness of circulation produces "bliss."

This is something I explain in *Internal Martial Arts Nei-gong* including various ways to get rid of channel obstructions. Try to cultivate everything in your body completely through all these "generation practices" remembering that the ultimate target is to produce an etheric body double, or copy of your body. This is the meaning of the "generation stage" in Vajrayana. You can only generate this subtle body, which is like the Qi body that leaves everyone's physical shell when they die, if you can cause your Qi to pass through all its atomic bonds and form a new copy or coherent whole. This takes a lot of work and years of effort.

To do this you can use Nyasa practice, but you have to use many other cultivation methods as well, especially meditation right after Nyasa practice is performed; you are not supposed to do Nyasa without being followed by meditation. You must work at this for years, sometimes several hours per day. Eventually your Qi will begin to rotate or circulate through your Qi channels, which feels like a type of rolling, at which time you should stay in meditation for hours to continue the process.

Many different types of Nyasa practice are available, each belonging to a different family of past individuals who achieved enlightenment, meaning they achieved a stage well beyond the subtle Qi body and can therefore use the energies of their higher bodies to help move your own energies. Through their assistance, this is how you "purify" your Qi channels. For instance, it isn't Ganesh who helps you with the Ganesh Nyasa but a regular person who succeeded and masquerades as Ganesh. Ganesh himself is a fictitious invention.

As another example, in the Masashogha Nyasa a practitioner places planets, constellations, sacred sites and other elements on his or her body while reciting mantras. The planets, constellations, sacred sites actually have nothing to do with the practice because it is your own efforts or higher beings that are helping you achieve the purification process of your energy. Nevertheless, enlightened masters who have previously succeeded (we call them "Buddhas," meaning they achieved the Supra-Causal body at minimum) have created all sorts of Nyasa with such correspondences knowing that a wise researcher, such as yourself, might discover some analogs with their body organs or main limbs (like the toes, knees, hips, back, chest, shoulder blades and head) that they might use as a helpful adjunct to cultivate their body parts in turn. Also, unusual correspondences motivate some people to practice who otherwise would not do so.

A practitioner who wishes to cultivate the Qi of their body is advised to practice all these Nyasa until they find one they really like, after which they can use the mantras on any body segment after having established a relationship with the practice, meaning the enlightened beings who oversee it. This is the same rule for "testing" a mantra. Always a Buddha and his students respond by trying to help you change your Qi channels, and if you find that one stirs your Qi better than another than that is one to use for awhile.

NYASA DERIVATIVES

If you practice yoga or martial arts, you are advised to work on cultivating each body part using stretching (physical movement) together with visualization (light), mantra (sound) and sensation (feeling the energy of the stretched body part). Knowing the basic sounds used in Nyasa Yoga, you might also attempt a strategy such as reciting "Om Kam, Kham, Gam, Gham, Nam" for the right arm to hands as you stretch those muscles, and recite each of these syllables on the relevant section of the arms or *marma*/acupuncture points. A similar practice would be to recite "Om Cam, Cham, Jam, Jham, Nam" for the left arm to left hand.

For the legs, while stretching/straining them (such as by standing in the horse stance posture of martial arts) one might recite "Om Tam, Tham, Dam, Dham, Nam," for the right hip to the right foot, appending the sounds to within the limbs. For the left hip to the left foot you might use "Om Tam, Tham, Dam, Dham, Nam" at the relevant sectional parts, reciting the sounds as if from within the body to further help stir the Qi in those areas.

Since the head contains sixteen mantra points, another Nyasa practice would be to practice pranayama in a sitting posture while pressing/touching each of these locations one by one while trying to feel the Qi and hold it at the respective location. You can also try to *guide the Qi from location to location to open up these regions.*

This principle can be used for any body section to bring energy into the region and open up its various sections, such as repeating the sound Im along with your breathing to bring Qi into the eyes, or repeating the mantra Pam, while focusing on the right side of the belly, to bring more energy into the abdomen. Countless other derivative methods can be constructed.

As to the sixteen mantra points for the head you can use the following Nyasa:

Om Am – Top of head
Om Am – Forehead
Om Im – Right eye
Om Im – Left eye
Om Um – Right ear
Om Um – Left ear
Om Rm – Right nostril
Om Rm – Left nostril
Om Lm – Right cheek
Om Lm – Left cheek
Om Em – Upper lip
Om Am – Lower lip
Om Om - Upper teeth
Om Aum – Lower teeth
Om Am – Upper palate
Om Ah – Lower palate

When you get good at Nyasa practice you can string together several of the mantras in sequence in order to cultivate a section of your body like this. The whole point is to activate your Qi, and after it is activated to start meditating and feel that Qi flowing everywhere in your body. The Nyasa Yoga practice stirs up your Qi, but immediately afterwards you must engage in meditation, which is the time that the Qi can start flowing in its circuits/orbits without you having to push it at all.

MAHASHODHA NYASA

Since we showed how to use mantra sounds for the face, you should understand that there are very abbreviated Nyasa Yoga practices for special areas of the body. Most mudras, for instance, do nothing supernatural but simply help to exercise the Qi channels of the fingers to help open them up. They are like Yoga practices just for the hands and fingers. As thermography pictures show, the fingers and fingertips are very difficult to open which is why, as done in Taoist cultivation, you should spin your Qi in various ways for all the joints and bones and skin of the hands in order to help open up their channels.

Some Tibetan masters who attain the Rainbow body - where they are able to turn their entire body to energy upon death by shrinking it away as the process is performed – often leave behind fingernails or toenails not as relics but because they could not completely cultivate those sections. Cultivating the body completely is hard to do and these sections are amongst the most difficult just as thermography pictures show. The Mahashodya Nyasa was therefore developed to help practitioners cultivate their hands and fingers:

Aim Hrim Shrim Am Kam Kham Gam Gham Nam Am Aim –
    Thumbs
Aim Hrim Shrim Im Cam Cham Jam Jham Nam Im Klim – Index
    fingers
Aim Hrim Shrim Um Tam Tham Dam Dham Nam Um Sauh –
    Middle fingers
Aim Hrim Shrim Em Tam Tham Dam Dham Nam Aim Aim – Ring
    fingers
Aim Hrim Shrim Aum Pam Pham Bam Bham Mam Aum Klim –
    Little fingers
Aim Hrim Shrim Am Yam Ram Lam Vam Sam Sam Sam Ham Lam
    Ksham Am Sauh – Front and Back of Hands

Once you understand the method of Nyasa and the use of sounds, which is called the science of Mantrayana, many other such techniques can be created or simply understood. To comprehend more about the Sanskrit sounds used for these practices you might turn to David Frawley's *Mantra Yoga and Primal Sound: Secrets of Seed (Bija) Mantras.*

YAJNAVALKYA'S *PRATYAHARA*

A final aspect of Nyasa Yoga practice to note is that you can consider it as a type of *pratyahara* practice. When you study the

Yajnavalkya's description of *pratyahara* you can understand how Nyasa really means that you withdraw your attention from your external senses and concentrate internally as you draw your Qi from one area to another to open up Qi channels in particular regions of the body. The lists of body parts you find in ancient texts, with attendant mantras, just provide a sequence you can follow for the task of sending Qi to body parts one-by-one in turn. The whole body, of course, must be purified by the Qi channels everywhere being opened.

The sage Yajnavalkya explained the instructions for an eighteen part *pratyahara*, which is essentially a Nyasa yoga for the big toes, ankles, mid-shanks, calves, knees, thighs, anus, the center of the body (*dehamadhya*), generative organ, navel, heart, neck pit, palate, nose, circular orb of the eyes, center of the eyebrows, forehead, and crown of the head:

> The following pratyahara is the greatest yogic practice and is praised and followed by yogis always. Having drawn the prana from one point to another, holding it in the eighteen vital points (*marmasthanas*) is spoken of as pratyahara. The Asvini Kumaras who are the best among the physicians of the celestials (devas) have spoken thus of the vital points in the body, for the attainment of liberation from yoga.
>
> I shall explain all of them in an orderly manner. Listen, disciplined [Gargi]!
>
> The big toes, the ankles, in the mid-shanks, the root of the calves, the knees, middle of the thighs, the root of the anus, the center of the body (dehamadhya), generative organ, the navel, the heart, and neck pit, Gargi. Then, the root of the palate, the root of the nose, circular orb of the eyes, the center of the eyebrows, the forehead, and crown of the head. ....
> These are the vital points. ...
>
> Some skilled yogis speak of [another] pratyahara. Listen beautiful [Gargi], I will tell you [about] it. During the practice of pranayama, the prana must be held by the mind from the big toe to the crown of the head, like a totally filled pot. Drawing [the prana] from the crown of the head, one must focus it in the forehead. Drawing [the prana] from the crown of the head, one must focus it in the forehead. Again, drawing

the prana from the forehead, one must focus it between the eyebrows. Drawing [the prana] from the center of the eyebrows one must focus it in the center of the eyes. Drawing the prana from the eyes, one must focus it in the root of the nose. From the root of the nose, one must focus the prana in the root of the tongue. Drawing [the prana] from the root of the tongue, one must focus it in the base of the throat (neck-pit). Drawing the prana from the neck-pit, one must focus it in the center of the heart, from the center of the heart one must focus it in the center of the navel, again from the center of the navel one must focus it in the generative organ and then from the generative organ one must focus it in the abode of fire (dehamadhya), from the dehamadhya (center of the body), Gargi, one must focus it in the root of the anus and from the root of the anus in the [mid-] thighs, then from the mid-thigh in the center of the knees. Then, [from the knee] one must focus the prana in the root of the calf, from there in the middle of the shank, and drawing [the prana] from the middle of the shank in the ankle. From the ankle, Gargi, one must focus it (the prana) in the big toes of the feet.

The wise one who, drawing the prana from point to point, focuses it in the above said manner, will be freed from all bondage and will live as long as the moon and the stars exist (will attain liberation). This [pratyahara] is praised as the means for the fruition of yoga even by Agastya (one of the great sages). Among the pratyaharas, this one is considered as the best by yogis.[2]

If you can now take your knowledge of typical Nyasa principles and sequences you have learned and match it with these descriptions of Yajnavalkya's *pratyahara* technique you will now have yet another way of cultivating your Qi according to his instructions of drawing the Qi/prana from place to place.

The idea of Nyasa or *pratyahara* is the same principle of drawing your Qi from one area to the next in order to open up the Qi channels in that region. Nyasa Yoga is thus a body cultivation

---

[2] *Yoga Yajnavalkya*, trans. by A.G. Mohan with Ganesh Mohan, (Svastha Yoga Ote Ltd, 2013), pp. 75-79.

practice meant to help you transform all your *nadis* or Qi channels in a logical sequence.

Despite all the fanciful talk about the powers/energies of deities and divine protection, you must practice Nyasa Yoga with this in mind. It is a prana cultivation practice, a *nadi* cultivation practice. It is a nei-gong inner energy work practice designed to help you open up your Qi channels. It essentially accomplishes what the (restricted) Tibetan Vajrayana tantric empowerment practices are meant to help you accomplish. It eventually enables you to cultivate the deva body, which is the first milestone of the spiritual path regardless of your tradition. This is True Yoga.

CHAPTER 7
MANTRAYANA

Now we turn to the typical spiritual practice of mantra recitation, or Japa practice, which can become thousands or even hundreds of thousands of times more effective if you use it in a special way. How? By combining it with the principles of Nyasa Yoga where you recite the sound while simultaneously focusing on different parts of your body in consecutive sequence. This combination becomes a form of Mantrayana practice.

Previously we saw in the *Vairocanabhisambodhi Sutra* that the two sounds Rah and Vah (or Ram and Vam) could be used to cultivate the body in a dualistic fashion of top and bottom, left side and right side, or front and back. This is cultivating the body in two parts whereas Master Hakuyu's soma egg cream method is cultivating the body as one single part or whole.

This idea can also be expanded to work on three sections of the body using a simple three syllable mantra, as well as four or five syllable mantras to be used on four or five segments of the body. You can cultivate the body in a different number of sections like this, such as the seven sections of the body normally identified by the seven chakras. Here are some examples of how this works.

OM AH HUNG

A common mantra used throughout the world is "Om Ah Hung" attributed to the Buddha Samantabhadra who has vowed to accomplish great deeds that help people succeed in their spiritual cultivation.

Typically a practitioner might mindlessly recite Om Ah Hung (or Hum) millions of times hoping to acquire some spiritual result. The typical result is to attract the attention of enlightened individuals and their assistance to help you open up and purify your Qi channels as well change your fortune for the better by giving you thoughts that help you solve problems in your life. When your Qi channels open people often feel warm in the body area where that happens, such as after extended mantra practice.

Now let's take a moment to investigate the sounds of this mantra. Please stop a moment and recite the sound "Om" several times. When doing so, try to feel the sound and vibration it causes within your body. Where do you feel it most – in your head, chest or abdomen?

Most people will feel it in their head, and secondarily in their chest but mostly in the head. Om is a sound that can be appended to any part of the body, but when you pronounce the syllable you will usually feel the vibrations most strongly in your head.

Now recite the "Ah" sound several dozen times and try to feel where the sound resonates most in your body. Where do you feel the most energy – in your head, chest or abdomen?

Most people will say in their chest. The Ah sound – which appears in numerous mantras such as "Alleluia," "Om Shivaya Namaha," "Allah" and so forth – is the major sound used to open up the Qi channels in the heart (chest) region of your body. "Rah," "Ha," and so on are al forms of the Ah sound.

Now recite the forceful "Hum" or "Hung" sound (which is spoken with force as you exhale) several dozen times. Where do you feel it most within your body – in the head, chest or abdomen?

Most people will say in their abdomen or belly. This is a sound frequently used to move (cultivate) Qi within the abdomen and belly of the body along with the legs. Only people who have done a lot of stretching and other leg cultivation techniques will be able to feel it in the legs.

You have now established that by reciting the sounds Om, Ah and Hung you tend to feel the energy in your head (and arms), chest and then abdomen (and legs) respectively.

If you take this understanding, and now forevermore try to feel the energy in your head (and arms), chest and then abdomen (and legs) when you recite the Om Ah Hung mantra, you will be using the sounds and resultant vibrations to open up the Qi channels in three sections of the body! This is the purpose of Nyasa practice, only in this case you do not have to touch the body sections or think of anything such as a Buddha or deity while reciting the sounds. This secret method just taught is 10,000 times more effective than simple mantra practice alone.

Reciting the mantra Om Ah Hung while feeling the vibrations in these three different body segments - the head and arms, the chest, and the abdominal cavity and legs - is called Mantrayana practice.

If, when feeling the sound in an area (which helps to open up the Qi channels in that region) you also visualize that area becoming a different color, as is done in Vajrayana and some other tantric schools, this is "adding light to the sound" to help activate your Qi and channels.

For instance, during Vajrayana Nyasa practice for your fingers you recite mantras on their joints while visualizing that your thumb, first, second, third, fourth and pinky fingers are the colors red, blue, yellow, green and white, respectively. This not only helps you "seize" the Qi of each finger, but also builds your powers of visualization which are useful for manipulating Qi when you finally attain the deva body.

In India women paint their finger tips the color red, which is supposed to remind people to concentrate on moving their Qi to their finger tips in order to complete the Qi purification in the fingers since thermography pictures prove they are the most difficult part of the hands to transform. Some Tibetan masters achieve the "rainbow body" by transforming their physical body into energy before death. They often leave their fingernails behind as their body shrinks during the multi-day process. However, this is not due to the fact they compassionately left them behind as "relics" for students but because they weren't able to cultivate their fingertip nails completely because that section of the body is difficult to cultivate unless you pay it special attention.

In any case, Om Ah Hung can be used to cultivate the body in three large sections, which is an alternative to whole body cultivation or seven-section chakra cultivation. If you now search for an internet picture of nerve zones in the body ("dermatone map"), you will find that there are roughly three segments to the body – the head together with the arms; chest; and waist, abdomen or belly together with the legs. Using such pictures as a guide, you should logically conjecture that for the most help in opening your energy channels that the Om should be felt in the head and arms, the Ah sound in the chest, and Hung sound down from the waist to the feet.

If you recite the mantra Om Ah Hung while focusing on feeling the Qi in these different areas, reciting the sounds as if from within those areas (perhaps also adding visualization to your effort so as to stir up the Qi) and matching the sensations in each area to the sounds then you will have increased the effectiveness of your mantra practice manifold.

Other tripartite mantras that can be used this way include "Hring Shring Kling," "Hreem Shreem Kleem," "Hreem Kleem Shreem" and other variations.

OM AH VAH LAH HUM TWAY

Indian culture also partitions the body into five cavities according to the workings of the five Prana (Qi) or Vayu (winds) – Udana, Prana, Apana, Samana and Vyana. According to Yoga theory, Udana resides in the head and arms and legs, Prana in the chest, Apana in the pelvic girdle of the waist (excluding legs and upper spine), Samana in the belly or upper abdomen, and Vyana encompasses the whole body.

The Vairocana mantra "Om Ah Vah Lah Hum Tway" can therefore be recited by feeling the Qi in each of these body sections respectively – Om (head, arms and legs), Ah (chest – heart area), Vah (navel), Lah (pelvic girdle and legs), Hum (legs) and Tway (entire body and then space). The Vairocana mantra recitation recipe is therefore Om (head and throat), Ah (chest and head), Vah (navel), Lah (pelvis), Hum (legs) and Tway (entire body and then space).

Some schools replace the Tway with Kai, and the rule is that if you have an enlightened master who teaches a different mantra sound then you just go along with that. Each mantra connects with a different enlightened teacher, Buddha or tradition whose devas will work on helping you transform your Qi and channels, so by changing the sound you are connecting with a different Buddha family of volunteers to work on your channels. If you don't have a teacher, you can just try several mantras and see which ones "work best" for you. That's the general rule when trying to choose between mantras and wondering which ones to practice/use.

The more complicated mantras rarely correspond to using the best *bija* or root sounds (as with Om Ah Hung for the head, chest and abdomen) to open up the Qi in a particular body region. They are usually sounds or sentences telling a Buddha family to work on helping you open up your Qi channels.

If you truly want to move the Qi within your body to open up your Qi channels, you can create many different appropriations of mantra seed sounds, or *bijas*, to areas of the body and then use them to stimulate the Qi in that area. The important thing when mixing them up is to feel the sound in a new area so as to ignite, stir or activate the Qi in that region. If you don't move your Qi then your are getting little benefit from the mantra.

Some spiritual schools try to stir your Qi through emotional fervor and extreme emotional states (such as exhilaration, joy, unbounded happiness, etc.), but the Mantrayana practices try to stir your Qi through the use of mantra sounds. Adding emotions to this effort will also help to move your Qi. Obviously, the more types of stimulation you add to your effort (sound, light, vibration, stretching, Buddha help, etc.) the more powerful the possibilities for opening your channels if you learn how to do this correctly. That usually requires an expert Tantric teacher as your master.

OM MANI BEI ME HUNG

The popular manta for Avalokitesvara (Kuan Yin), "Om Mani Bei Me Hung," has many possible Mantrayana routines for cultivating the Qi of your body. As with using other mantras, you can create your own sequence of placements of these sounds as you feel necessary to help open up different body areas.

As you already know, sometimes the vibration of a sound within an area will stir up Qi in a region and help open up the blocked channels in that area. This is the general principle of Nyasa practice and Mantrayana, which is "appending syllables" to any part of the body to move the Qi. Therefore you should try to feel mantra sounds, or recite the mantra sound as if from within a particular body area if you want to affect its Qi channels very quickly.

Unfortunately, no one has ever created a Nyasa where the sounds used are the perfect, best ones to resonate the body cavity of that section of the body. Mantra sounds (*bijas*) can help open up Qi channels in the body, but they are rarely specifically useful to a particular body part. Only a very few sounds like Om, Ah and Hung can be highly appropriated to certain body locations, and this is why they are commonly found in many mantras and prayers (since all spiritual schools want to open up the channels in those locations).

It takes a while to develop the habit of associating a sound with a particular body region you are trying to vibrate/affect when you recite a mantra, which is why this technique needs practice. It requires deep, deliberate practice. You have to do it *slowly and deliberately many, many times* until you establish the habit energy of doing this correctly. Two books, *The Talent Code* and *Talent is Overrated,* talk about how to perform deep and deliberate practice to get better results in whatever skill or outcome you want, and you can apply their lessons to Mantrayana practices.

After you finally create this habit and continue forward with your mantra practice, it is inevitable that you will get sloppy over time. Therefore you must periodically use the principles of deliberate practice to refresh your practice by carefully relearning how to feel and visualize each body part in turn when reciting the appropriate sounds.

The rules of deep, deliberate practice teach that you should always practice a skill correctly, even if that learning process is incredibly slow, so that you don't end up repeating errors that become ingrained habits that you cannot change later. After you have it down perfectly then you can practice with increased speed.

GAYATRI, ZHUNTI AND VAJRA ARMORING

Longer mantras - such as the Buddhist Zhunti mantra, Hindu Gayatri mantra and "Vajra Armor" mantra of Padmasambhava - contain many sounds (syllables) that can be appended (used) all over the body as you are trying to cultivate your Qi and channels.

The Zhunti mantra runs:

Namah saptanam samyaksambuddha kotinam tadyatha
om cale cule cundi svaha.

The Gayatri mantra runs:

Om bhur bhuvah swaha
Om tat savitur varenyam
Bhargo devasya dhimahi
Dhiyo yo nah pracodayat.

Padmasambhava's "Vajra Armoring" mantra, which is recited prior to many Vajrayana practices meant to cultivate your Qi, can also be recited so that each sound is felt in a different section of your body. The mantra runs:

Humvajra Phat
Om Pema Shawa Re Phat
Nen Par Shig
Naga Nan
Tad Yatha
Sarva
Bere Ta
Hana Hana
Vajra Na
Raja Raja
Soha.

While past masters have worked out some very effective mappings of sounds to body parts for these and other mantras, the mantra sounds can be appended to different parts of your body as you feel appropriate. The important point is to try to feel the sensation of the sound within a body part when the sound is spoken, or the Qi of the body part itself. In other words, you want to use the mantra to move your Qi in different body sections.

Also, you can add visualization of that body part to the recitation routine and/or touching of the body part to help you focus and concentrate on that section. When working on any body part in this manner it also helps if you actually look at it, rather than just visualize it in your had with your eyes closed, and try to feel the Qi within it. You can also stay n a section for as long as you want until you open it.

When someone is stretching a particular muscle in yoga, for instance, they can amplify the usefulness of their asana through these techniques. How so? They can simultaneously visualize the muscles being stretched with the attempt to grab the Qi within them, recite a mantra as if from within the muscles to activate the Qi within them, flex the muscles to also help move the Qi and so on.

The principle is to perform any activities that will help you open up the Qi channels within a muscle. The purpose of all spiritual exercises is exactly this, which is to open up the Qi channels everywhere so that your entire body's Qi channels are eventually opened and you can then consequently generate a will-born deva body from these efforts.

You can use these principles when practicing all sorts of other mantras too, such as "Om Hreem Shreem Kleem Sou Aim," when you want to open up your Qi channels and change your fortune.

BAHA'I

In the Baha'i faith the invocation "Ya! Baha'u'l-Abha" (O Thou Glorious of the Most Glorious) is actually a mantra, and can be used according to the previous principles.

The "Ah"-rich phrase "Allah'u'Abha," which Baha'i practitioners are supposed to recite ninety-five times a day, is also actually a mantra that, because of the Ah sound, helps open up the Qi channels (*nadis*) in the chest and heart region of the body. In this way the Baha'i religion has skillfully incorporated useful mantras in its framework.

The *Kitáb-i-Aqdas* supplied the original instructions to repeat this phrase (mantra): "It hath been ordained that every believer in God, the Lord of Judgment, shall, each day, having washed his hands and then face, seat himself and, turning unto God, repeat 'Allah'u'-Abha' ninety-five times. Such was the decree of the Maker of the Heavens when with Majesty and power, He established Himself upon the thrones of His Names."

Most practitioners do not realize that the effectiveness of "Allah'u'Abha" is due to the predominance of the Ah-sound within the invocation. Actually, these instructions constitute the transmission of a mantra that will slowly, when performed on a daily basis, help to open up your Qi channels over time.

125

ISLAM

In Islam the Shahada, "La ilaha ill Allah," is also a mantra based on the Ah sound whose syllables can also be appended to (recited as if from within) most any region of the body, in no particular order, in order to move the Qi and open up the body's channel pathways too.

As with these other mantra practices, after your Qi is stirred up (activated or moved) by reciting this "mantra" you should then try to smoothen it out so that your body's energy feels harmonious overall, which people refer to as the sensation of "bliss." "Bliss" just means that your body feels more comfortable or pleasant. Unfortunately, meditation alone rarely makes the body feel blissful. What ancient spiritual texts fail to tell you is that you have to push, move, excite, enliven, stir up, vitalize, animate, energize, arouse, or exhilarate your Qi through practices like visualization and nei-gong, and then afterwards smoothen it out to feel physical bliss.

When your Qi is first stirred up and starts working through your Qi channels, it does not feel blissful at all, and yet the sensations you will feel of internal energy movement are exactly what some schools refer to as the bliss you are supposed to cultivate. However, the real bliss is after you next harmonize all of your awakened internal energy so that it feels comfortable and balanced. Unfortunately, the danger in arousing your vital energy is that you will give into sexual desires because of that energy, and then sexual dissipation that loses the very energy you need to keep opening up your Qi channels.

As stated, the call to prayer of Islam ("La ilaha ill Allah") is actually constructed like a mantra because of the sounds. Thus it is not only one of the pillars of the faith but can be used to help transform the Qi of your body and open its channels if you recite it on a continuous basis like a mantra. Islam has many other key phrases used in daily life that can be used like a Qi-mantra practice.

For instance, when praising something in Islam it is typical to say, "Subhanullah" (Glory to Allah). This phrase can also be used like a mantra. When appreciating something in Islam it is typical to say, "Masha-Allah" (As Allah willed). When saying this you can try to feel the Qi in your chest and heart region to open up the channels in that vicinity. Reciting "Masha-Allah" in this fashion is like reciting the Jesus prayer in the region of the heart to open up the Qi channels in that vicinity. When thanking someone it is typical to say, "Jazakullah" (Allah reward you). When so saying you can try to feel the different sounds of this response in different parts of your body such as your spine, chest and head.

When meeting someone it is typical for a Moslem to say, "Assalamu 'alaykum" (Peace be upon you). When so saying, a superior form of spiritual practice is not only to welcome the individual but to feel the Qi energy moved by each syllable in different parts of your body as well. As usual, this form of Qi cultivation from a welcoming phrase will slowly but surely lead to the opening of Qi channels, which is a superior form of Moslem practice. Replying to the above greeting, the syllables and sensations engendered by saying, "Wa 'alaykum assalam" (And upon you be peace) in response can also be felt within your body. Doing so is again a type of spiritual practice.

When hearing about a death or tragedy, the sounds of "Inna lillahi wa inna ilayhi rajiun" (To Allah we belong and to Him we return) can be felt in different parts of the body, too. As with all these sayings, a single time only provides the most minor of channel vibrations, which is why *dikhr* (Moslem mantra practice in conjunction with breathing) requires you to continually recite the same phrase over and over again as is done for mantra recitation in all religions.

When giving in charity, "Fee eemanullah" (In Allah's faith) can be felt in the heart/chest region, for offerings of charity tend to open up the heart area. This is one of the ways in which ordinary people, without any special spiritual practice, help to purify their inner etheric Qi body and thereby win the reward of heaven upon their death.

Whenever you practice some spiritual virtue (such as performing a selfless act of mercy, charity or kindness) and resultantly feel a warm sensation in your body, you should understand that the deed and your emotional response are opening Qi channels within your physical body. This is why you actually feel a warmth in your body after doing a good deed, such as practicing charity. The Qi is going through blocked channels, opening them, and the warmth you feel is the friction of that passage as the channels open.

SUMMARY

The smartest individuals within the organized religions recognize that many of their traditional religious prayers (ex. Alleluia or Hallelujah) constitute mantras whose sounds can help open up their Qi channels, and understand that they request help from higher beings for accomplishing the same task. This is another way in which praying can help you on the spiritual path.

Enlightened Buddhas devote themselves to helping people who recite certain prayers, mantras and religious texts from each and every tradition. Therefore continuous prayer recitation, such as reciting the rosary in Christianity, can *and is* a means to generate Qi energy sensations in your body and through that Qi activation can help you open up blockages in your Qi channels.

This form of Qi cultivation over time is like the practice of collecting pennies that can accumulate into a very large fortune, and is indicative of how Qi cultivation practice works. The big results only accrue over time after lots of consistent effort.

You must continually recite mantras over/within specific body locations for a very long time (while trying to move the Qi) to produce a definite result in channel purification, which is why the religious masters of the past turned this Nyasa Yoga practice into a type of daily prayer recitation. In that way people would undertake the necessary Mantrayana cultivation techniques without knowing what they were actually doing.

You can try to cultivate the body as a single unit, which is done via Master Hakuyu's soma duck egg technique. You can cultivate it via two sections, as taught in the *Mahavairocana Sutra* and *Yoga Yajnavalkya*. You can cultivate it via three sections, such as practiced in Taoism or Buddhism with Om Ah Hum. You can cultivate it in four or even five sections by various mantra, visualization, and nei-gong practices. If you use chakras as points of focus, you can cultivate the body in seven sections. If you use the white skeleton visualization method of Buddhism you can cultivate it according to bones, body appendages or sections and then as a single body unit.

Books like *Tibetan Yoga and Secret Doctrines* (Walter Evans-Wentz), *The Six Yogas of Naropa* (Glenn Mullin), and *Readings on The Six Yogas of Naropa* (Glenn Mullin) also teach various ways to cultivate the body. Helpful tantric techniques can also be found in *A Systematic Course in the Ancient Tantric Techniques of Yoga and Kriya* (Satyananda Saraswati), *Dharana Darshan: Yogic, Tantric and Upanishadic Practices of*

Concentration and Visualization (Niranjanananda Saraswati), *Kriya Secrets Revealed* (J.C. Stevens).

You can also cultivate your body according to channel lines, marma/acupuncture points and in many other ways as well until the real kundalini arises. The possibilities are endless for how to cultivate all the Qi/prana of your body so as to open up all the bonds in every cell, tissue, muscle, bone and organ. This is how you eventually produce a deva body. Many traditions have worked out cultivation sadhana to do this quickly, such as in the Asian religions, but it can be done in the western religions as well. It just takes wisdom and devoted practice.

CHAPTER 8
BINDUS, CHANNELS, GLANDS, LIMBS AND INTERNAL ORGANS

Again, the basic principle of advanced Mantrayana practice is not just to continually recite a mantra mindlessly but to focus your concentration on a particular location of the body when reciting and to mantra as if from within that area in order that the vibration shakes up the Qi energy within it. You should do this while seizing that area (trying to feel the energy) or while visualizing a color change or brightness change encompassing that region, or while stretching that area in order to bring Qi to the region. You basically try to grab an area with your consciousness so as to affect the Qi in that region. The next step is that you want your Qi to push through the local Qi channels.

Many methods can be used in your "grabbing" and "pushing" of Qi/prana to open up the energy channels within a region. You can simultaneously layer many methods upon one another for cultivating your Qi channels (*nadis*), and thus can vary the practice in different ways. The whole point is that you can use a variety of different cultivation efforts to purify your body's Qi and channels.

When the energy within you due to these efforts reaches a state of fullness all over, that state is called bliss though the feeling is by no means blissful. Initially it is just chaotic energy that is not peaceful. Within that state of fullness you can feel where the energy is blocked or restricted, and can try to move your Qi in those regions to open up the channels and smooth out imbalances. Due to the internal sensations, you will know where you need to do more qi-gong or nei-gong work to produce an internal state of equilibrium. After you harmonize the Qi everywhere in your body, you can thereby reach a *state of comfort* that is a higher stage of bliss than the excitement or excitation phase used for stirring up your Qi in the first place.

During the Twelve-year Period after the genuine Kundalini Awakening, during which time future masters are devotedly working on transforming their body's Qi channels to be able to generate the deva body (subtle body, impure illusory body, astral body, *yin-shen*, mind-born body, etc.) and yet higher stages of purified attainment, they are using many forms of Nyasa and Mantrayana practice as well as many other techniques to help quickly transform their physical body.

The more methodologies you *simultaneously* add to your efforts, the better will be your results if you do the practices correctly. It takes wisdom to determine which ones to do and with what strength and frequency. Here are several of the possibilities one might consider.

Qi Channels

To get things started, a wise practitioner can do Mantrayana or Nyasa while focusing on the *major* Qi channels of their body by using acupuncture meridian charts as a reference guide. There are twelve principal meridian Qi channels) in Chinese medicine that are associated with internal organs, and eight extraordinary channels. These have their own set of acupuncture points along their length that can also be used for mantra and concentration practice, too.

According to the tantric Yoga schools, there are 72,000 *nadis* and among them the ten most important are the *ida, pingala, sushumna, gandhari, hastijihva, pusa, yasasvini, alambusa, kuhu,* and *sankhini*. These are considered the primary support for all other *nadis*, or Qi channels. These *nadi* are also often taken as a basis for various Nyasa or visualization practices. The most important of these ten are the *ida* (left), *pingala* (right) and *sushumna* (central) *nadi* that are located in the spine, so most every cultivation school pays a lot of qi-gong and nei-gong attention on working to open up the channels in the spine. People think that the central channel, called the *zhong mai* in Chinese, runs up the center of the body but it is actually within the spine too.

The *ida nadi* of the spine is also considered to run along the left side of the nose, the *pingala* along the right side of the nose, the *gandhari nadi* is in the left eye, the *hasti jihwa* is located in the right eye, the *poosha* is situated in the right ear, the *yasawini nadi* is situated in the right ear, the *alampusa nadi* is located in the face, the *guhu nadi* is situated in the base of the genitals, and the *sankini nadi* is located in the muladhara.[3] Actually, this only focuses on termination points of the *nadi* because the *ida, pingala* and *sushumna* are in the spine and collectively called the back channel or *tu-mai* by the Chinese. In order to cultivate a quiet mind you must open up the Qi channels in the spine that lead to the brain as well as the Qi channels in the brain within the nerves. If one does visualization, qi-gong and nei-gong practices guided by DTI pictures of the brain, this will quickly speed your cultivation attainments.

For cultivation beginners the most important channels are those within the spine and down the front of the body (the digestive organs) as well as the two leg channels that proceed from the perineum down the inside of the legs to the big toes. When you have excess energy you should lightly move the Qi down the channels of the leg to your big toes, and when your energy is waning you can draw it upwards from the toes along the same channels.

Martial artists who are practicing the horse stance position, as explained in my book *Internal Martial Arts Nei-gong*, can make their practice many times more effective by visualizing the two channels running down the insides of their legs to their big toes when standing. The usefulness of this posture can be further amplified by visualizing the lines and by lightly reciting a mantra as if from along the channels. When extending the arms and holding them out in front of yourself for many minutes in Taiji practice, you can visualize the arm channels in the same fashion to help open them.

Obviously, many martial arts training postures and yoga asanas can be augmented by combining visualization efforts with the mantra techniques of Nyasa and Mantrayana.

Bindus or Acupuncture Points

---

[3] *Yoga Makaranda or Yoga Saram (The Essence of Yoga)*, Sri Tirumalai Krishnamacharya (India, Madurai C.M.V. Press, 1938), pp. 44-45.

As mentioned, a practitioner can also mantra on the acupuncture and acupressure points of the body, too, or they can focus on a simplified set of acupuncture points called the *marma* points as taught in India.

The *marma* points are the "*bindus*" or "points" mentioned in Buddhist Vajrayana yoga texts. These texts also mention "drops" that are supposedly substances that melt within the body when the Qi channels become warm, but this is just nonsense. This was a false explanation invented ages ago to guide aspirants in visualization efforts, and the incorrect information has proceeded forwards until now. If you ever see drops or bodhicitta in visions, it's just a visualization trick being played on you by devas.

The whole idea of substances melting within your Qi channels is nonsense. Basically, as your Qi energy goes through your channels to widen them there is friction, and with friction there is heat and warming. You can also say that you need warmth to open up your Qi channels or the process of opening them produces warmth. All stages of Qi purification will therefore involve heat or warmth in your physical and subtle bodies as your channels open although there are times when you will experience coolness or shivering cold when channels open too. There are indeed Yin Qi blessings that are accompanied by coolness rather than warmth, but there are no "drops" of special substances inside the channels which are being melted.

In any case, the early stages of spiritual practice constitute a process of purification or transformation of your Qi and Qi channels whereas Shakyamuni Buddha called it the balancing of the four (five) elements of your body.

Logical Body Segments

By now you should realize that a practitioner who wants to change his body can also take any mantra and recite it upon, or as if from within or along, any areas or logical segments/sections of his body such as the limbs separated by joints.

As an example, you might focus on your entire upper arm (thus feeling it), and recite a mantra from within the arm while trying to feel the length and internal flesh of the arm (which means *trying to feel the energy* of the arm). You might also try to change its color, or visualize the humerus bone of the arm shining inside it with a bright white light while you also try to feel the arm. There are many variations along these lines that you can try to master. All of them take lots of work.

All these extra activities simply help to bring Qi to that segment of your body, which thus assists in opening and purifying your channels in the vicinity of your concentration. This is why you try to feel the limb you are concentrating on, and why stretching exercises of that limb will help to open up the channels as well. This is especially important for the legs.

The best and highest practice is to stretch the individual muscles, such as through Pilates or Yoga, so that you can feel them. While stretching the muscles, try to feel the entire length or outline of the muscle and simultaneously use visualization and mantra to try to push, excite, or activate the Qi of that muscle. The same can be done for your bones and internal organs.

Internal Organs

For instance, another Nyasa method is to focus on the various organs of the body and to recite mantras as if from those locations. The famous "Six Healing Sounds" from Chinese Taoism is an example of how to use this technique for cultivating your body organs, and is a good example of a six section method.

The effectiveness of the Six Healing Sounds of Taoism can be exponentially increased if practitioners try to "feel" their organs when making the sounds, which are supposed to connect with the Qi of the organs. They can even visualize their organs changing color when making the sounds by using the classic colors of the Chinese medical schools – red (heart), green or blue (liver), white (lung), black or blue (kidneys), yellow (stomach and spleen). Another method is to try to feel a Qi pathway between a selected organ and other logical regions of your body such as the portions of the hand or foot that correspond to the organs via the theories of reflexology.

The idea of simultaneously using your breath, sensations, and visualization when using the Six Healing Sounds can be used for other non-traditional parts within the body, too, such as the small and large intestines or the brain. The best way to open up the brain, however, is by spinning or moving your Qi along the structure of the brain and major nerve pathways as revealed by DTI diagrams. This is very important for quick progress in meditation and spiritual cultivation. Please do this if you want to succeed quickly.

When focusing on a particular organ, you might even link the appropriate reflexology zones in the feet and hands to that organ, feeling a connection between all these regions (to help open up the meridians along these lines) while also focusing on any related processing centers in the brain, too.

THE SIX HEALING SOUNDS

As to the actual Six Healing Sounds practice itself for cultivating the Qi of your internal organs, it can readily be found in many Taoist books and on the internet. This is a method of cultivating six internal organs of your body, and thus six body regions that are normally ignored by other internal energy cultivation methods. One of the shortest but best explanations comes from Immortal Li Qingyun, who explained:

"The Six Qi are 1) Blowing [Chui]. 2) Exhaling [Hu]. 3) Giggling [Xi]. 4) Expelling [He]. 5) Hushing [Xu]. 6) Resting [Xi]. These are the Buddhist way of curing internal diseases. There is a chant that reads, 'Expelling breath controls the heart, blowing controls the kidneys, exhaling controls the spleen; resting controls the lungs; hushing controls the liver; and giggling controls the Triple Warmer.' Everyone who wants to know about the secrets for treating visceral diseases and longevity can listen to me to explain. Human viscera are the easiest to get sick. If not treating them right away, one would die. The Six Words of 'Chui,' 'Hu,' 'Xi,' 'He,' 'Xu,' and 'Xi' can treat all kinds of internal organ disease and cure them. If there is no disease, also use these six words to extinguish irrational thoughts and keep demons away. The method for self treatment is: every day between 11:00 a.m. and 3:00 p.m., close the eyes, sit quietly, knock teeth, swallow saliva, and read these six words softly.

"Heart disease patients should cross their hands and place them on the head, then intone *He* [pronounced 'ho,' the Expelling Breath] thirty-six times softly.

"Kidney disease patients should place their hands to surround the knees and intone *Chui* [pronounced 'chway,' Blowing Breath] thirty-six times softly.

"Liver disease patients should cross their hands and put them over the Jade Pillow [occiput], close the eyes, and intone *Xu* [pronounced 'shue,' Hushing Breath] thirty-six times softly.

"Lung disease patients should overturn their hands, place them on the back, and intone *Xi* [pronounced 'shee,' Resting breath] thirty-six times softly.

"Spleen problem patients should put their hands over the abdomen, bite their lips, and intone *Hu* [pronounced 'who,' Exhaling Breath] thirty-six times softly.

"For Triple Warmer problems [in the thoracic and abdomino-pelvic cavities], lay down, close the eyes, and intone *Xi* [pronounced 'she-hee,' Giggling Breath] thirty-six times softly.

"These are the best ways to treat visceral diseases. Only people who have done them can understand thoroughly and know the effects."[4]

There are other variants of the Six Healing Sounds too. For instance, the traditional sounds are Shoo or Xuu for the liver, Haww or Huhh for the heart, Hooo for the stomach, Sssss or Shhh or Xi for the lungs, Chuu or Chway for the kidneys, and Shee for the triple warmer. As you can see, the sound variants are many.

The important point is to find a sound *that works for you* rather than trying to be perfect in phonetically duplicating the teachings from some particular school. "Works" means that when you use a particular sound for an organ that you can actually feel the Qi of that organ or a connection with that organ. You can move that Qi to help transform the Qi channels within the organ.

You want to use a sound that works such that in the attachment to or gripping of an organ you can cultivate its channels. You need to find a sound for each organ that helps you connect with the Qi of that organ, which can then be used to help cultivate it. The Six Healing Sounds give you a basis from which to start testing different sounds to determine what works best for you.

ENDOCRINE GLAND VISUALIZATION

It is a basic fact that when you focus or concentrate on an area of your body and try to feel the region, you bring Qi to that area.

---

[4] Yang Sen, Stuart Alve Olson translator, *The Immortal: True Accounts of the 250-Year-Old Man, Li Qingyun*, (Arizona: Valley Spirit Arts, 2014), pp. 368-370.

This is because your Qi (vital energy) and mind (thought or consciousness) are linked. Your thoughts and Qi are linked such that the two "ride together" and your thoughts can move your Qi throughout your body. This is one of the basic principles behind Nyasa Yoga.

If you bring a sound (mantra) to an area in order to move its Qi, you can also nudge the Qi in that area after a long amount of practice and training. If you try to grab an area and change it in your mind through visualization efforts of some sort that affects its Qi, this will also bring Qi to the area and activate the Qi channels in the region.

While we have been discussing organs and body sections, your glands and endocrine system can all be rejuvenated through this technique too. By visualizing the glands of your body and sending Qi to those areas you can help activate them, which is a positive step towards *physical rejuvenation* that is highly encouraged.

On the road of cultivation you want to reach a state of hormonal balance, and this type of cultivation practice (visualizing your glands and sending Qi to them) will help you to do so.

First let's familiarize ourselves with the location of the major glandular organs within your body:

- The area of the brain stem that encompasses the pineal, hypothalamus and pituitary glands
- Salivary glands on the sides of the mouth
- Thyroid and parathyroid glands of the throat
- Thymus gland of the windpipe near the heart behind the breastbone
- Pancreas
- Adrenal glands atop the kidneys (just envision the kidneys)
- Ovaries and uterus (and breasts), or testes

To meditate on or cultivate your glands you mentally locate them within your body and then shine light on them or visualize them as if shining with light. You can also try to rotate your Qi within and around the glands.

You proceed by starting with the glands in your brain and then work downwards, visualizing the throat region, then thymus, and so on until you can visualize all the glandular regions simultaneously, feeling the Qi in these areas, and then you are finished. When starting with the brain, it is also very important to take the extra step of focusing on the brain stem and cerebellum.

This is a practice that will not only help you open up the Qi routes to your glands, which are some of the most important organs of your body, but help your hormonal system (once glands are reactivated) achieve a better and more proper state of balance. It can also produce some degree of physical rejuvenation.

CHAPTER 9
BETTER YOGA PRACTICE

Most spiritual paths, or cultivation practices, start with practices that purify your physical body. Your body is called the "form skandha (aggregate)" in Buddhism since it is a physical aggregate of solid form. Next most spiritual paths are commonly arranged in such a way that direct you to cultivating your Qi to purify and free your subtle astral body. Other practices work on cultivating your Mental (Causal) body that is attained after further purification of your Qi-based deva body, and next comes the Later Heaven Prana (Supra-Causal) body (Clear Light or Dharma body) achievement, which you can separate from the lower Causal (Mental) body after much further cultivation refinement and practice.

Once attained, each new body vehicle can always be separated from its lower shell so that it can come and go at will. They will all be tethered together, unless you use yogic means to detach from one that will then die. With more and more body attainments you train to learn how to use them independently of each other as tools (appendages) you can use where needed to do what you want in each realm. Then they become types of Buddha *nirmanakaya* attainments, although there are other *nirmanakaya* body emanations that are freely created and projected as needed.

As the Esoteric school of Vajrayana says, you need to cultivate a pure illusory body (Causal body or Mental body) in order to be able to realize enlightenment, which means being able to realize the clarity of mind that corresponds to the Supra-Causal body. The mind at this stage is often compared to an intangible clear light (without substance), but it is just the ordinary clear mind (though more clear than ours) of someone who has attained that body vehicle. It just exists at a different energy level than the energy level of the human stage of existence. This substance or essence of your body at this level of achievement is the natural, foundational substrate for the mind/body of the practitioner and this substance/energy is so refined that it transcends all subsequently lower or denser stages of matter.

Attaining this body and mind is equivalent to attaining the "fourth dhyana" of Buddhism. This is the stage of initial enlightenment, or *nirvana* with remainder (remaining dependency), that corresponds to reaching the *alaya* consciousness that is the foundation of the mind, but not ultimate foundation of all mind and matter.

The operations of consciousness and thoughts, at their subtlest most layer, are due to this level of ultra subtle energy but you can only reach it, or find it, after you have done a lot of prior cultivation work to purify your Qi and channels. You have to keep cultivating new bodies in turn until you finally attain a body at the level of this rarified material. Once you attain this stage it is superior to all the lower, coarser or denser substances, namely Shen, Qi and Jing – mental energy, vital energy and physical nature – that comprise the lower Causal, Subtle and Physical bodies. This level of subtle energy (called Later Heavenly Qi or Later Heaven Prana) transcends them all and is the substance of the Supra-Causal or Dharma body.

At this level of body purity (and therefore consciousness made of this substrate that transcends all the lower forms of materialization), you can feel the vibrations in these lower denser substances, and can cause vibrations in them as well since you have a body composed of their foundational substrate. Therefore you can know the thoughts of lower sentient beings having lower-level bodies and *give them thoughts as well* because your body and mental substance transcends theirs. Most of the superpowers of enlightened beings have to deal with affecting people's consciousness by entering into them and giving them thoughts to do good deeds or stop doing wrong deeds. If you listen to the quiet thoughts within, you can often change your fortune for the better by heeding such guidance. The problem is that you cannot tell what thought is yours or from someone else.

For instance, people often think they are becoming psychic when they start cultivating but what is really happeneing is that devas are going into their brains and practicing by giving them thoughts, which cause people to think that they are actually the psychic ones. The same goes for superpowers. People sometimes think they are developing superpowers from their cultivation work when they ae usually due to devas who are practicing with the individual.

The Supra-Causal level or "*alaya*" is also called "universal consciousness," "cosmic consciousness" or "unity consciousness" since all of consciousness (of lower bodied beings) can be known at this stage. With a Supra-Causal body made of Later Heaven Prana it is therefore easy to give thoughts to non-enlightened beings without them ever recognizing that the thoughts come from you, and that is one way in which Buddhas act in the world to help people.

Sometimes Buddhas give you thoughts, hunches, urges, intuitions, inclinations or inspirations to help you solve problems, such as the idea to call on the phone someone who might be thinking of you. If you know that someone has died it is because you have also received this type of thought projection. If you mantra or pray for heavenly assistance, this is also the type of help you can often receive. Sometimes these helpful notions can help you change your fortune, but sometimes the karma is so thick that they cannot.

The fact that you can "feel vibrations" in denser forms of energy because your body and mind are composed of their higher substratum substance also explains why someone who is enlightened can hear their name being called (or mantra being recited) even though they are a long distance away; if you think of an enlightened master they will know it. This is also why it is said that all the fully enlightened Buddhas can respond to the calls of sentient beings for help, such as why Avalokitesvara (Kuan Yin) can "hear the cries of the world."

When Hindus say that Shiva has omniscience and omnipresence, it is also because he has attained a body composed of a transcending (transcendental) substance that transcends all the lower worlds, and is thus omnipresent due to a body vessel composed of the substratum base substance and omniscient in the manner described. With this body you can therefore understand what people think and how they think, but it doesn't make you a master of their various types of expertise because you simply haven't developed those skills yourself.

If one trains sufficiently, someone in this higher body can even sense the thoughts someone has to form a difficult mudra with their fingers, which is another way that Buddhas (enlightened masters) can identify the spiritual practitioners who use their sadhana. Having a body composed of the very energy/substance that is the substrate of the consciousness of living beings gives you what we would consider miraculous powers. For instance, if you read a sutra or holy book that a master has written or vowed to protect, that enlightened master will know it and sometimes give thoughts to practitioners to help them understand difficult sections. Many Buddhas have vowed this and their testimonies are found in the Buddhist sutras.

The higher and more rarified or purified the substance of the body that you use, which you can only attain through continuous spiritual cultivation (which is called "penance" in India even though it doesn't have to hurt or be difficult), the greater your capabilities in these and other regards.

As stated, usually the spiritual path starts with the purification of the form skandha or physical body, and the result is the achievement of the subtle or deva body composed of Qi after all your energy channels have all been opened. It is an independent life that can leave the body and travel the world. If you continue cultivating that body then it can eventually generate a body of Shen, or higher energy corresponding to the finer thoughts of the conception skandha. This, of course, is just an analogy. This body is also called a Causal body or purified illusory body that can travel cosmic spheres or planes that a subtle body has no access to.

The superpowers of this body are much greater than those for devas who only attain the subtle body. In fact, if you attain a subtle body then you can control another person's physical body by entering it and overriding control as in possession. If you have a Mental (Causal) body you can control another person's subtle body. If you attain a Supra-Causal body you can control another individual's Causal body (as well as their subtle and physical bodies). An individual of a higher stage of attainment can control the bodies, mental functions and even superpowers on the individual below him.

There are more bodies still and attaining them all depends on your devotion to spiritual cultivation. The higher stage bodies can travel the cosmos whereas the lower stage Qi bodies are earth-bound and cannot. Buddhism explains that when people die and become spirits they are "confined to the Desire Realm," which has the same meaning. To be existent you must have a body, and to cultivate any of these bodies you always start with the flesh/form of that particular body. This means you start your cultivation/generation of each new body by working on opening the channels within its tissues.

If you examine the structure of muscles you will see that they are composed of long string-like fibers that are connected in bundles. Logically, if you were to stretch these fibrous tissues and thereby elongate them you would then free them of many internal knots, tangles and obstructions. This would then allow your Qi to flow more smoothly within your body, which is why all spiritual practitioners should take up stretching forms of exercise.

Thus the practice of Yoga asanas, the practice of Pilates, stretching exercises and the martial arts can all help you prepare for a better degree of Qi channel purification. Any sort of extensive stretching exercises can help you along these lines. However, if you don't engage in any activities that also cultivate your Qi at the same time, stretching practices simply constitute physical exercise rather than spiritual practice. You need to also practice pranayama, mantra and internal energy work *together* with stretching exercises to truly transform your Qi and channels. This is what makes Yoga the effective spiritual practice vehicle it is intended to be.

The father of modern Yoga, Tirumalai Krishnamacharya, who studied with Ramamohana Brahmachari and Sri Babu Bhagavan Das, has stated that mantra and *kumbhaka* (breath retention pranayama) practices should be practiced along with Yoga asanas. In this way, the combination of inner Qi movements achieved through mantra and pranayama, when combined with stretching, will serve to open the Qi channels in your muscles. Tirumalai Krishnamacharya suggested that those who wished to practice Yoga might also recite the Gayatri mantra, which you can do prior to or after Yoga practice.

Unfortunately, mantra and pranayama are rarely bundled together with Yoga anymore, and thus it can no longer reach its fullest potential. However, applying the principles of Nyasa and Mantrayana to Yoga practice will make it far more effective.

If you want to achieve big progress through Yoga you have to practice a lot of pranayama breath work and nei-gong practices to move your Qi. The *Geranda-Samhita* contains eight *kumbhaka* pranayama techniques, called pots, that spiritual adherents are strongly advised to master to help along these lines. If you combine these *kumbhaka* methods with the nine-bottled wind pranayama technique from Tibet (as featured in *Visualization Power*), it can help you transform your Qi channels so that you attain a subtle body very quickly.

The first recommendation for making Yoga practice more effective is that practitioners should have a clear picture in their mind of the muscles to be stretched during each posture. Whenever they are stretching they should try to *feel* the outline of those muscles *while also visualizing them*. Visualizing them means that you know their shape in your mind, and you use that to try and grab the Qi of that muscle shape and push energy through it.

If practitioners just visualize the muscles in their head but don't actually feel them, then they are not really cultivating the Qi and channels of the muscles. If they just recite a mantra and append it to a muscle without connecting with the muscle by feeling it, they are also not really cultivating the Qi and channels of those muscles. In many cases you may visualize a muscle or organ in your head and then find that your visualization does not actually match the anatomical position of the desired target area. Therefore, *you must always try to feel the target area being visualized.* If you look at it during practice while trying to move its Qi, that is even better.

To visualize something in your head is not the same thing as actually moving the Qi in an area of focus within your body. At times during mental practice you may even feel blocked in the sense that you to want to halt practice or want to skip over that region because it seems too difficult. When this happens you should double your efforts and change your tactic by trying to sense the area fully as if from inside it. Obviously, reciting a mantra as if from those tissues will help to activate the energy in those Qi channels too.

In short, you should always try to feel the underlying energies of a body region and try to affect that region directly with the gripping powers of consciousness to move the Qi in the area. Don't just move the Qi in your head but connect with the body's Qi and try to move it. For this reason, *it is useful to actually look at body parts when doing visualization practices* so that you end up actually cultivating that region's Qi channels rather than perfect a mental visualization.

Extremely valuable pictures of the actual muscles being stretched in Yoga asanas can be seen in *The Key Muscles of Yoga* and *The Key Poses of Yoga* by Ray Long. This is the type of image that must used by your mind when you choose to practice Yoga with visualization and mantra practice.

It would be helpful for Yoga teachers to project these pictures on a screen or wall while students are practicing asanas so that they can know the exact muscles to be stretched, might feel those muscles within themselves, can mentally grab them by referencing the pictures, and can recite mantras (cause vibrations) within those target regions. While Yoga teachers also tell students to push the Qi through their muscles when they hold an asana, westerners also sometimes use a technique where they get into a stretch, flex the muscle(s) being stretched, hold their breath to increase the intensity of the flex (while sometimes directing the energy to the muscle in this manner), and then release their breath while flexing at the same time.

For those who practice Pilates, visualization of your muscles being stretched is also encouraged to enhance its effectiveness. The most difficult muscles to open include those within the legs, feet and forearms, so it is important to use Pilates, weight lifting or yoga to work at defining the shape of the muscles in these body parts.

CHAPTER 10
OPENING THE SPINE

Countless Yoga, Ayurveda, and Chinese Medicine texts mention a large number of Qi channels in the body, some of which can be accurately seen in the pictures of acupuncture meridians. You can try to "open up a channel" but what you are actually trying to do is open up *all the channels within the muscle fibers, organs and bones along the route of the channel* just as you try to do when using the white skeleton visualization.

Putting it a different way, you are actually trying to flood/saturate your body with Qi to create an etheric body double, so the idea of opening up channels and pathways does *not* mean one or two lines here and there. It means having Qi flow everywhere in your body – all your muscles, flesh, cells and fibers get transformed. You only concentrate on specific channel lines to get started but you are trying to purify the etheric duplicate of your body that is already there for every cell and tissue of your body.

For some types of cultivation practice you concentrate on feeling or moving your Qi along a channel pathway while simultaneously performing a special visualization of the pathway or reciting a mantra along the channel. There are many ways of trying to move the flow of Qi in a certain direction so that this flow of energy opens all the channels aligned in that direction. You try to open all the parallel fibers of a muscle running in the same direction when you push Qi/prana through it. Sometimes, as in Taoist qi-gong, you also try to rotate your Qi through a channel's circulatory pathway in a way that constitutes a complete orbital circuit because this is an easy way to practice moving energy within you.

Chinese cultivation schools typically focus on opening up the front and back channels in the body through natural, effortless meditation. They typically use methods that don't forcefully push your Qi, but just let it arise and open channels naturally. Indian schools often focus on opening the spinal channels - which are the left, right and central channels - but use very forceful techniques to clear the spinal pathways. I recommend that people focus on the spine in some way, using the instructions of some school, for the quickest cultivation results.

The forceful techniques for opening the spinal Qi channels include *kumbhaka* pranayama techniques (breath retention practices where you hold your breath), special spinal visualizations that guide your Qi through the spine (as done in qi-gong), mantra (and visualization) practice on individual vertebra, and Yoga stretches.

Unfortunately, most practitioners do not realize that you cannot just cultivate the ascending Qi in the body through such techniques; you must also focus on the Qi pathways that descend within the body, namely the digestive and visceral organs. Most cultivation practices focus on sending Qi up your spine in order to open up the nervous system pathways, but you must always cultivate your body's descending Qi to complete the connective circuit of upwards and downwards flowing energy. The Chinese cultivation schools therefore emphasize that you must cultivate the back (ascending) *and* front (descending) Qi channels.

Therefore, you cannot just cultivate the Qi in the body that goes upwards through the spine to the brain. Your Qi must complete a full circuit by also coming down the front of your body to return to your pelvis and perineum, which is why Chinese cultivation schools focus on internal organs and glands in a descending sequence.

This need for a complete Qi circuit gives rise to the explanation that Qi must rotate through a circular orbit within your body starting from the perineum, rising to the head through the spine, and then descending to the perineum again via the front of the body and digestive organs. This rising and falling of the Qi, up the back and down the front channels of the body, is described in many religions. For instance, it is symbolized in the Bible by Jacob's Ladder where angels are supposedly seen traveling up and down a ladder.

An even better analogy of the cultivation process, other than Jacob's description of angels (Qi) climbing a ladder into the skies and then descending, is that the water of a lake (Jing) evaporates (turning into Qi), fills the empty skies full of with sunshine (Shen) and then falls back as rain (jing) again to replenish the lake.

Immortal Li Qingyun summarized another Taoist teachings that Jing converts to Qi, Qi converts to Spirit (Shen), the Spirit returns to emptiness naturally, and within this cycle there is a regeneration of Jing. He said that when the meditative mind becomes empty of random thoughts it responds positively by giving rise to Shen, or Spirit. When the Spirit is empty, it responds positively by affecting your Qi. When your Qi becomes empty (becomes pure, peaceful and still), it responds positively by regenerating your essence, Jing.

This is another way of describing the transformations between Jing, Qi and Shen that naturally occur when you start to meditate. Thus you have the sequence of replenishment for the essences of your body which happen due to meditation practice and other types of cultivation work.

RISHYASHRINGA

Indian culture explains this sequence of replenishment, and of ascending and descending Qi cycles, another way. A famous story runs that an accomplished yogi, Vibhandak, had a son, Rishyashringa, who was raised apart from all women and became a great yogi due to his cultivation and celibacy. Yogis practice such that the Qi in the body (which they often call "semen" as a way to warn aspirants not to sexually lose their Jing and Qi since they are needed for opening up the body's Qi channels) flows in the reverse direction up the spine into the brain. In Yoga the process is called *urdhva retas*.

One day, the sound of thunder caused Rishyashringa to drop a pot of water, which symbolizes that he lost his semen and thus his Qi. Annoyed at what had happened due to the thunder, using his superpowers Rishyashringa uttered a curse that rainclouds would no longer be able to form near his hermitage, which caused a drought in the lands around him.

In other words, if you just cultivate Yang Qi without its opposite, Yin Qi, your cultivation is incorrect because it produces a drought in the land. You need both positive and negative energies in your body, both ascending and descending Qi circulations. Your Qi has to both ascend *and then descend* in your body through your front channel, which is often called the body's water channel since it involves all your digestive organs.

In order to end the drought, the king of the land sent a courtesan to seduce Rishyashringa, who had never known sex with a woman, in order that upon having sex with the maiden the rainclouds would no longer be blocked. Upon the consummation of sex, rain fell from the sky again and the drought in the land came to an end, restoring the country to normal.

This story also implies that you cannot just cultivate your Yang Qi proceeding upwards in your spine, but must allow your Qi to descend in the front half of your body. You also need to cultivate Yin Qi, but in a way that balances your Yang Qi. Thus the various exercises promoted by Taoists on swallowing your saliva, or pausing and swallowing your breath during mantra practice, will let your Qi descend in your body so that you open these downward channels. If you just cultivate Yang Qi your body tends to get too hot, producing skin eruptions and other problems, whose only solution seems to be special types of acupuncture to remove excess internal heat. This is why Master Hakuyu advised a method of cultivating internal energetic harmony within your entire body to avoid the build-up of excesses and deficiencies. Herbs can sometimes alleviate these problems, but if internal heat builds up within the body you will usually have to search for cures through Chinese medical treatments.

To a wise reader this story also gives hints about the fact that sexual intercourse can be used to stimulate the body's internal Qi energies so that Qi starts moving through your channels. If you meditate after sexual intercourse, or afterwards relax while practicing witnessing practice that doesn't attach to any sensations, you will allow the Qi in your body to adjust itself by descending to the perineum (and feet as well) to complete a full body orbital circuit.

To help bring the Qi to run to the bottom of your feet, Taoism teaches people to flex the soles of their feet during sexual intercourse. This will help to draw your Qi to those areas from the leg channels. For someone who has deeply practiced pranayama and the white skeleton visualization technique (inner nei-gong for opening up Qi channels), every different sexual position can be used to help open up different Qi channels. These two cultivation exercises, along with merit, are the qualifying requirements specified by the Vajrayana school of Esoteric Buddhism for sexual cultivation practitioners.

The point is that you should not just focus on cultivating your strong Yang Qi ascending through the spine, but need to cultivate the gentleness of Yin Qi which descends within your body. Nevertheless, the spine is the primary pathway to open in cultivation because the first target is transforming your nervous system, which includes your spine and brain.

SPINAL VISUALIZATIONS

There are many ways of focusing on the spine to open the Qi channels within it, and the process has been symbolized in many cultural traditions.

In Taoism, practitioners often visualize the Qi running up the spine and down the front of their body, making a complete (microcosmic) orbit called the "River Chariot rotation." The analogy of a chariot to denote this pathway, which was also used in the Bible, is that the Qi rolls along from place to place as on a road or in a circuit.

In ancient Greece, the god of medicine Asclepius is represented holding a stick that is entwined with a serpent. This later became the caduceus, whose set of intertwining snakes does not accurately represent Qi flows going up the spine, but only illustrates a nei-gong practice of spinning the Qi in patterns between the spinal vertebrae so as to help open the spinal channel pathways. This is the secret of the symbology. It represents one of the many alternative ways to open up the spine.

Ancient Indians invented many Yogic, Tantric and Upanishadic practices, which employ concentration and visualization, for opening your Qi channels. Many of these practices, with instruction, can be found in Swami Niranjanananda Saraswati's *Dharana Darhan*, which is highly recommended. The excellent exercises in this book use various visualizations on the front and back channels, along with the sound So-Ham, which can help open up many channels within your body.

Kriya Yoga, which is a sibling of Kundalini Yoga, also focuses on removing blocks in the spine so that your Qi can ascend your spinal channels. One of the very best books on Kriya Yoga, which is also extremely useful to cultivators, is *Kriya Secrets Revealed* by J.C. Stevens.

This book presents the exercises of Kriya Yoga in condensed fashion, pulled from many different sources, and gives accurate and useful exercises for opening up the spinal Qi channels and chakras along its length. There is no need to duplicate a description of these exercises here since they are amply covered in these two books, which are highly recommended.

The practice of Yoga asanas, when done in conjunction with mantra, meditation and *kumbhaka* pranayama, can also help you activate your kundalini (Yang Qi) and open up your channels. This is a very quick road of practice, but without the mantra and pranayama to accompany Yoga practices, the spiritual results you can expect are limited. If you want to practice Yoga for spiritual results, your efforts must always be matched with pranayama, mantra recitation and meditation. The addition of visualization practices also helps your efforts. Thus you now have Nyasa Yoga teachings as well!

Yoga master Tirumalai Krishnamacharya, father of modern Yoga (and teacher of individuals such as B.K.S. Iyengar, Indra Devi, K. Pattabhi Jois, Srivasta Ramaswami), in particular recommended that Jalandhara Bandha Mudra, Sakti Calana Mudra, Aswini Mudra, Pasini Mudra, Ardhabaddapadmapascimottan asana, Bakasan, Ekapada Sirsasana, Triviramasana and Sarvangasana be used to help activate your Yang Qi (kundalini) and clean your Qi channels. Other masters have recommend different Yoga positions. Whichever asanas you use, you should also be practicing mantra, meditation, visualization and nei-gong exercises together with them for the quickest results. These are the additional practice instructions that most teachers don't tell you.

Martial arts are another way to help open up the channels in your spine, but once again they should be accompanied by spinal visualization efforts and qi-gong techniques as explained in my book, *Internal Martial Arts Nei-gong*. A very good collection of yoga materials is also found in *Roots of Yoga*, by Mallinson and Singleton.

CHAPTER 11
WHAT "CHAKRAS" REALLY ARE

If you look at thermography pictures of the human body you will see that the temperature drops off significantly in the hands and fingertips, feet, buttocks, top of the head, neck and underarms. The spine will glow as the hottest area of the body, making it one of the most important and yet easiest pathways to open. That's why spiritual cultivators always concentrate on opening up the spine (and brain) before any other body areas and then afterwards concentrate on working inwards to cultivate the rest of the body. Because your spinal nerves are part of your nervous system they also have a tie-in with the production of consciousness. That is what we are looking for because cultivation is ultimately about transforming consciousness in conjunction with the body.

To open up the Qi channels in your brain and spine to quiet/purify consciousness you must cultivate spiritual practices. Meditation, just by itself, will cause Yang Qi to arise within you and ascend up your spine, and then open up the channel pathways within the brain, thus quieting it because it becomes more efficient. Spinal "Qi channels" just means that the Qi or prana can pass through the nerve fibers of the spinal cord all the way through to the brain.

Many people have read Charles Leadbeater's book, *Chakras*, and actually believe in the fictitious pictures showing roundish Qi organs within the human body that are connected to the spine. These illustrations are utter nonsense that mislead people because no such round organs exist. The only thing that esoterically exists within your body is life force (Qi) that flows within your entire physical body structure. Because it permeates every atom, cell and tissue, it is part of the energetic composition of an exact subtle energy duplicate replica of your body that can leave upon death. After death and the emergence of the subtle body, individuals usually go through about three months (100 days) of orientation training for their new life in the subtle sphere until it ends.

Chakras just refer to sections of the body that must be entirely opened, purified or transformed – however you wish to word it. All the strange pictures of spoked chakras misleads people about the true nature of cultivation, which is why practitioners usually accomplish nothing by heeding such illustrations. Their only true use is for visualization practice.

The traditional images of chakra were useful symbols created in ancient times when anatomical images were not readily available. They represent sections of the body and were used to create areas of focus inside a cultivator's body for inner nei-gong practices. Today we can accurately visualize our internal anatomy to guide the opening of Qi channels because the internet gives us ample images for guidance, but in ancient times pictures weren't available. Therefore chakra images were invented. The availability of modern anatomical images gives us a big advantage over people of the past, especially if we use DTI scans of cranial nerves and apply qi-gong and nei-gong efforts to open those pathways.

When you die your astral body or "spirit" leaves your physical frame. This is simply a body of Qi, the subtle body or deva/deity body, and because it is made of Qi science cannot measure it yet. The prana subtle body that spiritual practitioners cultivate, which can leave the body at will, has a higher degree of purity and capability than the ordinary prana body that people leave with upon death, which is why people cultivate during life. This Qi body that a spiritual practitioner cultivates is classified as the beginning stage of the *sambhogakaya*, or Reward body attainment, which is an ultimate spiritual body of extremely rarified, etheric substance (higher level energy) that enlightened individuals develop.

Therefore you need to know that there are no spinning vortices called chakras inside your human (or deva) body or extra etheric organs that perform special functions. There is only an exact duplicate of your physical body with the same intricate structure and this etheric duplicate permeates your body completely. In short, spinning vortex chakras do not exist. The ancient Yoga books that describe chakras only used them as symbols to help cultivators focus on body areas in order to help open up all their Qi channels in those regions. Mos of the other dialogues about them cheat people.

Once again, chakras, as special internal organs having petals or spokes that offer superpowers when opened do not exist. Chakras were simply invented as focal points for inner visualization practice so that you might bring Qi to those regions to open Qi channels in the vicinity, and so that through concentration you could also develop stable powers of visualization. The idea that they provide superpowers was simply a fable designed to motivate diligent spiritual practice.

Since spiritual enlightenment has to do with consciousness and consciousness has to do with your nervous system that runs through your spine and brain, certain chakra symbols were invented ages ago to represent segments of your spine and brain. These segments, and the horizontal body segments in front of them, stake out all the sections of the body whose Qi channels must be opened (purified or transformed) through cultivation.

In other words, all beings have an etheric duplicate of their present structure composed of Qi. Qi (prana) is the life force of your body so it impregnates every body cell and tissue. That life force has made an exact Qi duplicate of your body, which is your astral or etheric double. It can leave your body when you are extremely sick or weak, when you suffer a near-death accident, when you undergo an operation with anesthesia, or when you die. However, like the human physical body it is also a body that is impermanent and destined to perish because of the low level quality of that Qi substance. The only way to live longer is to purify its nature to separate out its more subtle higher energy state, which is a more purified substance than Qi energy, and to use that new body of Shen as your primary body vehicle.

When we apply this information to our present physical body we say we must "cultivate," "purify" or "transform" our Qi and channels in order to make progress at spiritual cultivation. This means cultivating both our Yang Qi and Yin Qi as a harmonious whole. If we do so sufficiently we become able to use that inner body as we like, which is the first stage of the spiritual path corresponding to the first dhyana attainment. One attains a deva body, which is at a higher stage (and thus has higher powers) than the normal spirit bodies (made of Qi) of those who die. Thus it is capable of small miracles.

Those in "Heaven" are all trying to cultivate their own bodies to a higher stage of purity to attain the first dhyana. When their cultivation is really good they can cause another energy level to separate out from the Qi body, thus creating another more purified body. This is the Mental or Causal body made of Shen (a higher level of energy/substance than Qi) that is more refined and free of any coarser Qi elements (impurities) found in the lower Qi body. If you attain a body composed of Shen then you can eventually separate out a yet higher body composed of Later Heavenly Qi substance/energy, and then afterwards an Original Heavenly Qi stage body that equates with the perfected *sambhogakaya* that is attained with Buddhahood. This is the body of Immanence within the Nath Yoga tradition.

And so on the process proceeds ad infinitum. Cultivation is a process of difficult, devoted Yoga that requires hard work, discipline and merit because you need higher beings to lend you their powers/energy so that you can cultivate these higher bodies.

We conventionally say that the spiritual path ends with five bodies with the fifth then corresponding to Complete and Perfect Enlightenment (Buddhahood), but doubtless there are yet higher levels of cultivation past these five bodies. You just have to work harder to attain them, and this is hard enough to reach this level of achievement so masters never discuss anything farther. How far you can ultimately take this purification process, however, depends upon your devotion to cultivation work and attainment.

Along the way, you have to start upon this process by cultivating all the Qi channels of your present physical body. Normally you do that in segments at the beginning of the process because segments are easier to cultivate. This can be in two segments as in the *Mahavairocana Sutra* (such as using the Ram-Vam mantra protocol or other methods), three body cavity segments such as the three *dantian* of Taoism (such as by using Oh Ah Hum with appropriate visualizations and energy work), or seven chakra sections of the body, and so on. The body can be partitioned into large horizontal chunks based on regions of the spine and these segments are represented by chakras simply because this teaching method was convenient.

155

You can therefore also cultivate the entire body as a single whole (Hakuyu's method), or by component pieces (such as done in Nyasa Yoga or through the white skeleton visualization practice), in body segments (as with Mantrayana), by internal organs or chakras (which entails segmenting the body into sections according to the nerves of the spine). With any method you use, you must work at purifying the energy channels of those sections in turn.

The root of your ascending energies is said to reside in your pelvis, which is where you have sexual impulses. For instance, many men will feel uncomfortable or irritated in their pelvic regions when their Qi begins to stir and starts opening up channels in that vicinity. Trying to push through the channels in the genital areas and pelvis, their Qi encounters obstructions and that internal friction from running into blockages causes uncomfortable feelings of irritation.

To solve the problem they look for release through sexual intercourse or masturbation. Consequently, men all too readily lose their Jing and Qi, which is exactly the energy needed for opening up their Qi channels! Once lost through ejaculation, that energy is no longer available to open up channel pathways, and thus spiritual progress remains out of reach.

Because sexual desires are some of the strongest urges for human beings, we often call them our "lower nature" or "base nature" when they are simply what they are – energies or impulses. They are not higher or lower but must be brought under our control and channeled to produce results based upon what they can do for us. Those energies can be used for higher spiritual progress or to satisfy natural longings. If you always deploy your energies to satisfy your natural longings you just won't be able to make any significant spiritual progress because the energy won't be there to open up your Qi channels. Therefore we call our natural needs and longings "base instincts" in order to beautify spiritual progress.

If your Qi energies are not lost but accumulated and allowed to work at opening your Qi channels, they will "progress through the chakras" (sections of your body) and open any obstructions in the channel pathways they encounter. This will improve your body's internal energy circulation, and thus it will become warmer, more flexible and softer over time.

In short, you should always just consider the chakras as sections of the body you must cultivate that are represented through colorful symbols corresponding to spinal segments. The spine, with its curvature, naturally segments off body sections due to the fact that it contains nerves running to various regions. Therefore here are the real meanings of the chakras and parts they represent.

Root Chakra (Muladhara)

The Root Chakra refers to your pelvic girdle, specifically all the muscles (and nerves, arteries, veins, ligaments, lymph channels, bones, etc.) in your body around your genitalia, asshole and perineum. This chakra is said to have four petals and is usually represented by a four-sided square, a four-legged elephant or a four-armed deity.

If you have ever looked carefully you will have noticed that most mandalas also contain a square because that four-sided shape represents the root chakra. This is where the vital energy arises within your body. The rest of the mandala's geometric figures usually represent other chakras in the body.

A stupa is usually square at its base because stupas also represent the physical body with the base being the root chakra. The next higher section of a stupa is usually circular in shape, representing our round belly. The next higher section of a stupa is typically triangular in shape, representing the chest and heart region that points upwards. The next higher section is usually a half circle, half moon or series of concentric rings (like the vertebrae of the neck or bones of the jaw) representing the throat upwards to the bottom of the head. Finally there appears a crown on the top of a stupa, which represents our head and specifically our brain. The construction of a stupa therefore represents the human body in physical form, and at its base lies the four-petalled root chakra within the pelvis.

Why the emphasis on four petals or the four sides of a square? What does the figure four actually represent?

When you look at the perineal muscles of both men and women viewed from below, the major muscles around the perineum clearly form a square. For instance, men and women have two ischiocavernosus muscles that form a corner of the square whose center is the perineum and whose diagonal is the superficial transverse perineal muscle. The ileococcygeous muscle is also bent in such a way as to complete the square.

These muscles are not the root chakra, but represent the idea of the root chakra since there is no such actual thing as an esoteric "root chakra." There are only regions of the physical body whose Qi channels we need to stretch open and we use the nomenclature of "chakras" to identify these regions since this inspires people to cultivate practice.

All the muscles of the body have Qi/prana energy within them and it must flow through them just as does blood. As stated, when Qi starts to move through the muscles in the pelvic girdle there is normally friction or irritation that gives rise to uncomfortable feelings that we associate with sexual longings, and therefore we satisfy those impulses through sexual intercourse or masturbation. If that energy isn't lost (because we don't lose our Jing and Qi through the outlet of sex) then it will accumulate. When conserved it can then work to penetrate through the closed Qi channels within those fibers and thus that energy can finally be used for spiritual cultivation.

One way to reduce sexual desires and assist our cultivation efforts is therefore by stretching these muscles, as is done in Yoga, Pilates, the martial arts, dancing and athletics. If children can *stretch these muscles before or when passing through puberty*, such as by learning leg splits, forward toe-touching bends, the pigeon pose and so on then the channels in these muscles will be stretched free of jumbled knots. The children will then have less problems with sexual desires when the Qi starts flowing through those regions. Therefore they will have an easier time cultivating any spiritual path. This is important for parents to know, and great information for any parents who want spiritual and healthy children.

Sacral Chakra (Svadhisththana)

The sacral chakra refers to the sacrum, which is naturally shaped like a triangle. The sacral chakra is said to have six petals so it is often represented by a six-petalled lotus flower or six-pointed Star of David formed by two intersecting triangles. Sometimes it is also represented by a hooded cobra's head, which also has the shape of a triangle like the sacrum, while the snake's long body refers to the spine. A snake generally connotes sexual energies that must be transformed into spiritualized Yang Qi that runs up the spine during spiritual cultivation. The crocodile is also used to represent the chakra because the sacrum has bumps on it and a crocodile has scales on its back whose ridge-like nature bears a resemblance to these bumps.

Why does the sacral chakra have six petals? Because the sacrum has six sets of nerves coming out of it - S1, S2, S3, S4, S5, and C0. These six sets of nerves are the six petals of the chakra. Thus the chakra refers to the sacrum, these nerves, and all the muscles and tissues in the body in front of this region.

In Indian chakra diagrams, a four-armed man is often shown riding a crocodile to jointly symbolize the sacral chakra and root chakra regions together. The picture basically represents all the muscles, bones, nerves, etc. in the entire pelvic girdle that have to be opened during the course of spiritual cultivation. Remember that any chakra picture does not just represent the nerves and energies localized in that region of the spine, but all the areas controlled by those spinal nerves as well as all the flesh, bones, etc. surrounding that chakra location.

Ganges Devi, who represents the chief goddess deity of Ganges River in India, is also often represented as having four arms and riding a crocodile on the flowing Ganges River. The symbol of this female Buddha riding a crocodile on the river represents the Yang Qi energy traveling through the pelvis (root and sacral chakra areas) up the spine into the brain. Most every cultivation school will tell you that you must awaken the energies in this region, and has your Qi ascend the spine (rather than get lost through sexual release) in order to succeed at spiritual cultivation. In actuality you don't need to refrain from sex to succeed at cultivation, but must simply open up the Qi channels in this region without detrimentally losing your energies.

A Buddhist symbol that represents the two chakras while also encapsulating the idea of sexual energy is the image of the Buddha Samantabhadra riding on a white six-tusked elephant. An elephant has a head with two large ears, and this shape represents a man's penis and scrotum (sexual energies). In addition to the fact that an elephant's head and strength can represent the genitalia and strong vitality, one can also take his four legs as representing the root chakra as well. However, because your sexual energies must be purified on the road of spiritual cultivation, Samantabhadra's elephant is always shown as white in color to represent purity.

Another way of saying it is that the six-tusked white elephant represents the strong sexual energies of the pelvic region that are used for spiritual cultivation rather than sex, and thus those energies are purified (white in color) because of a higher usage. Samantabhadra rides upon them illustration how to devote them to spiritual cultivation.

In the commonly used mandala symbol of a six-pointed star, made of two triangles, the sacrum itself is represented by the downwards pointing triangle due to shape similarity whereas the ascending Qi going up the spine is represented by the upwards pointing triangle. Together the two triangles then produce the six-pointed Star of David. Since the pubic regions of men and women are shaped like triangles, both Yin and Yang or sexual activity can also be represented by a six-pointed star. Ascending Qi (Yang Qi) is represented by the color red in almost every cultivation school, and thus the two triangles together are another way to represent the sacral, or sex chakra.

Yoga practices like Mula bandha, Ashwini mudra, and other stretches are very useful for opening up this region of the body. They are good for learning sexual control as well. Had I known this information when younger I would have practiced these exercises as well as leg exercises everyday, which I highly encourage.

Navel/Solar Plexus Chakra (Manipura)

The navel chakra simply represents the area of the belly (abdomen) containing the appendix, large intestine, small intestines, liver, stomach, pancreas, spleen kidneys and so on. This is the "hara" of Japanese martial arts or lower *dantian* of Chinese medicine and martial arts.

This chakra is often represented as having ten petals, which is because it corresponds to the section of the body served by left and right nerves L1, L2, L3, L4, L5 coming out of the lumbar spinal vertebrae. Five times two (left and right) equals ten, and thus we have ten petals.

Sometimes the navel chakra is represented as having many more petals, so the actual number used is not important. What is important is knowing that it points to the need to cultivate the Qi channels of the belly on the spiritual path. However, it is very difficult to cultivate the belly region since it contains the curving intestines; you cannot accurately visualize Qi moving along this curvy pathway so it is hard to guide it in the abdomen using nei-gong or other practices. Usually people just try to spin their Qi in various ways within their belly to help open up the channels inside.

Another way to open these pathways is to soak the entire lower abdominal area in energy just as you would soak a piece of meat in sauce overnight before cooking it the next day. As a spiritual practice you therefore always imagine that the belly is always warm due to being soaked in Qi energy. This is why many cultivation and martial arts schools tell you to *always* keep your energy in the belly region. This was one of the cultivation methods used by Japanese mountain master Hakuyu who taught this technique to Zen master Hakuin.

Heart Chakra (Anahata)

The heart chakra is said to have twelve petals, corresponding to the T1 through T12 thoracic vertebrae and nerves you must open through Qi cultivation. Naturally it also refers to all the tissues in the chest cavity in front of these nerves, including the lungs, heart, ribs and associated muscles/tissues, but we usually just simplify matters by referring to the heart even though the heart chakra represents this greater region. Some people will see a vision of little flames in the heart when they start to successfully cultivate this region through nei-gong Qi work. By concentrating on this region through visualization exercises, mantra or by spinning your Qi in the vicinity, the various efforts will start to open up the local channels. This may temporarily produce pain in the area, and thus frighten a practitioner, nevertheless the region must be opened.

In some cultivation traditions, such as Japanese Shingon, nine petals are used to represent the heart chakra. For instance, in the mandalas used for Shingon visualization practice – such as the Womb Realm mandala - you will find a square of eight Buddhas and Bodhisattvas surrounding the central Buddha Vairocana. This mandala is supposed to be visualized in your heart. Vairocana at the center of the mandala represents the center of your heart while the other Buddhas represent the eight petals of the heart chakra. Some people take Vairocana to represent the *sushumuna,* or central channel, but there is no central channel in the center of your body because it is located in the spine.

WILLIAM BODRI

In general, the heart chakra symbolizes the entire chest cavity containing your heart, lungs, ribs, spine and all the surrounding tissues. The entire chest cavity surrounds the twelve thoracic vertebrae, which is where we get twelve as the number of heart chakra petals. As stated, the "heart chakra" therefore doesn't represent just the heart but *the entire chest cavity including the lungs*, ribs, esophagus, thymus and spine. Every Qi channel within this area must be opened through cultivation work such as *kumbhaka* pranayama, visualization of the rib bones, spinal vertebra and soft tissues (heart, lungs, etc.), mantra, qi-gong, nei-gong and so on.

Throat Chakra (Vishuddha)

The throat chakra, which corresponds to the cervical vertebrae and surrounding tissues of the neck and portions of the face and upper chest, is said to have sixteen petals due to the dual sets of C1, C2, C3, C4, ... C8 nerves extending out of the cervical vertebrae.

This chakra is often symbolized by a many-storied stupa since the levels correspond to the bands of the trachea, which is segmented like a stupa. This region of the body (the neck) is particularly difficult to open due to the complicated construction of muscles, ligaments, glands, bones, arteries and other tissues in the region.

Third Eye Chakra (Ajna)

The Ajna chakra, said to have two petals, represents the two halves of the nasal cavity and two lobes of the brain, which is why it has two petals shaped like two large wings. It also represents the two halves of the brain stem, which is its highest representation. The brain stem is represented by the Ardhanarishvara of Hinduism, a Shiva-Shakti composite of Yin and Yang that also symbolizes the Ajna chakra. When the Qi finally pierces the channels in the brain stem, it is temporarily painful.

In some religions an owl is used to represent wisdom because it is a smart bird whose two wings and small size can together represent the brain. For instance, the Goddess Lakshmi of India is often featured together with an owl whose feathers represent Qi channels. The goddess Athena also owns a pet owl and carries a spear to represent the idea that the spine and brain (spear and owl) have to be opened during the course of cultivation. The tip of the spear represents the brain stem at the end of the spine, which is the critical structural feature to open. The owl not only represents the brain, but its two feathered tufts (plumicoms or horns) represent the two nerve bundles that project upwards into the left and right sides of the brain respectively.

When the Qi first penetrates the brain stem to open it there is tremendous pain for about one minute, and then never any pain again in that region. For instance, when the Zen master Huike felt pain in his head during the Twelve-year Period of transformation he heard a voice in the sky say that he should just bear the pain because his bones were opening. Actually it was the channels in his brain stem that were being opened because a Buddha was passing Qi through them.

In some cultivation schools the two-winged owl also represents the cerebellum, which is also difficult to open in cultivation. It is hard to come up with a visualization routine or method of spinning Qi that quickly opens up the cerebellum's Qi channels.

In many cultivation traditions you are taught to focus or concentrate on the "third eye" region between the eyebrows above the nose, which many know will help bring Qi to the head from the spine and open up some Qi channels in the inner vicinity. It is also said that the upper opening of the central channel is at the forehead at this spot between the eyebrows. This is taught so that you focus on these regions.

Actually, concentrating on this area is meant to help open up the hard to reach sinus cavities behind this spot, which must be transformed through Qi like all other body tissues. If you want to make an etheric duplicate of your body able to leave it at will, you need some way to open up the channels in this hard-to-reach area, which is yet another reason that why many spiritual schools have you concentrate on the forehead. Unfortunately, that method is not good enough by itself, which is why visualization and other practices for your sinus cavity will help in its cultivation.

If you buy a piece of 3D anatomy software, like "Essential Anatomy" for the iPad and Mac, you will be able to see and rotate pictures of the entire sinus cavity to get a feel for its shape. The Qi channels in all these tissues have to be opened, and one way to bring Qi to the area is by first concentrating on the point between the eyebrows. Later you can learn how to move that Qi into the soft tissues behind the nose so that they open.

When practicing alternate nostril breathing or other techniques you should also, at times, try to feel the Qi inside the tissues of the sinus cavity. That ability to feel tissues is one means to help open up the channels. It is unfortunate that a sinus drip into the throat often initiates when you start to open the Qi channels in this vicinity, and as *Tao and Longevity* explained (with many examples) the only way to deal with this possibility is to swallow the fluid until the stage passes.

The practice of pushing the tongue up against the roof of the mouth, or stretching it backwards in the mouth while pushing upwards, also helps to stretch the muscles in both the throat and nasal cavity. Thus it helps to open the Qi channels in those areas. There is nothing special about tongue exercises other than exercising all those internal muscles – stretching them – so that it is easier for the Qi to penetrate them, just as it must penetrate all the other muscles and tissues of the body as well. Stretching always makes this easier because it physically untangles knots and obstructions within the tissues.

In Yoga people sometimes cut the frenum membrane under the tongue to help do this, but this is unnecessary. For some inexplicable reasons, Indian practitioners have adopted the strange notion that cutting the frenum leads to higher spiritual states when there is no spiritual benefit to it whatsoever. Nothing! All of these methods are simply to help you exercise some muscles so that it's easier for Qi to pass through them. Since people attain the deva body in all sorts of traditions without doing this, why do you think there is any need to cut the frenum? It certainly is not necessary nor does it make a higher stage possible nor lead to a higher stage of attainment.

Crown Chakra (Sahasrara)

Most people have seen pictures of Buddhas with a strange curly-cue hairstyle representing the crown chakra. Therefore they believe that the 1,000-petalled crown chakra is some etheric, esoteric anatomy that somehow sits on top of the head or above the head. This is incorrect.

The crown chakra, with 1,000 petals, simply means your brain and its nerves. It is represented as having 1,000-petals because the large number stands for all the nerves (and thus *nadis*) in the brain that have to open through your cultivation. Purifying or transforming all the Qi channels in your brain means opening up the countless channels within its neural tissues and nerves, which is so many that we see numbers like 100 or 1000 to represent the large number of the crown chakra petals.

Due to our modern capabilities of diffusion tensor and diffusion spectrum brain imaging (high density fiber tracking), DTI or DSI, the motion of water molecules can be mapped in the brain to give us pictures of the actual nerves that run throughout it. These pictures are invaluable and should be used by you in advanced visualization and qi-gong/nei-gong practices to help open up the most important Qi channels in the brain! They are one of our modern world's best contributions to the science of spiritual cultivation.

The brain has thousands of nerves, and it is only today through the powers of DTI (please google "brain DTI" to look at available images) that we can actually see the nerves in the brain. Of particular importance from such pictures is to note how the spinal cord splits upwards into two ascending branches located in the left and right hemispheres of the brain.

This pair of nerve bundles extends the highest in the brain, and you must open the Qi channels in these two pathways. This is why some tantric visualization practices teach you to visualize a sun or Buddha over the top of your head. When you concentrate on a point above your head this pulls your Qi upwards through these two nerve bundles, thus helping to open them. Concentrating on the forehead, as another example, helps to draw Qi up your spine through the cranial nerves as well or simply floods the area behind the forehead with Qi too..

Most religions picture the two ascending nerve bundles as horns that associates them with signs of wisdom, spirituality or accomplishment, but scholars rarely understand the reason for this. The two wisdom horns of Moses in Judaism, horns of Yamantaka in Vajrayana Buddhism, two horns of Isis holding a sun above her head, and two horns of Kamadhenu (the Hindu Wish Giving Cow) are examples of how these two Qi pathways, or nerve bundles, are represented in different religions.

Pictures of Hinduism's Kamadhenu Wish Fulfilling Cow, which is also mentioned in Buddhism, contain many secrets of spiritual cultivation. Kamadhenu is a "Wish Fulfilling Cow" because the cow represents our brain, which is the instrument for how we think (make thoughts) and thus the organ for how we make wishes come true. The brain is our wish fulfilling gem.

Pictures of Kamadhenu show that the cow has four teats that the sage Gorasknath named Ambika (mother), Lambika (eyes at the summit), Ghantika (sound) and Talika (floor). Few know that these four teats represent the two nodes of the superior colliculus and two nodes of the inferior colliculus that process visual and auditory information in the brainstem, which is why they were so named. It is paramount to open the Qi channels in the brain stem along the road of spiritual cultivation and the brainstem is represented as the hump on the back of Kamadhenu. Many fictitious spiritual animals are pictured as having a single horn to represent the brainstem as well.

The Mahasiddha Nagabodhi, who was a student of Nagarjuna, was called the "Red-Horned" thief because the red horn represented his opened brain stem. In the Buddhist *Avatamsaka Sutra*, many Bodhisattvas are named using the word "topknot" to symbolize that they opened their brainstem or the brain itself. In addition, whenever you see a Buddha or deity holding an umbrella, the handle represents the brainstem while the fabric of the parasol represents the nerves in the surrounding tissues.

Cultivation masters, who via their deva body can shrink themselves to go into a human's brain (which is the ten-foot square room in the *Vimalakirti Sutra* and the "Palace chamber" in the *Avatamsaka Sutra*), can observe thought processes in real time to see what thinking functions are performed in different parts of the brain. This is something a new master must undergo as devas train in his/her brain during the Twelve-year Period of transformation. Because anyone with a deva body knows how to use Qi to activate thought patterns in the brain and know how it works, this is how the ancients were able to provide accurate names for the cow's teats.

In many Buddhist sutras the countless neurons of the brain are described as "nets of the finest jewels" that "reflect images of Buddhas and their teachings" since it is within the neurons that memories are stored. This is why, for instance, the *Avatamsaka Sutra* talks of the Buddha teaching within a Palace Chamber (the brain of an individual) where there were "fashioned nets of the finest jewels, from which came forth all the realms of action of the spiritual powers of the Buddhas, and in which were reflected images of the abodes of all beings."

Descriptions of multicolored lights and waving banners in Buddhist sutras are often disguised descriptions of what happens when thoughts or emotions occur within the brain. There is a surge of energy and chemical reactions in the neurons when someone has a new thought realization because neural pathways are newly fashioned from learning something new (a realization) or old pathways are activated with energy due to prompting.

The career of a deva is partly occupied by trying to give humans thoughts to do good deeds and cut off evil ways. They must be taught how to do this by demonstrations that take place within a person's brain, and the logical "volunteer" is a spiritual aspirant during the troublesome Twelve-year Period since that will also be part of the future master's activities when his deva body is finished.

The eighteen powers of an Arhat include the ability to cause living creatures to become subject to one's will, remember what they forgot, equip beings with fluidity in expression and bestow joy on people. These powers are all due to the fact that anyone with a deva body can affect the thoughts and emotions that are processed in the brain. The superpowers of spiritual seeing and hearing (clairaudience) mentioned in Buddhism, Hinduism and Yoga texts are also due to the fact that a human possessing a deva body can project it to wherever they want to see and know the events in that location.

As to Kamadhenu, her two colorful wings represent the two lobes of the brain with their many nerves channels (Qi channels), and the cow's hump represents the brain stem. Because of the brain's anatomical structure, cerebral spinal fluid is always flowing down into the cerebellum, which is why Goraksnath said that nectar is perpetually streaming down from the cow's udder. In pictures of Kamadhenu this "stream of nectar" (cerebral spinal fluid) is usually represented by the four teats (superior colliculus and inferior colliculus) issuing milk that flows to a Shiva Linga.

In Hindu culture the Shiva Linga is commonly taken to represent the phallus and yoni, male and female sexual energies, or the ascending energies of Creation (hence erect phallus) arising from Emptiness. However, in pictures of Kamadhenu it actually *represents the brainstem and cerebellum* that must be opened on the spiritual path if you want to become enlightened. This is a little known but correct meaning of the Shiva Linga. It represents our major thought centers of the brainstem – our wish fulfilling jewel - which is why it is paid homage.

Unfortunately, not one in a million Hindus know this and the higher meaning it represents that would inspire them to perform more spiritual cultivation and practice of the correct type. If you do not open up the Qi channels in the brain stem then you will never be able to fully open all the channels in your brain.

As explained, there are many benefits to your spiritual practice if you try to move your Qi along the nerve paths revealed by DTI brain images. Doing so as a daily practice routine will enable you to finally open up the Qi pathways within your twelve cranial nerves, which are represented as the twelve-petalled Kalachakra or Lalana chakra in the brain. There are many alternative chakra names for these twelve nerves as a group and for other sections of the brain. Basically, many areas of the brain, whose channels must open on the spiritual path, are symbolized as chakras.

Another fact few know is that the Kamadhenu has its equivalent in the Sphinx of ancient Egypt, who could ask questions of humans since the sphinx also symbolizes the brain. The hairs of the Sphinx represent the nerves or Qi channels in the brain (just as the owl's feathers represent Qi channels), its wings call forth the two brain lobes, and the four paws represent the four sections of the brain that you can clearly see in pictures.

The tail of the Sphinx represents our spinal cord. The Lamassu or Sadu of Mesopotamia (Sumerian and Akkadian) mythology also represent the Kamadhenu, which evidences the fact that all these ancient cultures had enlightened masters who put into art the fact that the brain's Qi channels must be opened during the course of spiritual cultivation practice.

The Chimera of Greece is another cultivation symbol similar to the Kamadhenu, Sphinx and Lamassu. It represents the brain as well. Its two goat horns represent the two hornish nerve bundles in the brain (as with Yamantaka), its serpent tail represents the spine and triangular sacrum, its two wings symbolize the two cranial hemispheres, the lion's hairs represent all the many cranial nerves or Qi channels of the brain that you can see in DTI images, and the fact it breathes fire represents the warm Yang Qi (kundalini) needed to cultivate all the Qi channel openings. Typically the animals used to represent Yang Qi (lions, bulls, horses, etc.) rather than Yin Qi (snakes, crabs, rats, etc.) denote the process of spiritual cultivation in some way.

The two-lobed brain stem and the two hornish nerve bundles are also represented in figures of Apis, the Egyptian divine cow. When you look at pictures of Apis' head you will clearly see a representation of the two halves of the brain stem that end in the left and right thalamus.

The strange animal called the Navagunjara found in the *Mahabharata* of India also represents the brain. It is another equivalent of Kamadhenu. Furthermore, the Tibetan Windhorse (Lung-Ta) that carries the Wishfulfilling Jewel of Enlightenment, which of course is the brain stem, is also just another symbol of the brain in a different form as well.

A key message from most of these symbols is that our brain stem is important enough to be singled out in brain representations. It is our primary processing area for thought, and because we have thoughts we can perform activities that materialize our wishes. That is why it is a wish fulfilling gem. The other important thing you can realize from these symbols is that there are many strange notions about chakras that predominate in society, but few touch upon the real meaning of what these symbols actually represent.

All the cells and tissues of your body have to be purified on the road of spiritual practice. That purification or transformation can only happen if Qi *freely* runs through, without encountering knots or other obstructions, all the Qi channels that etherically duplicate our physical structure as the underlying energy matrix within it. That process of purification – of the Qi opening those channel pathways – is considered a "spiritual process" that always involves warmth due to the warmth of Yang Qi and the friction that arises when obstacles within the channels are encountered and pushed aside. As the Qi channels are opened, the physical body undergoes detoxification (purification) and all sorts of skin conditions and other phenomena are normally produced.

This is another reason why you commonly visualize the red fire element on the cultivation trail since this tends to energize all the Yang Qi in a region, thus making it easier to open up those channels. When you visualize water, which is cool and settles downward, it helps to cultivate your Yin Qi and the downward flowing channels in your body, especially in the digestive organs.

You can use pranayama, visualization, meditation, Nyasa, Mantrayana, cosmic or environmental energy absorption, stretching and many other practices to help open up your Qi channels, and a few methods have already been described. If you don't open up your Qi channels you won't transform your physical body of Jing to be able to generate the deva body of Qi, attain any of the samadhi or dhyana mentioned in spiritual texts, or achieve enlightenment. You won't sufficiently purify the physical vehicle that supports consciousness (the brain) so that you will be able to realize the root energy source of consciousness. Meditation, without purifying the physical body, will get you nowhere on the spiritual trail.

Our consciousness involves energy, and if the physical structure that it runs through and operates within (the body vessel and brain) must also become cleansed and purified of obstructions so that consciousness can become calm and pure. That is why you need to cultivate to the purified Qi level of the Causal body, also called the purified illusory body (as opposed to the *impure* illusory body that is the subtle body), in order to be able to realize a more refined and more subtle purity level of consciousness that is one step away from the Later Heavenly Qi of the Supra-Causal body and enlightenment.

Vajrayana Buddhism says that only the purity of the pure illusory body is high enough to enable you to realize enlightenment, which means that this is the precursor step to attaining the Clear Light Dharma body composed of Later Heavenly Qi. Another way of saying it is that only the subtlest energy-wind supports the clear light mental activity of an enlightened Buddha, so you have to end up cultivating a body composed of that level of energy-wind. The winds or energies you always cultivate through spiritual cultivation are always related to the operations of consciousness within your mind.

The attainment of the Supra-Causal (Dharma) body constitutes enlightenment, which is also called the fourth dhyana attainment in Buddhism. Since there is one more body to be attained, it is only *nirvana with remainder.* Nevertheless, this is the body of Union or Unity. Ramalinga Swamigal calls it a body of Wisdom Light whose concomitant stage of consciousness seems infinite like space, where there seems no distinction between That and the What, and where one identifies with universal life. With this body you become "oned" with eternity and a witness of the universe.

Once you have that achievement, you have to cultivate beyond to the next stage, which is cultivating the body composed of Primordial Heavenly Prana that Ramalinga Swamigal calls the body of Immanence. This achievement corresponds to attaining the 9th or 10th bodhisattva bhumi and is the perfect *sambhogakaya* Reward body in Buddhism.

Most schools of cultivation don't talk about the body in an understandable nature like this. If you miss the point and think that enlightenment only involves consciousness and some sudden type of "Zen awakening" without prior dhyana work (which means attaining these other bodies ahead of time) you will miss the meaning of the spiritual path and probably waste years cultivating incorrectly. You will entirely miss the importance of the spiritual transformations involved with cultivating the *sambhogakaya* Enjoyment body (Reward body) that is necessary for enlightenment. This is a body that lives a very long time, so its attainment is almost like a no-death stage of immortal living.

Spiritual teachers commonly say that upon enlightenment you attain the *sambhogakaya* but this is wrong – upon attaining the *sambhogakaya* you attain enlightenment because that level of consciousness is the natural attendant consciousness (ordinary mind) of that body vehicle. The first step towards the complete *sambhogakaya* is the deva body, or subtle Qi body, and this achieved is sometimes considered the first stage/step of enlightenment. However, for *nirvana* (even though with remaining dependency) you must cultivate the Supra-Causal Dharma body or Clear Light body composed of Later Heavenly Prana.

When you cultivate the subtle body you can say that this is the first stage of the *sambhogakaya* achievement,. With this achievement you can attain the first dhyana. If you purify your deva body to a higher degree you can attain the second dhyana. If you then work even harder and cultivate the Causal/Wisdom/Mental/Shen body out of the subtle body, which enables you to attain the third dhyana, this is a higher stage of the *sambhogakaya* attainment. If you work yet harder and attain the Dharma Body or Later Heavenly Qi body (Clear Light body) this is a higher stage of the *sambhogakaya* achievement. At each stage of body purification you can attain a higher stage of enlightenment.

In order to achieve enlightenment the achievement involves

consciousness, which in turn is based on your nervous system. This is why the Qi channels in your brain and nerves must be opened fully so that those pathways contain no entanglements, knots, blockages or hindrances. Consciousness can only become more pure if there is a corresponding purification of your nervous system and your nervous system can only run better/quieter if the Qi channels within the nerves are cleared of all blockages.

The coarse physical body is far too impure for you to be able to realize enlightenment, which is why you must cultivate the higher subtle bodies that develop into the perfect *sambhogakaya*. The *Surangama Sutra* says that upon attaining the deva body you will then have the potential to achieve the sixty stages of development towards Buddhahood, which involve different degrees of *sambhogakaya* attainment, in addition to being able to freely assume any form at will or travel anywhere without obstruction. The deva body is the immediate cause for the network of form bodies of a Buddha.

You therefore have to open up all the Qi channel pathways in your nerves and your body so that as a first step you can produce an independent deva body. Once you have that body, then like the devas you have to work to produce a higher Causal/Mental body, which is composed of a yet higher type of purified energy/substance we call Shen. This body is the immediate precursor stage to *nirvana*, the *alaya* consciousness realization or Supra-Causal body attainment that is also called enlightenment or self-realization. In Vajrayana, to "realize the fundamental essence of the mind" therefore has a physical correlate of producing a body vehicle of rarified energy called a "fundamental wind."

STAGES OF MATTER

Let's illustrate this dialogue through an example to make it more clear.

Think of an ice cube. It is a solid, correct?

If you add energy to the ice cube, it melts and becomes water. Water is therefore at a higher energy state than ice. As liquid, it is less dense than the solid ice. Let's think of these characteristics by saying it is more "subtle" than ice.

Now add energy to the water and you get steam, which is like air. It is even less solid than liquid. It is even more subtle.

What is the next stage higher than steam? What is more subtle than steam? Space is more subtle than steam. Space is empty of even steam, so it is more etheric, refined or subtle than air. It is more pure of pollutants.

Now the hard question. What is more subtle than space? The answer is consciousness.

Why is consciousness more subtle than space? I'm going to use a trick explanation only so as to help you make progress in letting go. The space that you are seeing between your eyes and this book appears in your consciousness. You can see this space, but you cannot see your substance of consciousness that the space appears within. You can only see images, and the image you see is space. Therefore, consciousness is more subtle than space. Empty space appears within consciousness, but you cannot notice the substance of consciousness that it is made of – whatever it is - so consciousness is more subtle than space. You might even say that space somehow appears as an evolute within consciousness, so consciousness is more subtle/finer/etheric.

The instruments through which consciousness is produced in the body are the brain and nervous system. The brain, in particular, is your thinking organ just as the eye is your visual organ and the ear is your hearing organ. The brain's operations involve chemical reactions and energy to produce thoughts, i.e. consciousness.

Because the brain is the seat of consciousness, you must cultivate the purification of your nervous system in order to develop a more peaceful mind of non-jumpy clear consciousness. You have to open up the tiny Qi channels (*nadis*) in the brain so that energy can flow through its circuits without obstructions, and the pathway for doing so is through spiritual cultivation.

By generating bodies that are progressively more pure/subtle in their compositional substance, you also can finally attain one whose substance is so refined that it is the ultimate/fundamental energy type/level that underlies the human body and its consciousness. This is the "fundamental wind" of Vajrayana and the Yoga schools, but not the ultimate energy of the universe. That fundamental wind belongs to the level of the Supra-Causal body, but there are higher levels still. This description of the spiritual path is from the aspect of form rather than consciousness. If we were to speak of this level using the vernacular of consciousness then we would speak of the *alaya* consciousness or volition skandha.

Since the pathway to this level of enlightenment is through spiritual cultivation, and since purifying the Qi and channels of the nervous system is crucial to this eventual achievement of higher bodies and enlightenment, thus the ancients always emphasized the spinal Qi currents through teachings involving the left (*ida*), right (*pingala*), central (*sushumna*), back and front Qi channels. They also segmented the spine into logical segments that reflect the curvature of the spine and different types of cervical vertebrae. However, they named them "chakras" since this helped with concentration practice whereas they just refer to entire body segments that must be cultivated on the spiritual path.

When these segments have been cultivated (their Qi channels opened up) the energies are available for spiritual cultivation, and that's why we see India's Lord Surya (the solar deity) having a chariot with seven horses. We also see Buddhas being surrounded by seven dragons or protected by a naga hood of seven snakes. The chakras don't represent seven different energies, but just seven different sections of the body that you cultivate in order to cultivate the whole. In fact, most schools usually don't even discuss the *atala, vitala, sutala, talatala, rasatala, mahatala* and *patala* sections of the legs that need to be opened as well, and which are called the lower chakras of the body.

Again, the chakras just represent segments of the spine along with the sections of the body in front of them. Whenever you cultivate a spinal section you should always cultivate the internal organs and flesh in front since the entire body must be cultivated. Various methods have been developed to help open up your Qi channels everywhere, and your entire body must be cultivated so that its underlying etheric structure is cleansed out. This is why adepts rotate their Qi through muscles, organs, channels and body sections using all sorts of methods and sadhanas.

No one likes to say anything, but this is the big physical secret to spiritual cultivation, and during the twelve years that a master is cultivating his body after a kundalini awakening this is what he is working on. All the effort prior to that time is considered *preparation*.

Sometimes masters (both men and women) have attained enlightenment from a previous life and are reborn on this earth. Certainly they must *still cultivate every part of their body for their present human incarnation* but their task is easier than yours since their higher bodies still exist and will be donating Qi to their efforts to help them open up the channels of their new physical body. That's why they can attain the subtle body in heir early twenties and claim enlightenment.

Upon this success as a foundation, they can then go on to generate the Causal body, Supra-Causal body, Immanence body and so on. All these bodies remain linked together, as well as to the bodies of the previous life, like a large tree or vine. This will end up creating a network of multiple bodies that masters can use across realms and planes; as the *Hathatavakaumudi* says, a master never severs his connection of his original body with any of the new bodies he creates.

The way it works is that on the spiritual road you generate and then can use multiple bodies made of multiple substances. When the physical human body of a master dies then the subtle body, Causal body, Supra-Causal body and so on still survive. The subtle deva body only lives a few hundred years, but the Causal (Mental body or purified illusory body) body lives much, much longer and th Supra-Causal body longer still. The higher bodies are not immortal but so long-lived that they are described that way. When the subtle body dies a master usually incarnates again as a human in order to generate a new physical body, subtle body and extra set of Causal, Supra-Causal and yet more bodies (linked to the old ones) so that they can do more things in the cosmos.

When a master dies on the human plane he continues to live in all these upper planes according to how many bodies he has cultivated, and when his subtle body dies his yet higher bodies also still live. He might then – keeping the higher bodies as a base – project a new body to be reborn on earth (a *nirmanakaya*) that must go through this entire cultivation process again, yet which is still linked to his remaining heavenly bodies. The method to do this (generate a *nirmanakaya*) is not explained to the uninitiated who lack the requisite gong-fu.

Because an enlightened master still has his higher heavenly bodies, he can use their energies to quickly open up the channels of his new physical earthly body much, much faster than a regular person and achieve a new deva body quicker than you, but no one would know of this accomplishment. To anyone he would look and seem normal just like everyone else.

This explains why some masters reborn on earth start working at spiritual cultivation from as early as five or six years old. It is because the master still exists (retains bodies) on a higher plane and this new body is actually a projection like a new appendage of the old. Thus the still living master influences the mind of this new appendage to start cultivating early. These are some of the very high level tantric secrets of the spiritual path and explain some of the phenomena you encounter in the lives of saints of various traditions.

The masters, saints, prophets, gurus, sages, sadgurus, and so forth of all the world's religions are all doing this very same thing even though you don't know about it. Once they attain the subtle body due to their religious practices they are taught the rest of the path. The saints within Islam, Christianity and Judaism, for instance, are all cultivating these higher bodies even though those traditions lack these explicit teachings. This is why saints attain superpowers and higher wisdom.

When you finally escape from the physical shell with a subtle deva body you are extremely joyful and now have access to heaven, so the physical life doesn't matter anymore, especially when you find out what is real and false in terms of the world's religious dogmas. Much of what goes for religion is just wrong information that cheats people, and many deceptive things have been added to religions on purpose in order to lead people to better lives. The point is to use your chance in this world to escape by finally generating an enlightenment Supra-Causal Clear Light body that transcends all the material realms and can live nearly forever. As stated, above that attainment is the Immanence body or perfected *sambhogakaya* of Buddhism. This is the body corresponding to Complete and Perfect Enlightenment.

CHAPTER 12
THE 12-YEAR PERIOD

Once someone undergoes a Kundalini Awakening, which is when the *real* Yang Qi of the body arises en masse to kick off a whole sequence of deeper Qi and channel transformations, it is typical for a cultivator to go into secluded retreat. The whole process of Qi channel transformation from this point onwards takes about twelve years to complete, and sometimes longer. In Tibet this is called the period of Completion stage yogas.

During this time many strange, unusual and sometimes uncomfortable things will happen, so masters rarely speak about what they went through during this period. Shakyamuni explained many of the delusive states they go through in the *Surangama Sutra*, whose relevant translation can be found in *Meditation Case Studies*. Together with this book it tells you what to expect on the spiritual path.

Read any biography, autobiography or interview and you will rarely hear a spiritual master describe what they cultivated and what they experienced during this twelve-year period. Everyone is silent on the topic because of the trials and torture you must go through in dealing with devas who work on helping you purify your channels while training on how to affect people's thoughts at the same time. Some of those devas are actually the masters of your tradition as well as fellow students and friends who attained the subtle body before you. What happens is that a practitioner during this time eventually transforms (opens) all their Qi and channels, becomes able to generate the subtle deva body, masters the superpowers that become possible from this body, and starts working on generating even higher bodies based on the yogic process they now understand completely.

Usually a master will undertake many different types of nei-gong practices during this time, and will often be taught in their mind by "higher beings," meaning saints and sages who have previously succeeded, since they will soon have a subtle body that can join them. Of course, the aspirant is kept ignorant about who is really helping them and what is happening so that they don't know what is going on.

How do we know it takes twelve years of practice to fully open up all the Qi channels of your body after the genuine Kundalini Awakening? The direct teachings and stories of great masters all tell us this fact.

Ramana Maharshi said, "The sastras say one must serve a guru twelve years for enlightenment."

Taoism also says it takes twelve years to transform your body.

Sai Baba of Shirdi said, "I stayed with my master for twelve years."

Kabir meditated for twelve years and then finally got superpowers.

The sage Matsyendranath, the traditional founder of Hatha Yoga, is said to have cultivated within a fish's belly, and then emerged after twelve years of practice.

In *The Truth Is* the Hindu sage Papaji explained, "Kundalini is lying dormant in everybody in the muladhara chakra of the astral body which is in the heart of the physical body. This energy is sleeping and you give rise to it by concentrating on different chakras one after the other. ... focusing on the chakras will cause the energy to start traveling upward through all the chakras. Finally, it reaches the top and then you will feel that you are not the body, but that you are out of the body. This is a difficult process and takes at least twelve years in a quiet place with a good teacher."[5]

Mahavira, the founder of Jainism, meditated as an ascetic for twelve years and then attained enlightenment.

Vardhamana Mahavira, the 24th Tirthankara who founded

---

[5] *The Truth Is*, Sri H.W.L. Poonja, (Weiser Books, York Beach: Maine, 2000), p. 447.

Jainism, undertook ascetic practices for twelve years before becoming enlightened.

Shivabalayogi attained self-realization after twelve years of arduous cultivation practice.

Swami Sivanandaji Maharaj did vigorous cultivation work for twelve years in order to attain enlightenment.

Ramakrishna spent twelve years in practice and Asanga spent twelve years meditating in his cave.

Kancharia Gopanna (Goparaju) was imprisoned for twelve years after reconstructing a famous temple, at which time he was released due to the intercession of Lord Rama.

The Vajrayana master Naropa is said to have endured twelve hardships in order to meet his teacher Tilopa. There are also the Twelve Labors of Hercules, each of which represents a stage of Qi cultivation that took one year to perform (see *The Little Book of Hercules*).

The planet Jupiter takes twelve years to complete one orbit around the sun, and since Jupiter represents the Prana or Qi of our bodies (the wind element), perhaps this twelve-year orbit explains why it requires the length of twelve years to perfectly complete the subtle body's transformation until it is ready to emerge. Perhaps this is because it takes Jupiter, the planet representing our Qi, twelve years to complete the twelve zodiac signs and thus twelve years for our Qi to mature.

The initial years of this transformation are marked by chaos as countless Qi channels open and Buddhas (together with their deva students) work hard helping practitioners normalize their Qi flows and channels. One after another, teams of Buddhas and their students will enter your body to accomplish this thankless task. Naturally, you cannot open all the millions of Qi channels of your body at once, which is why it takes many years of devoted cultivation work on your part and their part to accomplish the feat. It takes twelve years for the rolling of Qi through your channels to become continuous, and this requires the work of countless masters and devas to get this going. Obviously you have to have a lot of merit for them to do this for you.

Since there has to be some reward on their part for all this hard work and effort, at the same time they are working on you the devas are being taught how to alter someone's thoughts (using you as the guinea pig) since this involves entering someone's brain and activating selected neural pathways. This is a skill one must develop in order to help human beings. Giving thoughts to people is relatively easy while affecting their emotions is a bit harder, but countless devas are taught how to do this, using you as the test subject, during this Twelve-year period. At the earliest stages of the process, until the practitioner finally catches on, they usually think they are being attacked/possessed by devils or demons when it is really just angels and devas.

During this time, devas are taught how to use their energy to activate the biochemical neural pathways of the brain, using their Qi bodies in a sort of possession, to bring up specific thoughts and emotions. During instruction they are often tested by seeing if they can make an individual fill in neurons with new content that becomes memories. They might cause someone to run through impossible scenarios in their head over and over again in order to see them create neural pathways. They might laughingly have contests with one another to see whose methods can cause you to say something you would not, despise someone you like, or do hundreds of other things against your nature and societal norms. A common contest is to see who can find out memories quickest in your brain, and who is strongest at giving you a thought while another tries to block it. All sorts of painful games for you go on.

The justification for the pain and anguish you go through during these twelve years is that once you have a deva body (that is actually higher than an ordinary deva's in terms of powers since born from this process), you will be doing this to humans, too, in order to help them change their bad behaviors and perform meritorious acts. When people call on God or Buddhas for help in solving situations, this is what devas and Buddhas do to intervene so you have to learn how to do this too. All devas (who are human beings who have died or residents naturally born in the local subtle plane) do this, entering your brain to give thoughts and read memories, so there are no secrets in anyone's mind hidden from heaven.

The unfortunate and torturous part of the process is that the devas test themselves by impelling you to do negative deeds that you normally wouldn't do, while their teacher opposes them with his/her greater power. The master, who is usually enlightened, opposes them during these efforts using his or her multiple higher bodies and *nirmanakaya* projections. Can I make you do something you normally wouldn't do? One will be tested thousands of times like this and needs tremendous willpower to avoid doing what is wrong to avoid harm. The Twelve-year Period of transformation is thus a time we can only refer to as a period of trial, tribulation, mental abuse, anxiety, vexation and torture.

During the Twelve-year Period it might seem like only one "demon" or group of demons is involved, but actually tens of thousands of heavenly devas and their teachers will be working on helping you purify your subtle body over time – one group after another while one or more voices will remain constant (giving you the impression it is always the same characters) - and in return for the help you receive they will use your brain (Vimalakirti's room) as a training vehicle. This sounds cruel, but because you are on the way to even higher powers (once you attain the subtle body first stage of enlightenment), the long period of painful trial and tribulation during the purification transformations of your channels is a reminder not to cause humans to do things you want them to do just because you have the power to do so.

Power corrupts and absolute power corrupts absolutely (as the Milgram experiment and Stanford prison experiments showed), so you cannot control the devas during this process. Devas tend to excess, and in their joy at being able to cheat you and play with your thoughts they will cause all sorts of troubles. Some schools say they will "consume you" as they put you through terrible anguish during this Twelve-year Period. If you have already cultivated your Yin Qi through other methods, however, you might be able to avoid some of the normal negative emotional extremes brought on from devas during this period since it won't be necessary to put you through many Yin emotional states.

This short synopsis explains why individuals going through the Twelve-year process, such as St. Anthony of Desert, Padre Pio, Saint Jean-Marie-Baptiste Vanney, Seraphim of Sarov, Yeshe Tsogyel, Jesus, Socrates, and many others reported hearing voices of spirits and/or being tested or tormented by demons, which were heavenly devas *pretending* to be devils. As the "Fifty States of Delusion" chapter of the Buddhist *Surangama Sutra* explains (see my book *Meditation Case Studies*), these are actually devas learning how to affect people's thoughts in conjunction with a variety of other events going on at the same time. They are simply devas masquerading as demons in order to arouse your Yin Qi, which strongly activates when you get frightened.

During this process individuals are often caused to give rise to excessive pride, arrogance, bravado (courage or bravery) and anger so that the emotions evoke their body's Yang Qi too, and so devas can see what happens when such emptions arise. The practice of wrathful *yidam* deity visualization practices in Tibetan Buddhism are meant to raise your Yang Qi in a related manner. The emotions of fear, anxiety, sadness, grief, and loneliness are also sometimes evoked so that your Yin Qi arises, and thereby the appropriate Yin channels can be identified and more readily opened.

Some individuals report hearing and seeing angels or various deities during this period rather than devils - such as having visions of Krishna, Buddha, Jesus and so on - and as explained in the *Surangama Sutra* this is actually due to devas as well who are practicing their visualization powers in your brain. Ramakrishna's visions were more along these lines of positive images. The book *Meditation Case Studies* explains all these different types of visions and voices in detail. You are advised to get it and also give it to someone who is going through spiritual experiences as it will help guide them.

You cannot even reach the Kundalini Awakening (called the "opening of the central channel" in Vajrayana Buddhism) unless you have first performed lots of preparatory cultivation work such as the Nyasa Yoga, Mantrayana, visualization, pranayama, meditation and Yoga exercises in this book. In Buddhism these fall into the stage of "intensified yogic practices."

Spiritual cultivation is basically a process of devoted Yoga practice (such as these exercises) that essentially involves cultivating your Qi. All the talk about emptiness, consciousness, original nature and so on all comes down to doing special forms of Yoga (especially pranayama and nei-gong) in order to first generate the subtle body, or deva body that equates with the first dhyana. Once you can pop out of the physical body with a subtle body made of Qi, then the rest of the teachings can be easily obtained.

This is what happens to many Christian, Jewish and Islamic saints who achieved the Tao through prayer and other traditional religious practices, but who were lacking these yogic teachings. Once out, everyone gets oriented by all the other heavenly residents as to the true spiritual path. Upon attaining the deva body, all the false dogmas held by religions are revealed as the rubbish they are.

Now once the Kundalini Awakening appears, the attainment of the independent deva spiritual body will lead to the Completion stage of spiritual practice whereas the preliminary spiritual exercises and cultivation work you do prior to this point (the preparatory practices) constitute the Generation stage practices of learning, preparation and intensified yoga efforts. The Vajrayana schools may have a different definition of the Generation and Completion stage yogas, but this is the definition I like to use.

While the initial years of this Twelve-year Period represent very energetic channel openings ("coarse dredging work"), the final years of this twelve-year transformational period involve advanced Qi and Qi channel cultivation. The sage Vallalar, also known as Ramalinga Swamigal, has written about some of the transformations that happen to the body during this time as it is "burnt out" through the continual application of the fire of yoga. The physical body of impure elements is purified enough to produce a purified body that has siddhi powers, namely the subtle deva body. From that body a higher body is then produced, and so on. Ramalinga Swamigal left 40,000 lines of verse describing many stages of transformation. Everyone goes through these same stages regardless of their religious school or path.

As regards these Qi and Qi channel practices, many masters during this time focus not just on emptiness meditation but on various ways to cultivate the Qi channels in every individual section of their body – every muscle, bone, organ, joint, nerve and tissue. They learn how to move the energy in different body parts by using their mind to guide their Qi. This is a skill that will later enable them to heal other people, and open up the Qi channels (*nadis*) of other spiritual practitioners too.

Masters during this time learn how to cultivate a single piece of the body by moving the Qi along it, practice the movement to perfection, and then move on to do another piece. They eventually link all these qi-gong/nei-gong movements together into a single seamless routine just as you would do in stepping through the parts of the body specified in a Nyasa practice. In this way they cultivate the Qi and channels throughout all their body parts. The end target is to feel the Qi of the body as one united single whole, and then the emergence of the subtle body.

Wouldn't it make sense to do as much of this cultivation work as possible now? After all, this type of Qi cultivation is what devas are preoccupied with doing in Heaven as their own form of spiritual cultivation. It is said that the Kundalini Yoga teachings (that got turned into Tibetan tantric teachings, Taoism teachings, Nath Yoga teachings and other traditions) and sexual cultivation teachings both came from the Desire Realm deva heavens. All these teachings involve cultivating your Qi and Qi channels through unusual energy techniques.

It makes absolute sense to get started ahead of time at cultivating your Qi and channels, which is the road of spiritual cultivation. Most people are unwilling to put in the required efforts and simply follow the religious road of worship and performing good deeds. This will cultivate and purify your Qi a little bit, but not enough for you to attain higher spiritual progress. For definite spiritual progress you have to work harder. Nyasa Yoga is one of the ways to approach the final result.

APPENDIX 1
CULTIVATING YOUR FEMININE ENERGIES

Most cultivation practices work on cultivating your Qi and Qi channels, and after enough channels open you will eventually experience a Kundalini Awakening.

This rare event, which only occurs to those who work extremely hard at spiritual cultivation, marks the beginning of a twelve-year period of difficult transformations that will result in the deva body, and then other stages of the spiritual path. If you attain the deva body you can eventually develop a network of other bodies that culminate in the *sambhogakaya* body attainment of Complete and Perfect Buddhahood. This attainment (a fifth body in addition to the other four you already possess by this stage) is actually the result of both merit and practice, and all the practice can be considered Yoga. Nyasa Yoga can help you attain this.

Whether they tell you or not, the accomplished saints and sages of all schools who succeed all equally pass through the Kundalini Awakening difficult stage of practice. It is mentioned in many spiritual traditions.

The experiences you undergo during this Twelve-year Period, and practices you might undertake to cultivate your Qi, are things most people would not understand, so nearly every master holds to silence about what happens during this time.

One event that happens is that your body's Qi starts to become clearly differentiated into its Yin and Yang components. Prior to this stage the two Qi are mixed together, and people cannot feel one or the other except in extreme emotional states of joy, love, passion, pride, courage, anger and devotion (Yang) or fear, anxiety, sickness, depression and grief (Yin). In other words, the most that anyone (even a spiritual aspirant) can usually feel within their body is the general sensation of Qi energy moving about, while its differentiation into Yin and Yang energies typically goes unnoticed.

There are many meditation practices that can help you purify your Qi enough to the extent that you can begin to discriminate between its Yin and Yang energies. Such practices include visualizing that your body becomes fire (Yang) and then water (Yin); that it is bright (Yang) and then black or blue (Yin) in color; that you age regress and become younger (Yang) and then older (Yin); that your body becomes like a strong male hero (Yang) or you change gender and turn into a woman (Yin); that it absorbs sun energy and/or becomes the sun (Yang) and then the moon (Yin).

All these practices constitute "cultivating your Qi." There are many other variations along these lines. At advanced stages of practice some Tibetan monks sit in the cold ice and snow while trying to raise the warm Yang Qi of the body while some Hindu sadhus sit in the center of a extremely hot circle of burning cow dung in order to cultivate the cooling Yin Qi of the body. These are advanced practices that force you to cultivate the Yin and Yang Qi of the body in great depth and can only be accomplished with the spiritual help of a master, otherwise the adherents would hurt their bodies.

At a certain point in time, due to enough cultivation work your Qi begins to sufficiently purify that it finally becomes clearly differentiated into separate Yin and Yang energies. This happens because enough Qi channels have opened and you can then feel separate Qi circulations within you.

In spiritual cultivation it is not just important that you can discriminate Yin Qi from the Yang Qi. Both your Yin and Yang Qi energies must become purified (refined) and then reach optimal states of balance within your subtle body. It is not right if either is deficient or in excess. For there to be harmony all your channels, comprising your etheric subtle body double, must open. This is why Nyasa Yoga and other spiritual exercise have you flooding your body sections with Qi over and over again until the kundalini process kicks off and starts doing this automatically due to the intervention of devas and Buddhas.

To help in cultivating the Yang Qi or Yin Qi of the body when deficient or in excess, Chinese Medicine and Ayurveda have certain herbal formulas available. Acupuncture may help as well.

Specifically in regards to Yin Qi or feminine energy, there are also certain mantras that can also be used to help restore balance to the Yin Qi of your body, regardless as to whether your Yin Qi is in excess or deficiency. One tantric body cultivation method for doing this, from India, is to recite the Lalita Tripura Sundari Nitya mantras that are paired with the phases of the moon, indicating that they help with Yin Qi cultivation. The help rendered to practitioners from this practice usually comes from female Buddhas.

Thus we have the fifteen Lalita Tripura Sundari Nityas that represent fifteen types of bright Yin energy. Lalita Tripura Sundari ("She who plays" or the "Red Goddess") is a female Buddha who is often represented as a sixteen year old maiden, which symbolizes the purity of her energy, and is one of the female Buddhas in charge of overseeing this type of Qi purification assistance. Actually, many accomplished masters, who become Buddhas, masquerade as Lalita Tripura Sundari in order to respond to all the practitioners using her sadhana, and this type of masquerading is done for every notable Buddha, Bodhisattva, saint, sage and deity in existence.

For this sadhana (practice), each of the fifteen phases of the waxing moon, the Nityas, is matched with a mantra. These have been translated by Mike Magee and are available at ShivaShakti.com as well as Astroyoti.com. You can recite these mantras, one for each day of the lunar month, to help cultivate Qi as well as transform all the five elements (Qi channels) of your body.

1 - **Kameshvari (Lady of Desire) Nitya** - Aim Hrim Shrim Am Aim Sa Ka La Hrim Nityaklinne Madadrave Sauh Am Kameshvari Nitya Shri Padukam Pujayami Tarpayami Namah

2 - **Bhagamalini (The Flowering Yoni) Nitya** - Aim Hrim Shrim Am Aim Bhagabuge Bhagini Bhagodari Bhagamale Bhagavahe Bhagaguhye Bhagayoni Bhaganipatini Sarvabhagavashankari Bhagarupe Nityaklinne Bhagasvarupe Sarvani Bhagani Me Hyanaya Varade Rete Surete Bhagaklinne Klinnadrave Kledaya Dravaya Amoghe Bhagavicce Kshubha Kshobhaya Sarvasatvan Bhagodari Aim Blum Jem Blum Bhem Blum Mom Blum Hem Blum Hem Klinne Sarvani Bhagani Me Vashamanaya Strim Hara Blem Hrim Am Bhagamalini Nitya Shri Padukam Pujayami Tarpayami Namah

3 - **Nityaklinna (Always Wet) Nitya** - Aim Hrim Shrim Nityaklinne Madadrave Svaha Im Nityaklinna Nitya Shri Padukam Pujayami Tarpayami Namah

4 - **Bherunda Nitya** - Aim Hrim Shrim Im Om Krom Bhrom Kraum Jhmraum Cchraum Jraum Svaha Im Bherunda Nitya Shri Padukam Pujayami Tarpayami Namah

5 - **Vahnivasini (Dweller in Fire) Nitya** - Om Hrim Vahnivasiniyai Namah

6 - **Mahavajreshvari (Vajreshvari) Nitya** - Um Hrim Klinne Aim Krom Nityamadadrave Hrim Um Mahavajreshvari Nitya Shri Padukam Pujayami Tarpayami Namah

7 - **Duti (Shivaduti) Nitya** - Aim Hrim Shrim Shivadutyai Namah Shivadutinitya Shri Padukam Pujayami Tarpayami Namah

8 - **Tvarita (Devi Totala) Nitya** - Om Hrim Hum Khe Ca Che Ksah Strim Hum Kse Hrim Phat

9 - **Kulasundari Nitya** - Aim Hrim Shrim Aim Klim Sauh Kulasundari Nitya Shri Padukam Pujayami Tarpayami Namah

10 - **Nitya Nitya** - Ha Sa Ka La Ra Daim Ha Sa Ka La Ra Dim Ha Sa Ka La Ra Dauh Nitya Nitya Shri Padukam Pujayami Tarpayami Namah

11 - **Nilapataka (Sapphire) Nitya** - Aim Hrim Shrim Phrem Strum Krom Am Klim Aim Blum Nityamadadrave Hum Phrem Hrim Em Nilapataka Nitya Shri Padukam Pujayami Tarpayami Namah

12 - **Vijaya (Victorious) Nitya** - Aim Hrim Shrim Bha Ma Ra Ya Aum Aim Vijaya Nitya Shri Padukam Pujayami Tarpayami Namah

13 - **Sarvamangala (All Auspicious) Nitya** - Aim Hrim Shrim Svaum Om Sarvamangala Nitya Shri Padukam Pujayami Tarpayami Namah

14 - **Jvalamalini (Garlanded with Flames) Nitya** - Om Namo Bhagavati Jvalamalini Devadevi Sarvabhutasamharakarike Jatavedasi Jvalanti Jvala Jvala Prajvala Prajvala Hrim Hrim Hum Ram Ram Ram Ram Ram Ram Ram Jvalamalini Hum Phat Svaha

15 - **Chitra (Variegated) Nitya** - Aim Hrim Shrim Ckaum Am Chitra Nitya Shri Padukam Pujayami Tarpayami Namah

The fifteen Kali Nityas correspond to the fifteen days of the waning moon. Therefore they represent different degrees of Yin Qi that you can cultivate to make spiritual (and health) progress. Here are the Kali Nitya mantras for this useful practice:

1 - **Kali** - Om Hrim Kali Kali Mahakali Kaumari Mahyam Dehi Svaha

2 - **Kapalini** - Om Hrim Krim Kapalini Maha-Kapala-Priye-Manase Kapala-Siddhim Me Dehi Hum Phat Svaha

3 - **Kulla** - Om Krim Kullaya Namah

4 - **Kurukulla** - Krim Om Kurukulle Krim Hrim Mama Sarva-Jana-Vasamanya Krim Kurukulle Hrim Svaha

5 - **Virodhini** - Om Krim Hrim Klim Hum Virodhini Satrun-Ucchataya Virodhaya Virodhaya Satru- Ksayakari Hum Phat

6 - **Vipracitta** - Om Shrim Klim Camunde Vipracitte Dushta-Ghatini Shatrun-Nashaya Etad-Dina-Vadhi Priye Siddhim Me Dehi Hum Phat Svaha

7 - **Ugra** - Om Strim Hum Hrim Phat

8 - **Ugraprabha** - Om Hum Ugra-Prabhe Devi Kali Mahadevi Svarupam Darshaya Hum Phat Svaha

9 - **Dipa Nitya** - Om Krim Hum Diptayai Sarva-Mantra-Phaladayai Hum Phat Svaha

10 - **Nila** - Hum Hum Krim Krim Hrim Hrim Hasabalamari Nilapatake Hum Phat

11 - **Ghana** - Om Klim Om Ghanalaye Ghanalaye Hrim Hum Phat

12 - **Balaka** - Om Krim Hum Hrim Balaka Kali Ati Adbhute Parakrame Abhista Siddhim Me Dehi Hum Phat Svaha

13 - **Matra** - Om Krim Him Hum Aim Aim Aim Aim Aim Aim Aim Aim Aim Aim Mahamatre Siddhim Me Dehi Satvaram Hum Phat Svaha

14 - **Mudra** - Om Krim Him Hum Prim Phrem Mudramba Mudrasiddhim Me Dehini Bho Jaganmudrasvarupini Hum Phat Svaha

15 - **Mita** - Om Krim Hum Hrim Aim Mite Paramite Parakramaya Om Krim Hum Him Em So-Aham Hum Phat Svaha

The Lalita Tripura Sundari and Kali mantras can be used to help you cultivate your Yin Qi. The common practice throughout the world is to pay reverence to Lalita Tripura Sundari, Kali, Tara, the Virgin Mary and other female Deities/Buddhas or religious figures – such as through acts of devotion or by longing to merge with them and imagining this happens (through visualization practice) - in order to cultivate your Yin Qi.

There are many other ways to cultivate your Yin Qi, but most of them will seem strange to ordinary people who are not cultivators and lack the theoretical understanding of the process. They are simply methods that you use to accomplish a task. As Lalita Sundari's name indicates, they are just "play" to get a result you seek, which is the purification of your Qi and channels (prana and *nadis*) in order to order to produce an independent subtle body.

The cultivation principle is that you use a raft to cross a river and then you leave it at the water bank. You don't keep using it (carrying it on your back) after the job is done; it is just a technique or tool for helping you cross the river. Therefore you only use these methods to get the result you seek and then you stop using them.

In this case, future masters use many methods to cultivate their Yin Qi so that they can fully develop their subtle deva body (from within their impure human body) quickly. After that attainment they must use other methods to progress further. The story of Ramakrishna's many cultivation methods provides an idea of the many methods one might use.

For instance, various visualization methods that your body is water will help you cultivate your Yin Qi. Visualizing that it is the color blue, or cool in nature, will also help cultivate Yin. Imagining that you are made of pearl is also another method for cultivating Yin Qi. Hopefully you can understand the principle.

Trying to absorb the essence of the moon (rather than sun) is another practice meant to help you cultivate your Yin Qi. Many cultivation schools teach absorption of energy practices (of celestial bodies such as the sun and moon) along these lines in order to help you open up Qi channels and cultivate a subtle body. When you imagine that you absorb the energy of the moon you can imagine that you lose your body and become just lunar light; other derivative techniques are also possible.

Imagining that a female goddess comes into your body is also a practice for cultivating your Yin Qi. Imagining that a strong male deity comes into your body is a way of cultivating Yang Qi. An actor who takes a woman's role in a play can use that role to cultivate his Yin Qi while a woman who pretends she is a man will be affecting her Yang Qi. Imagining that you merge with a Buddha or your master, be they man or woman, is a way of cultivating the appropriate Qi as well.

Traditional Chinese Medicine and Indian Ayurveda also have formulas to help you balance your Yin Qi and Yang Qi energies. The target is to *achieve energetic balance*. If you are Yin deficient, for instance, the medicines work so as to help supplement your Yin Qi. If you are Yang Qi deficient, medicines can help you supplement your Yang Qi. If you are at a state of excessive Yin or Yang, appropriate medicines can help you return to a more balanced, normal level. The entire purpose of the medicines (including acupuncture) is to help your body's Yin and Yang Qi achieve balance.

When young men have dreams or sexual fantasies where they age regress or turn into a women against their will (and within the dream possibly have some type of *fear-inducing* limit they are up against), this activates their Yin Qi. Similarly, when women have fantasies that they suddenly have a penis and are driven to have sex, this is cultivating their Yang Qi. Any fantasy that stays in your head without actively moving (connecting with) your Qi, however, does nothing in terms of Qi cultivation.

Even during sex the position of couples can be reversed to help each cultivate their opposite Qi. This is the meaning of the time when Krishna and Radha exchanged roles in their love-making.

Krishna wore Radha's clothes while Radha wore Krishna's clothes. Instead of Krishna playing the flute, Radha played the flute and Krishna danced around her. Then Radha took the lead when they made love and occupied the active position, dominating him. This is all play, however, and to remind us of this fact Radha said, "Even then Krishna, you cannot understand me. You can dress like me, talk like me and dance like me, but you can never feel what I feel for we can never exchange hearts."

In other words, a man should always stay a man and woman always stay a women in thought and deed after all such cultivation activities. None of these activities of cultivating Yin by the man or Yang by the women is meant to turn the man into a homosexual or woman into a lesbian by habit, mindset, Qi or whatever. Neither should either ever develop transgender leanings either. These are just advanced ways of cultivating your Yin and Yang Qi.

On the road of advanced cultivation practice, as we will find with the case of Shariputra in the *Vimalakirti Sutra,* for a time it is common for men to imagine that they are women and women to imagine that they are men to help cultivate their Yin and Yang Qi respectively. Females also often imagine that they are warriors as exemplified by the Goddess Athena, huntress Artemis and the many Hindu female deities who were also skilled at warfare. Basically, you have to cultivate both your Yin and Yang Qi, and there are various ways you can do this under the watchful eyes of a wise master. The idea of all this work is to reach enlightenment so many methods are employed.

When you grieve severely or get extremely frightened or anxious, such as when seeing a scary movie or encountering a dangerous situation, this helps open up your Yin Qi channels. Hence, festivals on a mass public scale, such as Halloween or a day of mourning for the dead (Ching Ming Grave-Sweeping day or the Ghost Festival in Asia), are times when Buddhas can help many people cultivate their Yin Qi. Through this you can understand that there is a great benefit to mass scale public festivals that cultivate happiness and joy (Yang), reverence (Yang), and even sadness, grieving or fright (Yin). Buddhas can use these times to help people.

When going through the Twelve-year Period of kundalini transformation, it is common for you to be exposed to many Yin situations. It is common, for instance, to sometimes spontaneously burst out crying. You can also be thrust into depressing or fearful, grieving, depression or anxiety-prone situations for months so that your Yin Qi channels can be more easily cultivated. Buddhas will actually throw you into frightening, anxiety ridden or grieving scenarios in order to help you cultivate your Yin Qi. This is why the Hesychast tradition instructs people to pray until they weep and why some bhakti traditions espouse the cultivation of extreme reverence that can also turn into weeping. Emotional extremes can move your Yin Qi or Yang Qi and thus be used to help cultivate the internal generation of your subtle body. However, you can only do this under the influence of an enlightened master.

Many of these emotional situations are described in the second set of fifty Heavenly Mara (Delusion) skandha states found in the *Surangama Sutra*. They are difficult emotional situations you are put through in order to cultivate the various types of Qi of your body (and organs) in order to help you quickly develop the subtle deva body. Sometimes they are simply emotions that devas cause you to experience because they are training their compatriots how to produce them in human brains. When working on your subtle body (skandha of sensation), Buddhas and devas can suddenly cause you to cry with sadness, become angry, become boastful, arrogant or proud, suffer with prolonged anxiety or depression, feel unlimited joy in excess, or feel the urgings of strong sexual desire. These are methods that evoke Yin Qi or Yang Qi within your body.

Without telling others the method they were using, Hindu masters such as Ramakrishna and Papaji wore women's clothes for a short while in order to help themselves cultivate their Yin Qi. Of course, neither was homosexual or transgender-longing. They were simply using an advanced Yin Qi cultivation method that few could understand or publicly accept. Taking the herb Passion Flower (or chrysin), which normalizes estrogen levels in men, can help prevent any unintended excess estrogen that might result at that time due to such practices. It is a natural aromatase inhibitor that inhibits estrogen production.

The Greek story of Hercules wearing women's clothes and knitting (working on his Qi channels) for one year, Thor dressing in women's clothes to retrieve his hammer (cultivate his Qi) from a giant, and Krishna's student Arjuna (in the *Mahabharata*) dressing in women's attire for one year, also portray this method. A related story of the goddess Hera turning Apollo's prophet Tiersias into a woman, who afterwards changed back to a man, also refers to cultivating your Yin Qi in order to develop a subtle body and all its powers. Narada, Krishna's student in the *Bhagavata Purana*, also becomes a woman after bathing in water, symbolizing that he used the imagination of being a woman to cultivate the Yin Qi of his body.

Another story related to Krishna and Radha is that Sudyumna and his horse (representing his Qi) were also turned into females in the forest of Shiva-Parvati lovemaking (all men who enter this forest are turned into the opposite sex, which carries a meaning related to the tantric cultivation practices we are discussing). To cultivate Qi, this type of imagination can be used during sex or as a standalone sexual fantasy under the appropriate conditions, but you need to have an enlightened master to make sure you don't go astray.

In the portion of the *Vimalakirti Sutra* where countless Buddhas, Bodhisattvas and students enter Vimalakirti's small room, which symbolizes the subtle bodied devas, gurus and yogis (shrunk down to a small size due to the power of *anima* possessed by deva bodies) entering someone's brain during the Twelve-year Period, flowers fall upon and stick to the students who haven't yet achieved enlightenment. This symbolizes that the accomplished ones can use many methods to change their Qi but don't get attached to the methods. At that time Shariputra is changed into a women by a goddess and could not through his own efforts change back, so the goddess then changed him back into a man. The meaning is that young students who use sexual fantasies (imagining they are young girls or having sex with devas) as a cultivation method during the Twelve-year Period of transformation (to help develop the subtle body) often lose control of themselves and drop into the technique.

There is also the Greek story of Tiresias, the prophet of Apollo who Hera transformed into a woman for seven years after he found and started beating two copulating snakes. The two mating snakes represent the Yin and Yang Qi of his physical body that he had finally purified and differentiated due to his spiritual cultivation practice. After this the *real* kundalini of the body can arise, which is what Milarepa prayed to experience before he left his master Marpa and went into retreat. It is said that Tiresias was later blinded by Hera, but Zeus gave him the gift of clairvoyance (the ability to divine the future), and a lifetime of seven lives.

This long lifespan of seven generations symbolized that he attained the deva body, which lives for hundreds of years, as does his blindness since he then used his deva body rather than the eyes of his physical nature. Using the deva body one typically gains clairvoyance, which explains his gifts of foresight. Once Tiresias had initiated the Kundalini Awakening by separating and purifying his Qi (the two snakes), that's when he was able to use more advanced Qi cultivation and purification techniques symbolized by being transformed into a woman. Doubtless he used other Yang cultivation techniques as well.

In practicing the cultivation techniques attributed to Dhumavati - a female Hindu deity (enlightened Buddha) associated with "negative" or "unfortunate" connotations (all Yin Qi conditions) - in order to change your Qi and channels and ultimately attain enlightenment, in some Dhumavati sadhanas the practitioners are instructed to go to a cemetery (Yin location) at midnight (peak Yin time) while naked (Yin) to perform the tantric rituals. This is because the individual will be within an environment of maximum Yin Qi while performing Yang Qi practices, and thus can use both energies to transform their body quickly. You cannot just cultivate pure Yin Qi without also using compensatory mechanisms to cultivate or arouse your Yang Qi, such as mantras and special foods, otherwise you are likely to get sick. Yin Qi methods are therefore always cultivated in conjunction with Yang Qi methods.

Many tantric practices in India involve graveyards, crematoriums, death, sickness and aging, war, poverty and other phenomena (such as special foods or astronomical phenomena like eclipses) that throw off strong Yin Qi so that practitioners can absorb Yin energies and use them to transform the Qi of their subtle bodies. The Aghori sects of India, which most cultivators are advised against since they involve many socially unacceptable practices and sadhana practices deemed dangerous, especially involve crematoriums, ghosts and other Yin phenomena. They might seem frightening or strange, but under the benevolent watchful eyes of enlightened Buddhas the methods can be used to transform your body quickly. Rare, however, are the Buddhas qualified to oversee such practices.

In Buddhism, Ksitigarbha (the "Hell Buddha" monk who deals with sickness, death, hungry ghosts and the hells) is an equivalent to Yin-based Aghori practices, and appears in a form more socially acceptable to the public. Ksitigarbha is also called the "Earth

Womb," "Earth Store" or "Earth Treasury" Buddha to denote the Yin nature of *the physical body* symbolized by the earth. He was supposedly a young maiden in a previous life, which also hints at the Yin purification possibilities available through his cultivation. To cultivate assistance for people who are sick, dying or have passed away, as well as to request personal help in purifying your Yin Qi energies, his mantra is "Namo Dizang Wang Pusa."

One can also cultivate Yin Qi by reciting the mantras of other enlightened Hindu female deities, whose mantras are as follows:

Kali – Om Hreem Shreem Kleem Kali Kali Soha
Bhuvaneshvari – Om Hreem Shreem Kleem Maha Bhuvaneshvari
  Soha
Dhumavati – Dhum Dhum Dhum Dhumavati Soha
Saraswati – Om Aim Maha Sarasvatyai Namah
Kaatyaayani – Om Hreem Katyayanaye Soha
Bhavani – Om Shreem Shreem Om Om Hreem Shreem Hum Phat
Tara – Om Tara Turttare Ture Soha

Tibetan Buddhists typically have sadhanas associated with Tara (an enlightened female Buddha) for helping with Yin cultivation. Mahayana Buddhists turn to Zhunti (Mother of the Buddhas) and her mantra ("Namo saptanam samyaksambuddha kotinam tadyatha om! zhurlee zhulee zhunti soha"). The world's religions have prayers, ceremonies, and rituals to many other female gods, patrons, deities, Buddhas, etc. in order to cultivate Yin, such as prayers to the Virgin Mary. Ordinary people, of course, do not know that their Yin and Yang Qi must be purified throughout their lives in order that their subtle body upon death can last longer than average, which prolongs the time spent in heaven before an eventual human rebirth.

Basically, there are many ways for a man to cultivate his Yin Qi and for a woman to cultivate her Yang Qi. When women cultivate Yang Qi in these tantric ways it usually escapes societal notice, but men who practice these advanced tantric methods (which should only be done if you have an enlightened master) usually end up doing things that break societal taboos and norms, so they look strange to the uninitiated who don't know what they are doing. They are using unusual practices to transform the Yin or Yang Qi of their body quickly at a non-superficial deep level and in a quick fashion.

THE FOUR DHYANA

The stages of spiritual progress are actually the same across all the *genuine* religions since these are non-denominational stations. Buddhism explains them best through its classification scheme of the four dhyana, or four stages of an Arhat (enlightened being), and all their correspondences.

The first, second, third, and fourth dhyana are the progressive stages of enlightenment, or Arhatship. The fourth dhyana is the stage of initial enlightenment, or *"nirvana* with remainder," achieved by a full Arhat. The fifth higher stage is *"nirvana* without remainder (remaining dependency)," which corresponds to Perfect and Complete Enlightenment, full Buddhahood or the stage of No More Learning.

The four dhyana attainments exactly correspond to the four stages of Arhatship – the **Srotapanna** ("Stream Entrant") who attains the first dhyana and subtle body, **Sakrdagamin** ("Once More to Come") who attains the second dhyana, **Anagamin** ("No Returner") who attains the third dhyana and Causal body, and **Arhat** who attains enlightenment (the fourth dhyana) and the Supra-Causal body but who is not yet completely enlightened. The **Great Golden Arhat** is the next higher stage of enlightenment - a fully enlightened Buddha who has attained *nirvana* without remainder.

The **first dhyana** is called "The Joyful Stage of Leaving Production" in Buddhism because when you attain the deva body you are extremely joyful. Joy is the main characteristic of the first dhyana. It is the major characteristic used to describe devas since they are always happy and making jokes with one another.

The **second dhyana** is called the "The Ground of Joy Born of Samadhi." The stage of joy in this dhyana is more refined than in the first dhyana because it corresponds to the fact that your Qi is still energized, but less jumpy than in the first dhyana. Therefore the feeling of Qi excitation over your body (bliss) is smoother in terms of sensation. Your body's stage of Qi refinement is higher than in the first dhyana attainment.

The names of these dhyana indicate a secret that the first and second dhyana can be cultivated by exciting your Qi fervently while trying to feel joyful. Many methods can help you do this, including special types of singing, dancing and sexual cultivation, since they excite/stimulate Yang Qi all over your body. The need for joy and excitation is also why you use fire element visualizations (imagining that you are fire) and other methods, such as Nyasa and Mantrayana, to stir up your Qi during nei-gong practice.

The **third dhyana** is called "The Wonderful Blissful Ground of Separating from Joy." This is because joy is abandoned as a mental stimulant for your cultivation, and instead you cultivate a calmer state of mind and subtle blissful body feeling for this achievement. In other words, to cultivate the next level of Qi purification, which is the attainment of a body made of Shen, the joyful energization and exhilaration methods used as coarse excitation for attaining the first and second dhyanas cannot be used and are abandoned.

The Mental/Causal body to be attained for the third dhyana attainment is of an energetic substance more refined than Qi. To attain this dhyana the excitation stimulant of joy is too rough since you are now cultivating a more refined energy rather than coarse vitality. Therefore much smoother or more peaceful Qi cultivation methods are used to cultivate this dhyana. This is why Vajrayana calls this the "detached joy" state.

You can also think of it in this way. When a master injects his Mental body within your physical/subtle body shell in order to stimulate your Qi channels and energies, because his body is composed of a more refined energy the amplitude of energetic movement he produces within you will be far smoother than the more pronounced energetic ups and downs you will experience when a subtle deva body possesses your own in order to do the same thing.

The **fourth dhyana** is called "The Ground of Clear Purity from Casting Away Thought," and can be considered a realm of no thought because your mind is pure and clear at this stage. In Taoism this dhyana is called a stage of great emptiness; it is the stage of enlightenment where your mind is perfectly clear (empty) and you can know the minds of sentient beings since their body-mind complexes are composed of substances much denser than the Supra-Causal Clear Light body you now have at this stage. This enlightenment body transcends all lower (physical, subtle and Causal) body vehicles.

In Vajrayana Buddhism, you are taught to use many nei-gong, pranayama and other methods to cultivate the four stages of **joy, supreme joy, detached joy** and **innate joy** that exactly correspond to the four dhyana. Sometimes these four dhyana, which correspond to the body attainments, are described as progressively subtler levels of "bliss," which also refer to less coarser ways of exciting your Qi in order to cultivate the higher bodies.

The body attainments are also described as cultivating the four Vajrayana empties: the **empty, very empty, great empty,** and **all-empty**, meaning that your mind becomes progressively clearer as you progress in higher body attainments. While some Vajrayana teachers say these are not the four dhyana they *are indeed* the equivalent descriptions of the four dhyana. Many times teachers will say misleading statements like this so that they don't lose students or so that you don't go to another school.

Buddhism also teaches that we can cultivate the four immeasurables (Brahmavihara, divine abodes or sublime attitudes) on the spiritual path. The four immeasurables are infinite **joy, loving kindness, compassion,** and **equanimity**. If you look at these emotions with a critical eye you will see that each is progressively more refined in nature than the previous.

Few know that sitting in meditation and trying to generate an infinite mind of one of these emotions is a way to purify your Qi so that you can attain each of the four dhyana. The level of Qi energization or "smoothness" of Qi corresponding to each immeasurable matches with one of the dhyana. The instruction missing in most four immeasurables cultivation teachings is therefore that you must use a particular infinite emotion to evoke Qi movements within your own body. Thus the practice becomes a means of Qi energization.

Joy, being the most excitation-prone of the four immeasurable emotions, highly stimulates or activates Qi flows in your body. Hence, cultivating or meditating on immeasurable joy helps you to cultivate the Qi of the subtle body so that you can attain the first dhyana. "Immeasurable" means you try to feel the emotion and a corresponding Qi-type all over your body and not just infinitely in the environment. Don't repress the emotion but try to be bursting with it

The four immeasurables of **joy, loving-kindness, compassion, and equanimity** therefore correspond to cultivating the Qi of the first, second, third and fourth dhyana when you try to mix your emotional feelings of these states with the Qi of your body in a vast way. Some of the emotions are more refined than the others (ex. equanimity is more refined than joy, which is an irritation when compared to the peacefulness of equanimity) and those correspond to the higher dhyana attainments.

In Vajrayana Buddhism the tantric "blisses" and "empties" are progressive degrees of refinement, which are used to represent the four dhyana, but few know the secret that anyone can cultivate the four dhyana via the four immeasurables. Everyone thinks the four empties and blisses have to do with four chakras or four body sections but they really refer to these same four degrees of energy excitation you should cultivate to attain the higher spiritual bodies: (1) the subtle body (impure illusory body, deva body, *yin-shen*, astral body, first dhyana), (2) a higher stage of refinement of that same subtle body (second dhyana) which is designated separately so as to encourage devas themselves to cultivate even if they think they cannot attain the next higher body, (3) the pure illusory body (Causal body or Mental body of the third dhyana) and (4) the Supra-Causal or clear light body (of equanimous Qi pertaining to the fourth dhyana, the Arhat's body of enlightenment).

For instance, if you sit in meditation and try to feel **infinite joy** all over your body that also permeates the entire world or universe, and simultaneously try to energize your Qi and whip it up into a frenzy of joy in order to move it, this will lead to a type of Qi cultivation that will open up your channels. This coarse cultivation of vibrational joy will help you cultivate the subtle body and first dhyana.

If you try to cultivate a more refined emotion of **immeasurable loving-kindness**, where your mind and Qi are stimulated but to a smoother degree (less coarse) than joy excitation, you will be practicing the Qi excitation which matches with the second dhyana. Hence, you will still be cultivating the Qi of your subtle body but at a higher level of refinement. You must always try to feel the sensation of Qi energization all over every cell of your body in order to purify or transform your Qi and channels when doing these meditations.

The next higher emotion, which corresponds to less excitation but a higher degree of energetic refinement, is infinite compassion. When cultivating **immeasurable compassion**, you try to feel yet smoother Qi all over your body while your mind is absorbed in infinite compassion (that has less excitation powers than loving-kindness). The level of physical bliss (Qi excitation) cultivated in this way is more subtle or smoother than for the previous two infinite emotions. If you try to cultivate being a bodiless consciousness, and still feel a taint of physical bliss (the shape of your body), this will help cultivate the third dhyana. What will also help you attain this stage is cultivating that you are infinite, boundless compassion (without a body).

Some people feel that compassion and loving-kindness (benevolence) should switch places, and actually it is up to you as to which emotion is more refined (less excitation-prone) than the other. You would use the lesser excitation prone emotion to cultivate the higher dhyana.

The point is that you need to cultivate a body feeling – a sensation of Qi moving felt all throughout your body – that you energize, excite, activate or stimulate by the corresponding emotion when meditating on one of the four immeasurables. It has to be Qi practice, not just mind practice, which is the big secret.

The higher the dhyana you want to reach, the more refined your Qi cultivation must be; the sensation felt within your body must be smoother and more refined. Therefore the fourth dhyana, which is said to correspond to a very refined sense of bliss without much mental excitation (emptiness), is matched with cultivating **infinite equanimity** or **peacefulness**. See how they match?

In Taoism the stages of the first-second, third and fourth dhyana are called the **Earth Immortal, Spirit Immortal,** and **Celestial Immortal** attainments respectively. Each of these grades/levels of Immortals has a different level of powers and abilities. The **Great Immortal** of Taoism, which corresponds to the **Great Golden Immortal** of Buddhism, represents the stage of Perfect and Complete Enlightenment.

The Yoga sutras of Hinduism call the first dhyana the *vitarka* (coarse grasping mentation) samadhi, the second dhyana the *vicara* (refined grasping mentation) samadhi, the third dhyana the ananda (bliss) samadhi and the fourth dhyana the *asmita* (existence) samadhi. This refers to the quality of your thought and consciousness (the attendant or concomitant consciousness) corresponding to each of the bodies you cultivate due to the refinement of its Qi. A wise student will realize that these names correspond to the Vajrayana descriptions of the empty, very empty, great empty, and all-empty minds which are the pointers to the first, second, third and fourth dhyana.

Buddhism describes the first dhyana as breaking free of the sensation skandha, which corresponds to obtaining a deva body. Many spiritual people, especially the heads of religious sects in the Hindu, Buddhist or Sufi traditions, have attained the deva body. The second dhyana represents a higher stage of Qi refinement (purification) for that subtle body. This appropriation of the first and second dhyana to the subtle body made of Qi is due to the fact that devas themselves, whose bodies are already made of Qi, were thus given an encouragement to practice through this designation.

The third dhyana attainment represents an entirely new body attainment - the Causal body or Mental body that arises out of the subtle body (and is composed of Shen, which is a more refined from of energy than Qi). This new body attainment corresponds to the description of "breaking free of the conception skandha" found in Buddhism.

The fourth dhyana attainment corresponds to attaining the Later Heavenly Qi, Clear Light, Supra-Causal or Dharma body, which means breaking free of the volition skandha (that contains both mental and physical factors) and the *alaya* consciousness that is the root source of both body and mind. While attauning the subtle body is considered "enlightenment," this stage is considered *nirvana* with remainder (remaining dependency), and hence sometimes only the Supra-Causal body is colloquially referred to as enlightenment (or initial enlightenment). This is basically the fourth dhyana attainment.

You can also describe this progression in terms of searching for the root source of your mind, which is how Buddhism phrases the path to the Supra-Causal body attainment of enlightenment. Typically religions that use the consciousness explanation totally ignore body attainments and trick people with words that mislead, but their spiritual instructions (i.e. meditation teachings) embody the intent to cause you to let go of consciousness and thus lead you upwards. Only if you let go of consciousness can your Qi begin to rotate so that you can eventually attain the subtle body.

Thus enlightenment is described on these roads as discovering a very empty, pristine, clear state of mind that is supposedly the bedrock of consciousness, but it is actually just the very clear but normal state of mind of an individual who has attained the Supra-Causal body attainment composed of Later Heavenly Qi that, as an energetic substrate, transcends all the lower essences/substances that comprise the physical universe. However, the attainment of this body is described by the Consciousness-only school as "realizing the *alaya* consciousness" since that is the concomitant mental state.

According to Consciousness-only teachings, within your mind appears your physical body. As a living being you also feel emotions and sensations, which are dependent upon the subtle body of Qi, and these too appear within your mind. Lastly, you also have thoughts that appear in your mind, which are termed the conception skandha in Buddhism. Thus, within your mind (consciousness) appears the phenomena of form, sensations and conceptions (thoughts). When the world around you appears within your mind, that appearance of images is due to your sense organs that link with your brain and produce mental images within consciousness. This is a mechanical thing that automatically happens. That sensory input is then interpreted by your discriminative thinking and memory (the sixth consciousness of Buddhism) that is also dependent upon the workings of your brain, and then images and understanding appear within a clear consciousness that is empty like light or space. But what exactly is consciousness itself within which they appear?

Ultimately, consciousness is what appears in a body vessel whose nervous system structure enables sentience (construction of thoughts), and which is constructed out of a certain type of matter (substance) and energy on that plane of existence. Consciousness isn't a substance but the ability to form thoughts and memories within that structure. A level of substance and its attendant energy composes your body *and* your consciousness, which is mechanically experienced within that vessel because of its structure. Consciousness (thoughts) automatically arises because the body structure permits it to arise and is designed so that this mechanical functioning arises. This is what has evolutionarily developed, that's all, whereas other evolutions of the original energy of the universe ended up producing rocks or trees or viruses or other things. It is all a naturalistic outcome. Luckily for beings with a high enough degree of consciousness, they have discovered a pathway to higher bodies that live longer and better. If you can spin out of this body structure a new body duplicate at a higher or more refined plane/level/sphere of energy-substance then you can live in that body.

That is the path of spiritual cultivation until you generate a body at the level of the Supra-Causal plane, which is called initial enlightenment (*nirvana* with remainder). If, as a human being, you finally generate a subtle body then this, too, is termed enlightenment but it is not the final enlightenment that one should seek. It is not full *nirvana* enlightenment. That is why the Supra-Causal body attainment is called initial enlightenment.

The whole spiritual path is the practice of Yoga to attain a higher spiritual body to arise out of the lower one, which requires the help of higher beings to circulate their own Qi inside yours for each body double to be created. If you are an unethical, immoral or nonvirtuous person they will not help you do this excep tot make your body healthy.

So what should you know about consciousness? The whole universe came from an original type of substance or energy that was pure, but somehow developed denser and denser evolutes. Your present body is in the lowest sphere of these evolutes. Some of the creations out of that original substance are insentient like chemicals or forces like magnetism. Some have become what we call living beings but without consciousness, like viruses. Some have become higher and lower sentient beings, such as fish and humans. You only know of your existence and beingness because of a highly developed consciousness. For instance, consciousness gives rise to the I-thought and thoughts, and sensory organs create images that replicate with similitude the outside world through images inside a brain. Without the centering I-thought you don't know of your existence.

Our consciousness is special in one fundamental sense over lower beings such as insects, fish, birds and so on. It is at such a highly developed level that we were able to find the path of spiritual cultivation that allows us to develop higher bodies on purpose out of lower sheaths (created out of denser energies), and we can follow this pathway. With those higher bodies we can then do good deeds in the world, such as acts of merit, by affecting the thoughts of beings with lower bodies, which is the career of a Bodhisattva and Buddha.

In terms of your experience of the world, there is no inside or outside to your consciousness you can ever know because you can only know, experience, or be aware of your own consciousness. Your consciousness *is* your world experience, and your mind is ultimately your consciousness whose functioning is dependent upon its body container. For example, your consciousness is dependent upon memories stored in brain neurons and neural pathways that form regular processing algorithms. It is also dependent upon the energy of life coursing through it and animating that life, which is cultivated to create a higher body of that energy substance. Your inner thoughts are your consciousness and the environment you see is also just your consciousness. Most people mistakenly forget that the world they see is just something appearing as thoughts within their mind (consciousness) even though it looks to be outside of you. They always forget that what they are seeing is just a picture in their brain.

When you see the world around you please remember that you are actually just experiencing thoughts *within your mind* – you are experiencing your consciousness only. It is not a world that you are experiencing but your own mental images of an outside world. You cannot experience that outside world directly because you can only experience your conscious images of that world.

Your consciousness is the only thing you can know and there is no experience possible outside of your consciousness *because you would need your consciousness to know it*. What you essentially are is the ultimate substrate of your consciousness and its body container, which means the ultimate substrate of the universe – its original essence that developed into everything. Everything you see/experience in your mind is really just *you* since it is just a construct of *your* consciousness appearing within your body that is part of your body complex, so it is you because it is a picture in your consciousness. The world outside of your consciousness is not you, however the world you see in your mind is you because that is your own consciousness, and your consciousness is part of you.

This is one of the meanings of the *maha-vakyas* or Great Sayings within the Hindu Upanishads "Thou art That." Thou art indeed That *which you see*. From another angle, since YOU are essentially the original essence which has become THAT, once again Thou art That.

The fact that the mechanism of consciousness evolutionarily arose in an appropriate body vessel out of an original nature, traditionally termed "Brahman" in Hinduism, also means that "All This is Brahman," and even "Brahman is consciousness." These are quotations given to people to help them let go during meditation so that their Qi/prana can arise and start opening their channels.

"I am Brahman" is another *maha-vakya* that basically says you are the original nature, namely an evolutionary product or development out of the original nature. In other words, every being who says "I" to himself is not actually referring to their body but to the original essence, for that is the true self or true I. When you say "I am Brahman" to yourself in meditation, it also helps you *let go of clinging to consciousness* so that the spiritual path of transformation can be quickened. You can use these sorts of sayings to help cultivate various states of mind such as the samadhi of infinite consciousness or the samadhi of infinite space.

As another example, the realization that you only ever experience your own consciousness (and nothing in the universe other than that) can lead to the realization that the "world you see hear, taste, etc." is *just your consciousness only* – it is thoughts and images somehow automatically, mechanistically created within your mind. An entire school within Buddhism has developed based on this. To you the world, your worldview, the world experience, existence or "presence" should be viewed as *just my "consciousness only."* Your experience of yourself is just a consciousness experience, something that happens within your mind. It is just a mental event within your consciousness. Without a brain you don't know that you exist. Of course there is still an existent world without you or your consciousness, but you need consciousness to know it.

There is no inside or outside to your experiencing of your consciousness. That is all you can ever experience. There is "no inside or outside" because your own experience of existence or beingness can only be just be manipulations (manifestations, images or thoughts) of your consciousness – thoughts and images you form - and not actually a world outside of it. Realizing this - that you and your world images are "consciousness-only" - can help you cultivate the samadhi of infinite consciousness when you realize that everything you see is just your personal mind. This can help you let go during meditation so that you detach from thoughts and let your Qi/prana arise to start opening up Qi channels.

When trying to cultivate the samadhi of infinite consciousness, the problem is that you are always clinging to the body and physical feeling states, which are also formations of consciousness in your mind (namely thoughts) and thinking they are you. You are always clinging to these manifestations of consciousness and by clinging to thoughts you impede the flow of Qi in your body since that flow and thoughts are interlinked. This is a basic rule of spiritual cultivation: thoughts and Qi/prana are linked, so to help your Qi/prana flow freely to generate the subtle body you need to practice detaching from thoughts when they appear.

To help you meditate and let go of thoughts, we colloquially say that consciousness is itself invisible and clear, like light or empty space, and that we miss the existence of the invisible background of empty consciousness that is the true untouched, unmanifest essence of consciousness. In a way this insinuates that consciousness is like a substance, but it isn't. It is a product of operations/functions within the brain.

In truth, when there is no such thing as consciousness (such as a rock) there is no clear light of consciousness at all, so such Consciousness-only descriptions are sometimes not exactly correct but just worded in a way meant to help you make progress in meditation so that you can eventually with practice achieve the first new body, the subtle body. They are meant to help you cultivate a state of presence, witnessing or pristine awareness where you let go of thoughts and body sensations so that your Qi begins to move and can start to solidify your inner subtle body by that Qi flow, which eventually turns into a rotation that brings about transformation. All the forms of meditation practice use different reasons as prompts to provoke you into trying to cultivate an "empty" mental state that detaches from thoughts so that your Qi/prana can begin to stir (it won't stir if you always attach to it, thus holding it in a way that prevents a rotation). You do not want to cling to your thoughts/Qi because then your energy can begin to move and start reinforcing the structural buildup of your inner subtle body.

Avalokitesvara's road of "cultivating hearing" mentioned in the

Surangama Sutra, where you suddenly hear a sound that appears within your consciousness without warning (a sudden event appearing out of nowhere that you cannot expect whilst mentally clinging), helps you break free of any *at-that-moment attachments* to your thoughts and body feeling states since the knowing of that sound is like a shot that jostles you enough to help you let go. It leads to a state of "open presence" where you are free of holding onto thoughts; you are never strongly attached to thoughts when they arise. The juxtaposition of clinging to a feeling state, even when you think you are not doing so, and then suddenly hearing a sound that unexpectedly appears out of nowhere, jostles consciousness and helps you to immediately drop that physical feeling state and rest in the "emptiness like space" that is the true nature of consciousness. Furthermore, by concentrating on hearing, just as anapana concentrates on physical body sensations, you can use this pathway to better cultivate your Qi development.

Another way of explaining matters entirely is that when there is an object in consciousness it is "objective knowledge"; you are experiencing knowledge of an object such as a sound or body feeling. On the other hand, when there is no object then what you are experiencing is objectless knowledge; you are still experiencing something.

Spiritual schools typically cheat people and say that objectless knowledge is pure consciousness, as if consciousness was a substance. They talk as if consciousness were a substance itself rather than the mechanical product of a nervous system. Thus they describe "pure consciousness" with various descriptions such as being like emptiness, clear light, no-thought, no-self, empty space, formlessness, a vacuum or void, or an unmanifest state. They use all sorts of linguistic trickery in order to help you let go of thoughts to cultivate a clear and empty state of mind. For instance, they say that we typically become fixated upon the phenomena that flash within consciousness and don't recognize the clear, empty movie screen of consciousness-substance within which they appear. That empty movie screen is actually still an image of consciousness produced by a movement of energy in the brain.

Consciousness or thoughts, emotions and sensations are formed when energy runs through the matrix of your brain in a certain way that causes certain chemical reactions happen. While clear consciousness is compared to the invisible background light or empty space within which objects appear, that is just a way of talking to help you let go of thoughts. Thoughts themselves are the creation of the chemical reactions in the brain and energy flowing through that nervous system. Whatever appears in the mind is like a picture that is flashing across a movie screen and the whole shebang of thoughts and picture screen is called consciousness. Everything appears within it, but how it is mechanically constructed cannot be seen unless you have a body of more rarified energy that can go inside a typical human brain and watch as thoughts and emotions form, which subtle-bodied devas do in order to learn how to guide the process. All heavenly residents are trying to cultivate ever higher bodies to be able to do this.

Now, to cultivate the fourth dhyana of enlightenment means attaining the Supra-Causal body that is composed of a very fundamental energy sphere - Later Heaven Qi. This substance is a type of energy just as physical matter (form), Qi and Shen are types of energy, each denser or more subtle than the next. To attain this stage of cultivation, you must train to be able to always let go of all the things that appear within your consciousness and let them arise and depart without attachments. Then the energy of that body will become able to rotate (due to the nonclinging) and eventually form a new higher spiritual body. You must therefore practice the freedom of "presence" - being in the moment - where you are not attaching to the I-identity but are just being pristine, clearly aware and letting whatever arises arise within your mind.

You always function with thoughts in your mind but you should be fluid with your thoughts because of non-clinging. Non-clinging or non-attachment does not mean that you should never practice concentration by holding onto thoughts for a long time. All the skills of using consciousness, such as for concentration or visualization or the proper thinking to reason out cause and effect, are the things you must learn and master for living. Detachment of thoughts does NOT mean that you don't hold onto thoughts when you are concentrating on something such as working on problems.

One reason to practice meditation (or anapana) is so that you learn how to let things arise in the mind without attaching to them, and in time your kundalini (*real* Yang Qi) will finally be aroused if you practice many other cultivation practices as well. Then your Qi will eventually set up a rotational flow within your body that over twelve

209

years will create the subtle body. This internal Qi flow cannot be initiated and sustained solely by your own efforts. You need the helpful intercession of enlightened masters and devas to make this possible. As explained in *Meditation Case Studies*, when they help you internally you are bound to experience all sorts of unusual phenomena such as visions.

Only by practicing witnessing or observation of the contents of the mind (vipassana), without clinging to those thoughts and the I-thought center that allows you to know experience, can you let go of the body being formed by the rotation/flow of Qi within you. The Supra-Causal body develops out of the Causal (Mental or Shen) body, which in turn develops out of the subtle (Qi) body, which you develop out of the physical body of form, and the generation process always follows this same procedure of a higher body of energy distilled/separated out of a lower.

When you attain the Supra-Causal body, or fourth dhyana attainment, the Consciousness-only school denotes this by saying you are at the level of the *alaya* consciousness that transcends lower states of matter and the attendant minds formed by that stage of matter.

To cultivate the Supra-Causal body you must practice meditation that witnesses whatever arises in consciousness without attaching to those manifestations of consciousness. This is the same thing you must do to attain the subtle body, which is the first of all subsequent spiritual bodies. Anapana practice is the witnessing of sensations brought about (stirred up) by arising Qi flows within the body while witnessing meditation (vipassana) is primarily the watching of thoughts. Kuan Yin's method of hearing is listening to sounds in a detached manner as well, which is related to these other practices. Since everything known within consciousness (objects or "others") is known due to an I-thought, you should not cling to the I-thought processes of your mind when pracricing such meditation efforts but should let all things arise without attachment, and yet without blocking them.

This is the explanation of spiritual cultivation from the aspect of consciousness, whose "purification" is normally the only path transmitted in most cultivation schools (see *What is Enlightenment?* for more examples). Most of the explanations in this book, however, deal with the body and Qi/prana aspects of cultivation since this discussion is usually neglected. In order to succeed at enlightenment quickly you must cultivate both emptiness and life force, both empty mind (a mind that does not cling to thoughts) and Qi/ prana. If you don't cultivate your Qi/vitality through various qi-gong and internal nei-gong practices then it will be impossible to produce the subtle deva body that is the basis for higher attainments.

You must cultivate both your Qi (life) and the essential nature of your mind (emptiness) to attain enlightenment. Through cultivating both you will attain the subtle energy deva body and other bodies very quickly, but please know that this also requires empowering blessings of other enlightened beings who must lend you energy to move your Qi. This is why you perform special practices that enlightened beings would know about when you cultivate them such as reciting mantras or holy texts, reciting the names of past enlightened masters, and visiting special places where enlightened beings are always paying attention in order to see people that they might be able to help.

If you follow schools such as Zen or Vedanta without knowing that *you must also cultivate your body (Qi)* then it is rare to become enlightened. Most people think that enlightenment is the result of some mental thought realization such as Archimedes' "Eurkea!," but this is wrong. They don't realize that anyone becoming enlightened through Zen, Vedanta or any other intellectual tradition were developing and using spiritual bodies but weren't telling people. Reading the teachings of these schools without realizing this fact will certainly mislead you, especially since these schools describe the spiritual path only in terms of consciousness attainments rather than the body attainments discussed.

To delineate spiritual progress, Buddhism also has the ten Bodhisattva bhumis, which are stages of enlightenment attainment. Few know the secret that each set of two bhumis represent a dhyana and body achievement, with five achievements in total.

Hence, the first and second bhumi, or **Very Joyous** and **Freedom from Defilement (Stainless or Pure)**, correspond to the Srotapanna Arhat, who has attained the first dhyana and the subtle body attainment. When you finally emerge in a deva (subtle) body you are extremely joyful, and hence the name Very Joyous. Stainless refers to your mind as compared to the mental state of a human. In Vajrayana this stage is simply known as "empty."

As you know by now, joy is also one of the roads you can take in order to cultivate the first dhyana attainment. When you stir up your Qi, you always try to be joyful. Thus joyful sex can be used on the path to help you attain the first dhyana (but not higher) if you learn how to use it to stir up your Qi while cultivating extreme joy at the same time. This is a method used in Taoism, Vajrayana and the Kaula schools of India.

The third and fourth Bodhisattva bhumis are called **Luminous (Radiant)** and **Brilliant Wisdom (Blazing)** respectively. The names refer to light because the Sakrdagamin Arhat (second dhyana attainee) can now reach the second dhyana heavens of Limited Radiance, Unbounded Radiance and Streaming Radiance. Their Qi refinement of their subtle body is a little bit better than that of the Srotapanna Arhat, but it is still a subtle body of just Qi.

Since the second dhyana is characterized by a more refined stage of joy, bliss and emptiness than the first dhyana, this is symbolized by the infinite loving-kindness meditation taught in Buddhism. If you cultivate a more subtle state of joy and bliss than just exciting joy (by using the route of immeasurable love or kindness meditation), this prepares you to attain the Qi of the second dhyana.

The fifth and sixth Bodhisattva bhumis are named **Difficult to Conquer** and **Manifesting Prajna-Wisdom**. The name Difficult to Conquer indicates that it is very difficult to attain the Causal or Mental body made of Shen from an effusion out of the lower subtle body of Qi that corresponds to the first and second dhyana. The jump to this body is difficult just as it is difficult to jump from the coarse human body to the subtle Qi body.

There is even a Buddha named Sudurijaya (Difficult to Conquer), who represents the fifth of the ten bhumis where an Arhat has overcome the worst difficulties to attain the Mental-Causal-Shen body from the subtle Qi body attainment. In Vajrayana Buddhism this is the "pure illusory body" attainment; only the pure illusory body is pure enough to attain the mind stream purity of the enlightened Arhat represented by the seventh bhumi.

The Mental body is composed of an entirely new substance than Qi, which is a higher energy substance called Shen, and corresponds to the third dhyana attainment. Once again, it is hard to reach this attainment from the second dhyana. Vast superpowers become available upon this attainment because you can then roam about in a higher subtle plane of existence. When you reach the highest stage of the third dhyana, you can attain the **samadhi of infinite space** that corresponds to the stage of Clearly Manifest; your mind is very empty (Vajrayana calls this the great empty, as explained) and quiet yet knows everything within it. When you try to cultivate yourself as bodiless awareness this is like trying to cultivate the samadhi of infinite space.

The seventh and eighth Bodhisattva bhumis match with the fourth dhyana of the Arhat and are named **Far-reaching (Proceeding Afar)** and **Attaining Calm (Immovable)**. Far-reaching refers to the fact that at this stage of enlightenment your mind is everywhere, which refers to the **samadhi of infinite consciousness**; those who attain enlightenment often speak of universal oneness, which is far-reaching or infinite since the Clear Light Qi energy (Later Heavenly Qi or fundamental wind) permeates everything as a fundamental substrate. The stage Immovable refers to the **samadhi of nothingness**, which is the Yin aspect of the moving *alaya* consciousness. It is a state of inert non-movement of consciousness, namely no-thought. In the samadhi of infinite nothingness the mind seems non-existent, like an absolute vacuum, and since there are no thoughts we call the stage Immovable. It is a stage of thoughtlessness, totally absent of thoughts, where the world seems to disappear.

The ninth and tenth bhumis are named **Finest Discriminatory Wisdom** and **Dharma Cloud**. For these progressive steps you attain the Earlier Heavenly Qi body that is higher than the Clear Light body, and which corresponds to complete Buddhahood. Ramalinga Swamigal calls this stage Immaculate. The attendant mental attainment that matches with this is said to be the Tao, or original nature – you have reached the most fundamental essence of the mind. At this stage you transcend the *alaya* consciousness but can still know the thoughts of all sentient beings. Your mind is also perfectly clear, so thus you have very Good Discrimination (Finest Discriminatory Wisdom). As a Full Buddha who has completed the path you can now teach everyone by raining down teachings everywhere; you become a Cloud of Dharma offering blessings and teachings.

Since the fundamental nature, Parabrahman, original essence, True Self or Tao is described as a foundational energy state being so pure it is empty of other energies, its opposite is the entire realm of manifestation, or Shakti. Shakti is also another name for the realm of manifestation, or Cloud of Dharma.

In the *Surangama Sutra* there are higher bhumis still, as well in Vajrayana Buddhism, which means there are higher stages you can cultivate past even this. However, but most religions only take people to the Early Heavenly Qi body and equate it with Perfect and Complete Enlightenment or Full Buddhahood. Actually the spiritual path extends onwards, but this is as far as masters describe until you reach the higher achievements, at which point the relevant teachings are given on how to progress further.

Thus you can see that Buddhism explains the spiritual path or stages of enlightenment in many different ways. For instance, the four dhyana match with the four immeasurables. They match with the four blisses and empties of Vajrayana. They match with the Bodhisattva bhumis (almost no one knows this). They match with body attainments.

The spiritual path is usually described through the aspect of consciousness so that people cultivate meditation and detachment of thoughts which gives rise to Qi movement, but this book has dealt with the body attainments that are also achieved. I believe the body vehicle explanation is superior and more motivational. In the end, however, attainment is just a matter of spiritual yoga.

You don't have to study lots of dharma to get enlightened, which is why countless individuals from Judaism, Islam, Christianity, Confucianism, Sikhism and other religions without deep cultivation teachings also attain the stage of a saint and gain the Tao. In essence, *the spiritual path is just a path of Yoga* so you don't need all these teachings. They are there only to help, but not absolute guides. What you really need is Yoga practice, and especially inner energy work.

In order to succeed you don't need to know a lot of theory about consciousness. You just need to let go of thoughts (practice detachment or non-clinging while letting thoughts always arise) because that is the primary requirement to progress from the physical body to the subtle body attainment, the subtle body to the Causal body and so on. You have to both meditate by letting go of thoughts while practicing witnessing, and also do lots of Yoga energy work to create a new body out of the previous body.

Only if you let go of all the things arising within consciousness can you cultivate a body that is a higher essence or energy substance than its lower manifestations and emanations. The spiritual path is therefore all just a path of devoted Yoga to change the Qi and Qi channels of your body at each and every level of existence.

If you just use the energy practices in this book alone, you have a greater chance to succeed than using most other pathways. You can also use these exercises along with any tradition since they are non-denominational.

APPENDIX 3
A LIFE GEARED TOWARD
SPIRITUAL CULTIVATION

If you really want to travel the spiritual path it is best to start as young as possible. Various activities or habits will speed your way, making progress easier, and will maximize your chances of succeeding. Use the assists yourself and teach them to others as young as possible, including your children.

First, get a **chiropractic adjustment** so that your skeletal structure becomes perfectly aligned. This will help with health and meditation. Do lots of qi-gong or nei-gong work on moving the Qi in your spine to open up channels heading into your brain, but always make sure that your skeleton is aligned and you practice good posture.

If you want to develop a subtle body that lasts for hundreds of years, you want an excellent body condition so you should practice healthy habits. Your skeletal structural alignment (posture, carriage and gait) determines your movement in the world as well as how your Qi flows and how people view you. Together with your breathing, heart rate and blood pressure, this total package affects the creation of thoughts within your brain. If your skeleton has a good alignment this will help with the taming of consciousness.

In advanced stages of cultivation practice you can practice permeating the environment with your Qi, Shen and Supra-Causal body energies. You can also link these energies to each of these processes (breathing, pulse, etc.) in order that you *automatically* flood the environment with positive impulses without having to think about it (since breathing, heart beat, etc. are autonomous processes). In other words, you might work on cultivating the dhyana-samadhi of friendliness by surrounding yourself with the feeling of friendliness, cultivating it within your mind at all times and projecting it into the environment.

You can also practice linking that emotion to your Qi so that it is projected into the environment on a vast scale and effortlessly refreshes with every breath you take. You can also practice flooding the environment with automatically projected feelings of peacefulness and compassion with every one of your heartbeats. Many people know that it is a yogic feat of an accomplished one to make their skin shine with light and thereby permeate the environmental with positive influences, but at even higher levels of cultivation one can train so that their energies are always naturally emitting beneficial influences into the environment, which can be on a small or vast scale.

In the *Avatamsaka Sutra*, the influences you can learn to effortlessly, automatically emanate from your presence are symbolized by things such as light (illumination), sound, fragrance, flavor, energy, clouds, winds, water currents, vitality or courage. Because the influences manifested can become effortless with practice, they are often considered as adornments you wear. Naturally, you must train to be able to emanate incredible beneficial influences. You do this by practicing concentration and projection along with perfecting the skillful technique you want. This type of effort or offering to others, when projected, is called bestowing peace, courage or happiness (joy) on sentient beings.

Second, **detox your body** to remove poisons from your system, which will slowly improve all health conditions and also your spiritual cultivation. Herbal and other detoxification regimens will help purge your body of poisons that are an impediment to health, the purification of your Qi and the generation of the subtle body. With less poisons in your body, your Qi must do less work to expel them from organs and tissues ("channels") to create a smooth flow and eventually generate the subtle body.

The early stages of cultivation always involve purging the body of poisons, as a sort of coarse level of detoxification. See my book *Detox Cleanse Your Body Quickly and Completely* and *Look Young, Live Longer* for ways to accomplish both coarse and refined detoxification of your physical body.

Third, start eating right and **eat the right nutritional supplements** that will help you with your health, energy and anti-aging efforts, and thus the spiritual path. See my book *Look Younger, Live Longer* for the right diet and supplements to take for health and anti-aging. This book will help you regain your health, live longer and prepare you for the spiritual trail. It even provides teachings that can be co-jointly used with Nyasa Yoga to help quickly transform the physical body. A key takeaway is to eat a daily scoop of red and green superfoods and let your body draw nutrients from the rich supply of nutrients they contain.

Fourth, an optimal thing to do is **stretch every muscle of your body to definition** while doing visualization and Mantrayana on each of them. This will help you not only become healthier but prepare a base for the successful generation of the subtle body. I like Pilates for this because it enables you to isolate individual muscles, and Yoga to a lesser extent.

The key is to *stretch each of your muscles so that they can be seen with definition*, and try to move your Qi through them. When you are practicing, it helps to have color-coded pictures of the muscles being stretched during practice to help guide your visualization focus. The soft martial arts like Tai Qi, Baguazhang, Xing Yi Quan and Akido (and the Slavic physical system Zdorovye) are also wonderful in teaching you how to develop and use your Qi energy in tune with muscles and movement, but you have to use the energy work, such as the methods in this book, to cultivate your Qi as well.

Fifth, **practice pranayama**. *Kumbhaka* (holding your breath) pranayama is one of the most important spiritual practices you can employ to make progress quickly.

Sixth, sex is an important part of life you probably will not want to do without. Therefore, as a lay woman **learn kegel exercises and mula bhandha** in order to open up Qi channels in the pelvic region. As a man, **practice mula bhandha** and train yourself for being able to do karezza, which is lovemaking without ejaculation. You need to learn how to make love without ejaculation but while generating joy and energetically moving your Qi throughout your body to help open up Qi channels. A monk or nun must still master mula mandha even though they refrain from sex.

You need to conserve your Qi and semen (Jing) on the path because if you lose it then that energy won't be available for opening up Qi channels. For sex that can help your cultivation, learn how to match the "immeasurable joy" meditation of Buddhism with the methods of moving your Qi taught within this book, and match it with your sexual technique. Then you have another way to open up your Qi channels for the spiritual path.

Seventh, **start cultivating** various spiritual practices and the earlier the better. You need to meditate for results according to the instructions in this book. You need to be doing internal energy work, like the Nyasa Yoga practices and traditional nei-gong, and consciousness-emptiness meditation practices.

The best advice I can give you is what I wrote in *Move Forward* – **simultaneously use several different methods based on different principles** such as witnessing meditation, mantra, visualization (such as the white skeleton visualization), *kumbhaka* pranayama, nei-gong and qi-gong (spinning or moving your Qi internally), Nyasa Yoga and Mantrayana, Yoga/stretching/martial arts, charity and offering, special types of singing, and sexual cultivation.

Success in spiritual cultivation is not about the number of books you read or what you learn about consciousness, superpowers, kung-fu and so on. *It is all a path of Yoga practices in the end, especially internal energy work Yoga practices!* Because of this, you need to set up a daily practice schedule and stick to it through thick and thin. Every day you need to recite mantras, practice meditation, practice visualization concentration and move your Qi through a variety of inner energy techniques. The inner energy work is most important. It takes years to build up the foundation of Qi channel cleansings before the real kundalini can awaken, but when it finally does then the deva body is assured.

The instructions in this book teach you how to move your Qi, but then you always have to sit in meditation and let the Qi flow everywhere by itself. These exercises are like a match that ignites a process; once ignited you let the Qi do what it wants and just witness or observe it without interfering. If you feel it stuck in any place, then you do extra work on that location afterwards or sometimes within your meditation session, but don't distract yourself from the rest of the session's completion. To succeed at cultivating the subtle body you must spend countless hours in meditation. The result comes from long meditation sessions after your Qi is energized, and from cumulative practice hours. The more work you do, the better.

Eighth, for the best results you should practice with **an enlightened spiritual master** who is devoted to practice. He or she can come from any tradition. Enlightened monks, gurus, sadhus, etc. whose only job is to oversee the training of other monks, and who from a respected tradition of many spiritual masters, will probably give you the best chance to succeed quickly because they are working *primarily* on helping people transform their Qi and channels rather than involved in other activities. The sole job they have chosen, despite any other activities in the etheric realms, is to help people gain enlightenment (rather than social or cultural work) and the first requirement is helping you attain the subtle deva body, which requires the assistance of many devas.

Thus it is often best to have a teacher who belongs to a monastic tradition because the deva helpers you will also need will come from that traditions. If the master is distracted by worldly activities you probably will get inferior attention on your Qi and channel cultivation.

If an enlightened master is not a monk, nun, priest, sadhu, etc. but doing regular worldly work as a layman, their worldly activities might distract them from a priority of attention on your practice and progress. This cannot be known for sure, so you have to judge a master by the results he achieves. My general rule is that an enlightened spiritual master who is not engaged in too many worldly activities with their higher bodies and is only taking care of a few disciples to help them succeed is probably best. To find one you must work hard and mantra to the accomplished past spiritual saints of the tradition you have chosen. They will then notice and try to guide you to an appropriate connection.

When you start cultivating it is common to feel many sensations in the body arising due to Qi movements. These internal and external sensations (other than just shaking, perspiration and so on) have been cataloged by Yoga and include the sensations of your body feeling coarse, itchy, cold, warm, light, heavy, dry, slippery (smooth), granular, lost, moving, light and peaceful, cold, hot, floating, sinking, solid, soft, or dreamy. All sorts of sensations arise due to spiritual cultivation and you are advised to ignore them.

Buddhism actually specifies nearly forty different sensations that can arise in cultivation due to Qi. Excusing the tense, during the course of spiritual cultivation you might feel that your body (or your

Qi) is cold, warm, light, heavy, rough/coarse, dry, granular, slippery (smooth), soft, tender, hard, brave, energetic, slow, hurried/urgent, sore, aching/painful, swollen, numb, stuck (an internal body feeling), jumpy or fidgety, thirsty, full, hungry, itchy, sticky, moving, quiet/peaceful, old, sick, dead, tired, restless, or resting.

Just ignore these feelings that arise as you make progress, and continue cultivating until you gain the initial fruit of the path.

ABOUT THE AUTHOR

William Bodri is the author of several health and self-help books including:

- *Meditation Case Studies*
- *Visualization Power*
- *Look Younger, Live Longer*
- *Quick, Fast, Done: Simple Time Management Secrets from Some of History's Greatest Leaders*
- *Move Forward: Powerful Strategies for Creating Better Outcomes in Life*
- *The Little Book of Meditation*
- *The Little Book of Hercules*
- *Internal Martial Arts Nei-gong*
- *What is Enlightenment?*

If you enjoyed this book you would probably enjoy his titles *Meditation Case Studies, Internal Martial Arts Nei-gong, Look Younger, Live Longer, The Little Book of Hercules, The Little Book of Meditation, Visualization Power* and *Move Forward*, all of which contain similar materials.

While this book concentrates on internal energy yoga work (nei-gong), *Look Younger, Live Longer* reveals different roads of physical body cultivation you can follow while the companion book on consciousness practices is *Meditation Case Studies* (and to a lesser extent *What is Enlightenment?*).

Made in the USA
Middletown, DE
02 September 2017